John Knox

A View of the British Empire

Vol. 2

John Knox

A View of the British Empire
Vol. 2

ISBN/EAN: 9783743353848

Manufactured in Europe, USA, Canada, Australia, Japa

Cover: Foto ©ninafisch / pixelio.de

Manufactured and distributed by brebook publishing software (www.brebook.com)

John Knox

A View of the British Empire

A VIEW OF THE BRITISH EMPIRE,

MORE ESPECIALLY

SCOTLAND;

WITH SOME PROPOSALS

FOR THE

IMPROVEMENT OF THAT COUNTRY,

THE

EXTENSION OF ITS FISHERIES,

AND THE

RELIEF OF THE PEOPLE.

By JOHN KNOX.

VOL. II.

The Third Edition, greatly Enlarged.

LONDON;

PRINTED FOR J. WALTER, AT CHARING-CROSS;
SHEPPERSON AND REYNOLDS, OXFORD-STREET;
W. RICHARDSON, ROYAL-EXCHANGE;
AND W. GORDON, EDINBURGH.

MDCCLXXXV.

CONTENTS

OF

VOL. II.

National Improvements recommended, particularly in the Highlands.

CONTENTS.

An Account of the Quantity of British Herrings and Cod exported from Scotland, from Christmas 1750, to Christmas 1782, distinguishing each Year, and the Ports from whence exported.

Ports from whence export.	Herr. White Barrel	Cod Dried. Cwt	Q.	lb.
1751.				
Aberdeen	84			
Air	6624			
Anstruther	31			
Borrowstoness	11			
Campbletown	6084	[illegible]		
Dunbar	—	38[illegible]	1	
Fort William	217			
Irvine	837			
Leith	1[illegible]			
Montrose	[illegible]			
Orkney	698			
Port Glasgow	2405			
Port Greenock	7595			
Shetland	1672	7312	3	
Total	15800	8040	0	
1752.				
Air	3558	97	2	
Anstruther	340			
Campbeltown	2773	1708		
Dunbar	—	47	1	14
Fort William	259			
Inverness	12			
Irvine	367			
Kirkaldy	39			
Leith	166	126	2	21
Montrose	184			
Orkney	196			
Port Glasgow	2214			
Port Greenock	6927			
Stranraer	156			
Shetland	810	6218	2	
Total	18003	8198	0	7
1753.				
Air	1067	509	2	
Anstruther	603			
Borrowstoness	20			
Campbeltown	6244	1426		
Fort William	—	108		
Inverness	238			
Irvine	107	207		
Montrose	90			
Port Glasgow	3276			
Port Greenock	10262			
Stranraer	1029			
Shetland	3482	7424		
Total	26420	9674	2	

Ports from whence export.	Herr. White Barrel	Cod Dried. Cwt.	Q.	lb.
1754.				
Aberdeen	4			
Air	686			
Anstruther	288			
Borrowstoness	30			
Campbeltown	6933	1837	1	
Dunbar	—	37	1	
Fort William	412			
Irvine	280	1022	3	25
Montrose	52			
Port Glasgow	3117			
Port Greenock	7570			
Stranraer	1690			
Shetland	5286	10178	1	
Total	26335	13075	1	25
1755.				
Aberdeen	264	9	2	21
Air	3830	130		
Campbeltown	24436	1196		
Fort William	1315			
Inverness	779	12	2	
Irvine	3754	550	3	1
Leith	250			
Orkney	1737			
Port Glasgow	4054			
Port Greenock	4675	185		20
Stranraer	1935			
Shetland	2599	5742	3	
Total	49429	7826	3	14
1756.				
Aberdeen	—	25	3	14
Air	2730			
Anstruther	286			
Campbeltown	13528	1153		
Fort William	1444	111		
Inverness	291			
Irvine	2930	240		
Leith	158			
Montrose	67			
Orkney	2003			
Port Glasgow	4519			
Port Greenock	9072			
Stranraer	951			
Shetland	3476	9287	2	
Total	41456	108[illegible]	1	14

Ports from whence export.	Herrs. White Barrel	Cod Dried Cwt.	Q.	lb.
1757.				
Aberdeen	—			
Air	1239	31	2	7
Anſtruther	743			
Campbeltown	3271	1064		
Fort William	1592			
Irvine	863	656	1	2
Leith	561			
Montroſe	33			
Port Glaſgow	2924			
Port Greenock	6257			
Stranraer	5924			
Shetland	1133	6170	2	
Total	24542	7922	1	9
1758.				
Aberdeen	—	—		
Air	1237	1022	1	
Anſtruther	177			
Caithneſs	—			
Campbeltown	5083	2467		
Dunbar	—	61		
Fort William	799			
Irvine	695	336	2	15
Leith	97			
Port Glaſgow	4326			
Port Greenock	11878			
Stranraer	13121			
Port Patrick	14			
Shetland	4173	9287	2	
Total	41602	13174	1	15
1759.				
Aberdeen	—			
Air	1513			
Campbeltown	2846	3637		
Dunbar	—	91		
Fort William	501	9	2	
Irvine	290	362		7
Port Glaſgow	1293			
Port Greenock	5422			
Stranraer	9025			
Shetland	1166	8480	3	
Total	22057	12580	1	7

Ports from whence export.	Herrs. White Barrel	Cod. Dried. Cwt.	Q	lb.
1760.				
Air	1789			
Anſtruther	14			
Campbeltown	1712	1103		
Fort William	111			
Irvine	365	97	3	14
Leith	61	123		
Port Glaſgow	4329			
Port Greenock	5512			
Stranraer	432			
Shetland	460	9815	3	
Total	14787	11139	2	14
1761.				
Air	4288			
Campbeltown	6026	1114		
Fort William	201	57		
Irvine	1495	196	1	14
Kirkudbright	480			
Port Glaſgow	4692			
Port Greenock	7514	41	2	
Stranraer	747			
Shetland	950	7133	2	
Total	26396	8544	1	14
1762.				
Aberdeen	—	34	3	8
Air	598			
Campbeltown	4895	982		
Fort William	283	63	2	
Irvine	809			
Port Glaſgow	752			
Port Greenock	4438	59	1	
Stranraer	460			
Shetland	1250	9931	2	21
Total	13486	10171	1	1

Ports from whence export. 1763.	Herrs. White Barrel.	Cod Dried. Cwt.	Q.	lb.
Aberdeen	—	28	3	21
Air	1997			
Campbeltown	10775	1170		
Fort William	985			
Inverness	500			
Irvine	1636			
Oban	13			
Port Glasgow	2574			
Port Greenock	5700	17	2	21
Stranraer	142			
Shetland	941	9841	1	
Total	25265	11057	3	14
1764.				
Air	333			
Campbeltown	2641	1211		
Fort William	11			
Montrose	—	58		14
Oban	1827	280	2	
Port Glasgow	1894			
Port Greenock	1692	83	1	15
Shetland	952	9974	1	
Total	9351	11582	1	1
1765.				
Air	74			
Alloa	26			
Borrowstoness	381			
Campbeltown	12300	352		
Fort William	297			
Irvine	2183			
Leith	198			
Oban	1028	165	2	10
Port Glasgow	1636			
Port Greenock	9628			
Rothesay	83			
Stronaway	1111	291		
Stranraer	73			
Shetland	1438	11062	2	
Total	30458	11871		10

Ports from whence export. 1766.	Herrs. White Barrel.	Cod Dried. Cwt.	Q.	lb.
Air	717			
Campbeltown	10675	631	5	
Fort William	461			
Irvine	889			
Leith	59			
Oban	1054			
Port Glasgow	2532			
Port Greenock	5270			
Stronaway	1885	297		
Stranraer	371			
Shetland	3119	7244	2	1
Total	27053	8173	1	1
1767.				
Air	57			
Campbeltown	6390	337	2	14
Fort William	178			
Inverness	3			
Irvine	591			
Leith	170			
Oban	381			
Port Glasgow	2509			
Port Greenock	6095			
Rothesay	193			
Stronaway	410	129	2	24
Stranraer	522			
Shetland	2565	7650	2	
Total	20060	8117	3	10
1768.				
Air	235			
Caithness	523			
Campbeltown	8474	865		21
Irvine	1018			
Kirkaldy	59			
Leith	429			
Oban	1024			
Port Glasgow	4687			
Port Greenock	7334	146	3	
Rothesay	234			
Stronaway	706	188		
Stanraer	929			
Shetland	2539	9853	3	7
Total	28184	10967	3	

Ports from whence export. 1769.	Herrs. White Barrel	Cod Dried. Cwt.	Q.	lb.
Air	35			
Borrowstoness	30			
Campbeltown	6476	560	3	7
Dunbar	272			
Irvine	954			
Kirkaldy	25			
Leith	1025			
Oban	1185	38		
Port Glafgow	1802			
Port Greenock	5811	187	2	2
Stronaway	3979	399	3	
Stranraer	1429			
Shetland	2600	5188	3	14
Total	25624	6374	3	23
1770				
Air	964			
Caithnefs	1159			
Campbeltown	16175	1360	3	14
Dunbar	521			
Fort William	65	200		
Irvine	1569			
Kirkaldy	60			
Leith	1028	25		
Oban	5132	56	2	14
Port Glafgow	3239			
Port Greenock	12574	1930	3	16
Stronaway	982	110	1	
Stranraer	1934			
Shetland	2039	5565		14
Total	47442	9248	3	2
1771				
Air	228			
Anftruther	56			
Caithnefs	1877			
Campbeltown	4313	297	2	14
Dunbar	105			
Fort William	194			
Invernefs	145			
Irvine	1212			
Leith	262			
Oban	1146			
Port Glafgow	1289			
Port Greenock	14176			
Rothefay	382			
Stronaway	2872	764	3	
Stranraer	912			
Shetland	1915	7740		7
Total	31086	8802	1	21

Ports from whence export. 1772.	Herrs. White Barrel	Cod Dried. Cwt.	Q.	lb.
Anftruther	299			
Caithnefs	3619			
Campbeltown	5538	622	1	17
Fort William	59			
Invernefs	12			
Irvine	424			
Kirkaldy	118			
Leith	690			
Oban	275	38	1	
Port Glafgow	497			
Port Greenock	8711	370	3	20
Stronaway	1433	141	3	
Shetland	14	6656	3	14
Total	21679	7830		23
1773.				
Aberdeen	203			
Air	150			
Caithnefs	2285			
Campbeltown	14638	751	3	7
Irvine	1312			
Kirkaldy	24			
Leith	719			
Oban	1656			
Port Glafgow	619			
Port Greenock	14575	63	1	23
Rothefay	206			
Stronaway	2198	522		16
Stranraer	866			
Shetland	325	6970	2	
Total	39777	8307	3	18
1774.				
Aberdeen	6			
Air	291			
Caithnefs	953			
Campbeltown	12137	1144	2	3
Dunbar	363			
Fort William	144			
Irvine	1312			
Leith	1639			
Oban	546			
Port Glafgow	2608			
Port Greenock	18535	751	2	25
Rothefay	570			
Stronaway	2968	1098	3	21
Stranraer	670			
Shetland	530	4417	1	14
Total	43275	7412	2	7

Ports from whence export. 1775.	Herrs. White Barrel	Cod Dried. Cwt.	Q.	lb.
Aberdeen		192		21
Air	151			
Anstruther	839			
Caithness	450			
Campbeltown	8122	925	3	81
Dunbar	173			
Irvine	1312			
Kirkaldy	143			
Leith	808			
Montrose	24			
Oban	1159	550	[illegible]	
Port Glasgow	1319			
Port Greenock	13702	102	3	
Rothesay	495			
Stronaway	3178	592	2	
Stranraer	977			
Port Patrick	184			
Shetland	43	8123	2	
Total	33082	10489	1	14
1776.				
Aberdeen		1439	3	23
Air	1326		1	
Campbeltown	14186	265	3	21
Dunbar				
Dundee				
Irvine	1173			
Leith	559			
Montrose		20		
Oban	797			
Port Glasgow	3721			
Port Greenock	22897	504	3	20
Rothesay	536			
Stronaway	3435	1144	1	14
Stranraer	1534			
Shetland		7642	2	14
Total	50165	11017	3	8
1777.				
Aberdeen		1522	2	
Air	301			
Campbeltown	9709	718	3	6
Dunbar		242		
Isle Martyn				
Irvine	1414			
Kirkudbright	196			
Leith	464	79	2	14
Port Glasgow	3800			
Port Greenock	21714	371	2	16
Stronaway	2197	2279		
Stranraer	1383			
Port Patrick	39			
Shetland		7088	3	
Total	41217	12302	1	8

2 2 3

Ports from whence export. 1778.	Herrs. White Barrel	Cod Dried. Cwt.	Q.	lb.
Aberdeen		1080		
Anstrucher	103			
Campbeltown	8004	385		
Dunbar	74	50	3	12
Isle Martyn				
Irvine	856			
Leith	20			
Oban	52			
Port Glasgow	5619			
Port Greenock	19393	670		18
Stronaway	546	654	1	
Stranraer	953			
Shetland		5866	3	14
Total	35620	8727		16
1779.				
Aberdeen		796		
Anstruther	25			
Campbeltown	10673	150	3	
Isle Martyn	88			
Irvine	691			
Kirkudbright	100			
Port Glasgow	5448			
Port Greenock	14096	1659		19
Stronaway	988	481	2	
Shetland		3495	3	
Total	32110	6583		19
1780.				
Aberdeen		[illegible]		
Campbeltown	5075	299		1
Dunbar	76	20		
Isle Martyn	22			
Irvine	23			
Leith		15		
Oban		628	2	
Port Glasgow	4071			
Port Greenock	14518	2431	1	3
Stronaway	1230	244		
Stranraer	106			
Zetland		9785	1	
Total	25122	13703		4

Ports from whence export. 1781.	Herrs. White Barrel	Cod Dried. Cwt.	Q.	lb.
Aberdeen		1600		
Campbeltown	1768			
Dunbar		23	2	14
Invernefs		804		
Oban		56	2	
Port Glafgow	2264			
Port Greenock	9150	2422	1	15
Stronaway	900	669		14
Shetland		8909	1	14
Total	14082	14485		1

Ports from whence export. 1782.	Herrs. White Barrel	Cod Dried. Cwt.	Q.	lb.
Aberdeen		379		
Anftruther	203			
Caithnefs	11			
Campbeltown	396	287	1	
Dunbar				
Invernefs		739		
Kirkudbright	9			
Oban		474	3	
Port Glafgow	2169			
Port Greenock	8819	1365	1	11
Stronaway	914	1712	2	
Shetland		9081	1	
Total	12522	14038		11

CATHCART BOYD,
Examiner of falt and fifhery accounts.

Cuftom-houfe, Edinburgh, 13*th Dec.* 1784.

The following curious treatise did not come to hand in time to be inserted in its proper place.—It is, however, too important to be omitted. The latter part, containing orders of the Netherlands for the better government of the royal fishing, is nearly the same with the rules and orders of the Dutch already inserted, and is therefore omitted.

The Herring-Busse Trade, expressed in sundry Particulars, both for the building of Busses, making of deepe Sea-Nets, and other Appurtenances; also the right curing of the Herring for Forraine Vent. Together with sundry Orders of the Netherlands, for the better Government of the Royall Fishing; as by the following Treatise doth more at large appeare. All which hath bin perused by the Parliament Committee, and is appointed to bee published for the general Direction of the whole Kingdome. Written by Simon Smith, Agent for the Royall Fishing. 1641.

Forasmuch as I finde divers Treatises published, that have sufficiently already invited unto the herring-busse-fishings, which some well-wishers of the commonwealth have bin thereby stirred up to set on the worke; therefore I shall not need to use any further inticements, unto the prosecuting so royall an imployment, then what is already extant, and as by my booke called *A true Narration of the Royal Fishings*, is expressed, to which I doe referre, and in this treatise onely apply my labours to the publication of such particulars, directions and orders, as have not heretofore bin published, whereby all places in the kingdome may be informed in a right way of managing the herring trade with busses, to their best advantage, which being observed in a way of good governement in all those places where this herring fishing shall be erected, will doubtlesse, with God's blessing, prove very beneficiall to all that shall have relation thereunto.

Directions for the building of a Herring Busse.

The length of the busse, from stemme to sterne must be 75 foot. That is to say, 45 foot the length of the keele, which must be, viz.

Eighteen inches deepe, the fore part of the keele.

Twelve inches deepe, the after part of the keele.

Fourteen inches the breadth of the keele.

Twenty-three foot the stem or rake, which must bee, viz.

Five foot crooked.

Twenty inches broad the fore stem.

Seven foot the sterne post must fall backwards.

The sterne-post must be 20 foot, and crooked in the inside 16 inches, square in the after side, and 7 inches thicke.

The fore stem must fall in length forwards 23 foot, 7 foot deepe beneath 16 foot and a halfe broad in the mid-ship, within the tymbers.

 Ten

Ten foot deepe from the keele to the uppermost decke.

Four feet 3 inches the lower deck from the keele, wherein are ten double roomes, besides the net roomes for stoage.

Five feet 9 inches between the decks.

The stoage will be for 412 barrels, viz.

	Barrels
Foure double roomes before the cabbins, will hold —	128
Two double roomes in the lastidge, where the nets are hail'd in — — —	24
Two double roomes before the cabbins — —	44
One single roome after the net roome, will hold —	28
One single roome under the cabbin, will hold — —	16
And under the cabbins, where the men lye — —	72
And betwixt the cabbins, in the fore stem — —	100
	412

Which 412 barrels, reckoning 12 barrels to the last, produceth 34 lasts and 4 barrels.

The Charge of the said Busse.	£.	s.	d.
The hull will cost for tymber and workmanship	300	0	0
The masts, yards, &c. — —	8	0	0
The iron worke and anchors — —	60	0	0
The standing rigging and other ropes —	17	0	0
The three cables, which must be of 100 fathoms a-piece, about, 8 inches, weighing 13cwt. a-piece, of one sieze — —	60	0	0
The sayles and ropes thereunto belonging —	32	0	0
The blocks and pumpes, &c. — —	6	0	0
The anchor stocks — — —	2	0	0
The boate and oares — —	8	0	0
The bricklayer and painter — —	2	10	0
The flags and ancient — —	3	0	0
The compasse maker — —	1	10	0
Totall is	500	0	0

The Charge of the 56 Nets, which the said Busse doth use at the setting out.

	£.	s.	d.
Four deepings of 70 masses a-piece, makes a net, whereof two cost 16s. a-piece, and two cost 10s. a-piece, which together is 52s. for a net, so the 56 nets amounts to — —	145	12	0
For twine making will cost 2s. a net —	5	12	0
For norsels at 8d. a net, being 130 to a net —	1	17	4
For 8 way-ropes, weighing 3cwt. 2qrs. a rope, at 30s. per cent.* — —	42	0	0

Carried forward

* *Every seven nets have a rope.*

	£	s.	d.
Brought forward			
For 7 coyles of 1⅛ inches, will be 1cwt. a coyle, which 7cwt. at 28s. per cent. being for feysons, the coyle conteining 64 fathoms, and each feyson must have 8 fathoms, which coms to — —	9	16	0
For 14 coyles of 64 fathoms a-piece, to make 56 net-ropes, weighing 10cwt. 2qrs. at 28s. per cent. †	14	14	0
For one coyle of 1cwt. to make bowlestraps —	1	8	0
For 60 bowles at 15d. a-piece, is —— —	3	15	0
For 6cwt. of corke, at 18s. per cent. is —	5	8	0
For 50lb. of marline to fasten the corks, at 4d. per lb.	0	16	8
For 80lb. of spunne yarne, to save the bowlestraps from wearing out, at 28s. per cent. —	0	15	4
For the tanning and beetler's worke, and pettie charges at 2s. per net, is — —	5	12	0
	237	4	4

The whole charge of the 56 nets amounts unto 237l. 4s. 4d. which breaketh out 4l. 5s. for every net.

The consumptive Charge in the two Moneth's Fishing.

	£	s.	d.
Ten weyes of Spanish salt is 400 bushels, water measure, which will make 470 barrels of herring, reckoning 6 bushels to make 7 barrels of herring, which doth cost with charges 4l. the weye, is —	40	0	0
Thirty-five lasts of herring cask, at 22s. the last	38	10	0
Two dozen of gipping knives, adzes, and other irons	1	0	0
For baskets and other petty necessaries — —	1	0	0

The Victualling for two Moneths.

	£	s.	d.
Of the master, at 5s. the weeke is — —	2	0	0
Of 15 men, 4s. a-piece for a weeke — —	24	0	0
Of two boyes at the same rate — —	3	4	0
Some is	29	4	0
The wages of the 16 men and two boys ——	36	0	0
The master his allowance of 1s. the barrell for every merchantable barrell of herrings, being on 400 barrells, the some of —— —	20	0	0
Some is	165	14	0
The allowance to make good the nets, which is usually reckoned at 25s. a net, is for 56 nets ——	70	0	0
The weare and teare of the busse at 10l. a moneth	20	0	0

† *The net-rope being 16 fathoms, so that a coyle will make four net-ropes.*

The whole charge that is consumed, is	—	255 14 0
So the sum of this two months imployment will be:		
The nett sales made of the 400 barrells,* is	—	400 0 0
Deduct the charge aforesaid	—	255 14 0
Remaineth cleer gains in two moneths	—	144 6 0

The Times and Places of the Herring Fishings.

To get unto the coast of Sheteland by the beginning of June, when the herrings do rise about Crane Head, which is the head-land or outmost part of Bratio † Sownde, within two leagues, sometimes more, where the herrings doe abide about 14 dayes.

From thence to Farry ‡ Island, which is within 7 leagues to the southward of Sheteland, where the herring continue about three weeks round about that Farry Island.

From thence to Buffin Nesse §, being about 30 leagues to the southward of Farry Island, the fishing places called Buffin Deepes, and is 20 leagues to the northward of the Frythe ||, where the herring abide about 14 dayes, and 14 dayes more on the fishing grounds under Chivet hils, and Chivet chace. ¶

Thence they follow them to the Doggerbanckie, where they stay sometimes a moneth, and sometimes six weekes, and then about the beginning of September they come into the Yarmouth seas, where they continue untill the middle of November, and from thence they fall to the southward, being followed with small fisher-boats, but dangerous for the busses to follow them.

There is also good fishing in the loughes, at the island of the Lewes, very commodious and profitable to those inhabitants, but not so for the busses.

Also on the coast of the Isle of Man, is great appearance of herring, which is most proper for those of Leverpoole, but unprofitable for busses to bee sent from other farre remote ports.

The several Sorts of Herrings, and Times of packing them.

There are barrels of herrings called sea-sticks**; and there are barrels called re-packed herrings.

The sea-sticks are all the fishing season as they come from sea,

* *I here doe reckon but 400 barrels, and not 470, as is mentioned in the calculate of the salt, because the 70 overplus is given in for waste, in making fresh pickle.*

† Bratio *Sownde*—*Brassa Sound.*

‡ Farrie *Island*—Fair *Island.*

§ *Buffin Ness*—Buchanness *in Aberdeenshire.*

|| *Frythe*—*the* Firth *of* Forth.

¶ *Chivet Hills*—*Near Berwick.*

** Sea-sticks *are herrings only once packed.*

which

which containe betweene 500 and 600 herring as they ſhall riſe in bigneſſe, which being repackt up ſure, 17 barrels will make but 12 repackt barrels, for the manner is to take out the herring, waſhing them in their owne pickle, and ſo lay them orderly in a freſh barrel, which have no ſalt put to them, but trodden downe as cloſe as may be, and ſo headed up.

The ſummer herring, which are taken from June to the 15th of July, are ſold away in ſea-ſticks, to bee ſpent preſently in regard of their fatneſſe, and will not endure re-packing, and ſo goe one with another full and ſhotten; but the re-packt herrings are ſorted, the full herrings by themſelves packed, and the ſhotten and ſick herring in barrels by themſelves, marking the barrels diſtinctly.

There are alſo a ſort of herrings called crux-herrings, beginning the 14th of September, being the day noted *exal. crucis*; theſe herrings are made with ſalt upon ſalt, and are carefully ſorted out (all full herring) and uſed in the re-packing, as beforementioned, and can pack but 10 barrels a day.

The corved herrings, which are to make red herrings, are thoſe that are taken in the Yarmouth ſeas, provided that they can bee carried on ſhore within two or three days after they be taken, otherwiſe they muſt be pickled.

The corved herrings are never gipped, but rowed in ſalt, for the better preſervation of them till they can be brought aſhore; and if any be preſerved for to make red herrings, they are waſhed out of the pickle before they be hanged up in the red-herring houſes.

Obſervations in the Fiſhings at Sea.

In the evening they caſt out their nets, and ſo drive all night, and in the morning they get them in againe, and gip, ſalt, and packe all the herrings before they ſet on the kettle.

And if ſo be they get not herrings, then they ſayle up and downe all that day, untill they find a hopeful place to take herring, and at the break of day hale in their nets.

All the day the buſſe rides by the anchor whilſt the nets are aboard, and if foul weather, then doe they put out all their cables at length, and ſo procure the buſſes eaſier riding and more ſafety.

The Diſpoſal of the Men and Youths in the laying out of their Nets, and haling them in againe.

Firſt; one net is caſt overboord, and ſo the buſſe driving away, the one drawes the reſt after it, and when-as all the 56 nets are out, the buſſe rides by the way-rope, every net hath one rope called a ſeyzon, whereby it hangs on the way-rope, which lets downe the net eight fathomes deepe into the ſea; to every ſeyzon belongs a buye, which is faſtned to the way-rope, and four whole herring barrels to the whole fleet of nets, whereby the better to find out the nets, in caſe they ſhould be broken off and loſt at any

any time through stormes; or by accident with some ships rudders comming over, may break them. *

The Imployment of the Men in their Offices, when the Nets are to be haled up.

There is six men at the capsten, then the first seyzon, comming in the hawse way; one man doth stand there and loosen it from the way-rope, and hee gives it to another man that brings the net therewith to the last way, where they hale in the net, and there are two men standing that pull in the net, then there are three men more that shake the herrings out of the net into the well, and one man takes the net from them and stowes it. There is one man with a chop-sticke, catching cods for the kettle, and the master he stands in the chaine waels with the ladnet, to save the herrings that drop out of the nets; in haling them in, there is one boy to hold on the way-rope, at the capsten, and one boy to coyle it, and stowe it from the capsten.

When the Nets are haled in with Herrings.

One man takes the herrings out of the well with the ladnet, and fills the gippers baskets.

Nine gippers which cut their throats, and takes out the guts, and fling the full herrings into one basket, and the shotten herrings into another.

One man takes the full baskets, when they are gipt, and carries them to the rower backe, wherein is salt.

One boy doth row and stirre them up and downe in the salt.

One boy takes the rowed herring, and carries them in baskets to the packers.

Foure men pack the herrings into the barrels, and lay them one by one straite and even.

One man when the barrel is full, takes the same from the packer, and it stands one day open to settle, and that the salt may melt and dissolve to pickle, and then fills them up, and heads up the barrels.

Nota, The master is to view and approve every barrel before it bee headed up, that it may be found merchantable; or in default thereof, the master is to make allowance accordingly.

For making of the pickle, the observation is, that it must be so strong as that a herring will swim in it, and then it doth so pine and overcome the nature of the herring, that it makes it stiffe, and preserves it; otherwise, if the pickle bee weaker then the nature of the herring, it will overcome the strength of the pickle, and so the herring will decay.

* *The Flemming is so carefull, that they suffer no ship to go out before the rudder be viewed by sworn men, that their rudders will not take the ropes.*

The

The Implayment of the Fishermen and Marriners, whilst they be in Harbor, and till they come to their Fishings outwards bound.

They are to rigge and fit the busse, and to stow the salte and beere, which is instead of the ballast; they are to take in the caske and victualling, and other provisions.

They are to take in the nets with the net-ropes, way-ropes, boyes, and all things thereto belonging; and having them aboard, they are to bring the nets to their ropes, and nolsel, and corke them, and make them in all respects fit, and in a readinesse against they come to the fishing grounds.

Homewards bound.

They are to wash out their nets, and take out the nossels and seyzons, and corckes, preserving them all they can in a profitable way.

And to unlade and rowle into the storehouse all their herrings, well conditioned in the chimes and hoopes.

And having unladen and cleansed the busse, and made the roomes fit, they are presently to take into her againe 56 fresh nets, and the like quantity of salte, and caske, and other provisions, and make all expedition to the fishing againe, receiving their wages and allowances according to the orders which are hereafter expressed.

Each Gipper must have

A paire of tanned leather sleeves will cost 18d.
A paire of bootes will cost 7s.
A paire of boot-britches will cost 4s.
A barme-skin or apron will cost 3s. 4d.
And sixe gipping-knives a man will cost 18d. *

The Plantation for a Fishing, where, and how.

In that part of the river or sea-towne, where these accommodations may be had, viz.

A good wharfe to build store-houses upon, where the busse may come close to the store-house, and so both lade and unlade with easier charge, and quicker dispatch.

Also where there may be made an arsinall or docke to harbor up the busses, and there to plant willowes † to make hoops for the caske, and reede for the busses.

To have ground for the twine-spinners and rope-makers to worke in, and to lay up sea-coales and tanning-barke for to tanne the nets with; also to lay up Norway short wood for the busses firing, for dressing their victuals.

The store-houses to be built with the lower-story open for the

* *The gipper is to pay for these out of his wages.*

† *The willow hoop is best for preservation of the pickle, for that the salt water will not rot it as it doth the other; for the pickle running out, the herrings spoyle.*

better

harter rowling in and packing of the herrings, and laying up the provisions of salt, with a large yard in the middle, for the coopers, to make and trim the caske. Also a convenient place to fix up a large copper to tan the nets, * to be of that sufficient bignesse, that it may tan a whole fleet of 56 nets at once. And there must be ground adjoyning to put in stakes for the drying of the nets as they are drawne out of the tanne fat, and hung abroad on those stakes, which is done with much ease and celerity by one man, and with lesse damage to the net then any other way; in the second story, the nets, deepings and twine to be safely kept, and there to be wrought by the beetesters; and in the upper story, to have the cables and ropes housed and coyled, and the sayles and other provisions laid up.

The Provisions to be made aforehand for furnishing the Magazine.

The best rine and rusband are these; hempe brought in by the eastland merchants from the parts of Lieffeland and Prusia.

Pitch and tarre from the Balticke seas and Norway.

Barrels, boards, and willow hoopes, from Hambourgh and those parts.

Deale-boards, masts and sparres, from Norway, and fire-wood.

Lixboan salt, and salt upon salt made in England.

Normandy canvas for sayles, and Ipswich canvas.

Pease and oatemeale.

Butter and cheese.

Bacon in gammons.

Aquavitæ and vineger.

Gipping-knives and chop-sticks, adzes and other tooles.

Leather for the gippers.

Barke of ashen trees for tanning the nets.

Seacoales for heating the copper for tanning.

Corke and rosen from Burdeaux.

Candles and other chandlery wares.

To have a good quantity of deepings or quarter nets always in readinesse, for to new the nets at the return of the busses.

And all the twine that can be gotten of the summer spinning, which is then best made both for spinning and drying.

The aforesaid provisions being made in dew seasons, will not onely prove very profitable unto the fishing stock, but likewise to whosoever shall be pleased to lay out his money in all or any of the said provisions, that so the fishers may be readily supplyed at their returne, the want whereof hath beene the chiefest cause of the ill successe that hath accrewed unto those former undertakers.

* *Which will be done with as few coales as a copper that will hold but half the nets.*

Some

Some queries having been sent to the Brassa Sound correspondent, for a further explanation in certain ambiguous passages, his answer is as follows:

"In answer to your queries respecting the herring fishing, please know, that the two apartments on the vessel's deck, like two meal-garnels, are temporary for throwing the herrings into, to keep them from among the mens feet, and for giving the men room to do what is necessary about the nets and vessel, without injuring the fish.

The method they use in cleaning the herrings is by cutting out a bit of the throat, or what is called the gip, with which the gills come out, and at which the gippers are exceeding quick and dextrous. They then rouse or driezle them in a tub among salt, and then salt them in barrels; and after they have laid a sufficient time, they repack them in the casks in which they are sent to market. This I hope will satisfy you in these particulars."

NATIONAL

NATIONAL IMPROVEMENTS

RECOMMENDED,

PARTICULALY IN THE

HIGHLANDS.

OF INLAND NAVIGATION.

HITHERTO the inhabitants of the Highlands, unable to avail themſelves of the bounty which their ſeas afford, have lived in penury, amidſt the ſources of affluence; I ſhall therefore ſpecify ſuch meaſures as ſeem moſt conducive to the purpoſes of general utility, in the full eſtabliſhment of a populous thriving colony.

The firſt object which preſents itſelf is the opening ſhorter communications between the Atlantic and the Britiſh Sea; the advantages of which are ſo obvious, that they may be conſidered as the groundwork of all ſucceeding improvements, not only in the Highlands, but over Scotland in general.

That nation admits of three artificial navigations:

1. The Southern navigation, between the Forth and the Clyde.

2. The Weſtern navigation, between Lochfine and the Atlantic.

3. The Northern navigation, between Fort William and Inverneſs.

Navigation

Navigation between the Forth and the Clyde.

Scotland is almoſt divided into two parts by the rivers Forth and Clyde. The Forth falls into the eaſt ſea below Edinburgh, and has an eaſy communication with the whole eaſtern coaſt of Great Britain; with France, Oſtend, Holland, Hamburgh, Pruſſia, Dantzic, Ruſſia, Sweden, Denmark, Norway, and Greenland. The Clyde falls into the Atlantic ocean below Glaſgow, and communicates with the weſtern coaſt of Great Britain; with Ireland, the ſouth of France, Portugal, Spain, the Mediterranean, America, and the Weſt Indies. Theſe two rivers, thus falling in oppoſite directions into the two ſeas, which environ our iſland, and the neck of land between them amounting ſcarcely to twenty-four miles, gave riſe to the idea of a junction, ſo as to open a communication acroſs the kingdom, and thereby cut off the long, dangerous navigation by the Land's End, and the Pentland Firth.

An object of ſuch general utility did not eſcape the notice of Charles II. who, amidſt all his gallantries, was the great promoter of every deſign which had the ſucceſs of trade and navigation in view. That monarch propoſed to open a paſſage for tranſports, and ſmall ſhips of war, at the expence of 500,000 l. a ſum far beyond the abilities of his reign; and the deſign was conſequently laid aſide. The affairs of the continent engaged the attention of ſucceeding princes, till the beginning of the preſent reign; when the earl of Chatham, endued with all the penetration and magnanimity of an able ſtateſman, propoſed to carry the deſign immediately into execution, at the public expence, on a ſmaller ſcale than the original deſign, but ſtill ſufficient to admit veſſels of burden. Unfortunately, the reſignation of that great man, among other cauſes, loſt to theſe kingdoms the only opportunity which Nature pre-

 ſented

sented, for giving security and expedition to the British navigation in the northern seas.

The business thus abandoned a second time by the state, was now taken up by individuals, some of whom were suspected of private views inimicable to the general welfare of the community; and, from this time forward, we are to consider this great work sacrificed to the hopes of gain, of influence, and to jobbing: first, in respect to the direction of the canal, and secondly, to its dimensions. Nature had pointed out * Borrowstounness on the Forth, and Dalmure Burn-Foot, six miles below Glasgow on the Clyde, as the two extremities of this inland navigation; but such was the force of influence, that, instead of opening the east end of the canal at Borrowstounness, where there is water, at neap tides, for ships of 200 or 300 tons burden, and safe lying, it was begun upon the river Carron, at the distance of a mile from its junction with the Forth, and four miles above Borrowstounness, where vessels of burden could not float at neap tides; besides the delay and inconveniencies in navigating the Forth, and the mouth of the Carron, from floods and contrary winds; also a circuitous navigation of at least two miles.

The depth of water, and dimensions of the canal, came next under consideration, and gave rise to much controversy, between the inhabitants of the east country on the one part, and a considerable number of the citizens of Glasgow on the other. When we consider that the space to be cut did not, with all its windings, exceed 30 or 32 miles, and that this short navigation would at once open a communication between the two seas and all the countries lying upon those seas, common reason pointed out the propriety of the greatest depth of water that the nature of the

* Borrowstounness is, next to Leith, the principal trading town on the Forth; Dalmure is a small village on the Clyde, washed by a rivulet called Dalmure Burn; at the junction of which with the Clyde the canal is to be carried.

country

country would admit. This was the desire of the nation in general; and it would have been the interest of Ireland, London, Bristol, Liverpool, and other towns in England, to have subscribed towards a design in which their commerce, especially in time of war, was materially interested.

This circumstance was however neglected by the merchants; and those of the Scottish nation, who were friends to a deep canal, seeing themselves overpowered by their opponents, submitted reluctantly to an imperfect navigation. Mr. Smeaton, an able engineer from Yorkshire, had estimated the expence of 4, 7, 10, and 14 feet water *. Certain merchants of Glasgow adopted the scale of 4 feet, which, though sufficient for the trade of that city, would scarcely have answered any valuable purpose to the nation in general; and it was surmised, no doubt invidiously, that those persons never meant that the canal should join the Clyde. While a bill for cutting the proposed ditch of 4 feet water was before parliament, and on the brink of being passed, the east country gentlemen and traders took the alarm, objected to the trifling design, and, fortunately for the public, obtained a bill extending the depth of water to 7 feet †. It now became

* Having asked Mr. Smeaton, if a canal of 14 feet was practicable between those rivers, he answered in the affirmative; adding, that with sufficient funds, he could carry a canal over hills or under them, of any depth. Another engineer declares that 15 feet deep was very practicable.

Canals in Germany, and the Low Countries, have frequently 20 feet water; a sufficient depth for the largest merchantmen. They were made, not at the expence of individuals, but by the respective states of those countries, who alone should undertake such great works.

† I have been well informed, that the establishment of this navigation, instead of a very small one for lighters to Glasgow, was chiefly owing to the unwearied endeavours of Mr. Chambers, merchant in Edinburgh, a person of extensive commercial knowledge, and great public spirit. He, and other persons of knowledge in trade and navigation, insisted long and strenuously for 9 feet water, so as to admit vessels of good burden to pass through without delay, or unloading

became neceſſary to open a ſubſcription to the amount of 150,000l. which was ſoon filled; and about 130,000 l. was actually paid.

Mr. Smeaton began the arduous work in 1768; overcame almoſt inſurmountable difficulties, till he had got to the extent of 9 miles, when, on account of ſome miſunderſtanding with the managers of the canal, he reſigned that buſineſs.

Two ſtrangers from Yorkſhire ſoon preſented themſelves, and with ſuch plauſibility of ſpeech, that they were immediately engaged to carry on the work. When theſe men had completed about 9 or 10 miles, they were diſcharged, and Mr. Smeaton was again employed.

The work was now conducted upon the original principles, till it came within ſight of the river Kelvin, and ſix miles from the propoſed junction with the Clyde; when the ſubſcription, and a ſubſequent loan, being exhauſted, beyond which the proprietors were unwilling to proceed, the work was ſtopped in 1775, and hath ever ſince remained in *ſtatu quo*. The inhabitants of Glaſgow, however, by means of a collateral branch, nearly 3 miles in length, have opened a navigable communication from that city to the Forth, and thus the emporium of the north communicates with both ſides of the iſland.

After the experience of ſeveral years, the navigation by the Carron was found ſo inconvenient, that a new ſubſcription was propoſed, for opening a com-

loading their cargoes at either end, knowing the great advantages thereof to trade; and the convention of the royal boroughs highly approved of their plan. They propoſed alſo, that the expence, which, by Mr. Smeaton's eſtimate, was only about 200,000 l. ſhould be defrayed by the public, and with no more toll than what might be requiſite to keep the works in repair; and there was not a doubt but ſuch aids would have been obtained, from the forfeited eſtates, and by lotteries.

muni-

munication from Borrowstounness to join the canal near Falkirk; and in 1784, a bill was obtained in parliament for that purpose.

This work, when finished, will affect the Carron navigation, though every possible effort hath been made to shorten that passage. Some years ago, a cut was made near the mouth of the river, to cut off a bend or reach; and, in 1784, the proprietor of the adjoining lands put himself to the expence of a second cut, by which the Carron river is now totally avoided. It is a mile in length, and navigable for vessels of large burden. Had this cut been made at the first setting out, there would have been no rivalship from Borrowstounness; but the whole business hath been a series of blunders and unnecessary expence, in which the public spirited proprietors are equally involved with those, whose selfish views hath proved so detrimental to the whole design in all its stages. The expenditure, down to 1783, amounts to 212,000l. No dividend hath yet been made, or can be made, until the debts shall be discharged, when it may be supposed, that the total expenditure will be increased to 220,000l. or 11,000l. per annum, while the tonnage, at a medium of years, doth not amount to 7000l. About 6 miles, and those the most difficult in the whole tract, remain to be finished; for which government hath allowed 50,000 l. from the forfeited estates. If to these sums we add the Borrowstounness expenditure, and the two subsequent cuts at the mouth of the Carron, this canal will cost 300,000l. or upwards, previous to the first dividend; while, at the same time, the tonnage is rated so high, that vessels carrying bulky goods, sometimes prefer the long passage by the Pentland Firth.

The dimensions of this canal, though greatly contracted from the original designs, are much superior to any work of the same nature in South Britain. The

 English

English canals are generally from 3 to 5 feet deep, 20 to 40 feet wide, and the lock-gates from 10 to 12 feet; but they answer the purpose of inland carriage, from one town to another, for which alone they were designed. The depth of the canal, between the Forth and Clyde, is 7 feet; its breadth, at the surface, 56 feet; the locks are 75 feet long, and their gates 20 feet wide. It is raised from the Carron by 20 locks in a tract of 10 miles, to the amazing height of 155 feet above the medium full sea mark. At the 20th lock begins the canal of partition, on the summit between the east and west seas, and which canal of partition continues 18 miles on a level, terminating at Hamilton-hill, a mile north-west from the Clyde at Glasgow *. In some places, the canal is carried through mossy ground; in other places, through solid rock. In the fourth mile of the canal there are 10 locks, and a fine aqueduct bridge, which crosses the great road leading from Edinburgh to Glasgow. The expence of this mile amounted to 18,000l. At Kirkintulloch, the canal is carried over the water of Logie on an aqueduct bridge, whose arch is 90 feet broad; which arch was thrown over in 3 different stretches, of 30 feet each, having only 30 feet of a center, which was shifted on small rollers from one stretch to another. Though this was a thing new, and never attempted before with an arch of this size; yet the joinings are as fairly equal as any other part

* From this termination of the canal, there is a descent to the Clyde of many feet, on which account there can be no junction of these waters at an expence less than 20,000 or 30,000l. though the distance doth not exceed a mile. Should that city recover itself from the losses sustained by the American war, and the revolt of those provinces, it is probable that this junction may be effected by a new subscription. With a view to this desirable object, it might be expedient to procure an estimate of the expence from Mr. Smeaton during his abode in that country, superintending the main navigation. The depth of the Clyde at Glasgow, in spring tides, is from 6 to 7 feet; and in neap tides, 5 feet.

of

of the arch. The whole is thought to be a capital piece of masonry. There are in the whole 18 draw-bridges, and 15 aqueduct bridges of note, besides small ones, and tunnels.

The supplying the canal with water was of itself a very great work. One reservoir is above 24 feet deep, and covers a surface of 50 acres, near Kilsyth. Another, about 7 miles north of Glasgow, consists of 70 acres, and is banked up at the sluice, 22 feet deep.

Upon the whole, this canal, when finished, will be one of the greatest works in Britain, since the time of the Romans. There are 20 locks already finished; the remaining 6 miles will require 19; but the most expensive work will be to carry the canal over Kelvin river, a considerable body of water, which, in wet weather carries all before it. The depth of the Clyde, at Dalmure Burn-Foot, in spring tides, is 15 feet; and, at Dunotter, half a mile below, there are 18 feet.

The proprietors are now more sensible than ever of their error, in not forming a cut of 10 feet water, and proposals have been made to raise the banks, so as to obtain 8 feet; but this, though practicable, would prove an expensive, and possibly, a fruitless attempt. Were we to speculate upon the probable increase of trade, commerce, and wealth in that part of the kingdom 50 years hence, 100,000l. may easily be raised to deepen the canal 2 or 3 feet, being a more effectual improvement than raising the banks; and, with that idea in view, I asked Mr. Smeaton, among other questions, Whether the remaining 6 miles might not be constructed for 9 or 10 feet water? "The banks, said he, can be raised a foot; but you have put another question that requires some consideration to answer with safety." If this depth can be effected, it would certainly be doing posterity an essential service, to put it into execution, though the extra-expence might amount to 20,000l. or 25,000l.

The canal at present, when clean, admits loaded vessels of 70 or 80 tons; when completed, it will na-

 vigate

vigate thofe of 100, or upwards, built and rigged on a proper conftruction. Ships paffing this canal ought to be built on the fame plan with thofe employed by the Dutch, Hamburghers, Dantzickers, and other towns on the Baltic; that is, long and flat bottomed with lee-boards. All veffels or lighters proper for navigating large canals, fhould be fitted out and rigged with one maft, either as a floop or galliot; having on yards aloft, they can take no wind-hold, fo that they can eafily pafs the canal, when a fquare rigged fhip could not attempt it, befides the detriment done to the locks and banks by high rigged veffels.

There are veffels at prefent in the London trade, from Leith, that carry 130 tons, drawing only eight feet water, and a fmall alteration in this model will bring them to feven feet; confequently, when the canal is completed, veffels of that burden may trade from the Clyde to the Baltic, Holland, and all parts of Great Britain, without unloading at the entrance of the canal, or any impediment whatever, except from occafional frofts in the winter, and droughts in the fummer, to which all inland navigations, whether natural or artificial are fubject.

Canals, unlefs frequently cleaned, are apt to fill up in certain parts, and though the above-mentioned cut was originally feven feet, no veffel drawing above fix feet and a half can navigate on it, unlefs the practice of fhipping in fhallow bar harbours be adopted. As moft veffels draw more water in the ftern than in the bow part of the fhip, they are trimmed on an even keel, till they have paffed the fhallows, and by this method, half a foot water may be gained.

Buffes, and other unavoidable fharp-bottomed veffels belonging to the Clyde, may alfo pafs the canal by means of lighters, the expence of which cannot be great, nor would any additional tonnage be charged.

 Upon

Upon the whole, this canal, even in its contracted state, will exceed the most sanguine hopes of the public, in general utility. The distance between the entrance into the Clyde and the Forth, is, by the Pentland Firth 600 miles; by the canal, scarcely 100. But this disproportion of distance in a sea voyage is trifling, when compared with the delays, the ship-wrecks, the positive and casual expences attending a passage by the Hebrides and the Pentland Firth, or even by Land's End, particularly in time of war, when insurance run from 15 to 20 per cent. while, by means of the inland navigation, it seldom exceeds 5 per cent.

Respecting the West Highlands; the utility of a short passage between that country and the Eastern seas, need scarcely be mentioned. Hitherto the navigation of the Highlands, and the petty traffic of the inhabitants, have not extended beyond the limits of Glasgow, which was carried on by means of the Clyde; but when the remaining 6 miles shall be completed, a new world will open to their view; the scene of action will be extended; vessels of a larger and better construction will be gradually introduced; the natives will not only take and cure all the various fishes which frequent their seas, but also embark upon distant voyages, as occasions may require, for a market. Those people who have hitherto been excluded from foreign intercourse with mankind, who have been left to prowl amidst their boisterous shores, at home, will now begin to trade with the various ports of Scotland; with London, Holland, and the Baltic, where the excellency of their herrings will generally command a ready sale.

The benefits to Glasgow and its neighbourhood, from the canal in its present state, almost exceed credibility, of which the annual tonnage to and from that city, of 6 or 7000 *l.* is a strong proof. During the scarcity of 1782-83, the quantity of grain conveyed thither from England, Germany, and Dantzic by means of the canal, prevented a real famine,

famine, and faved the lives of thoufands in that populous country. By this communication alfo, the trade between Glafgow and London, at all times confiderable, is carried on with great eafe and facility, much to the fatisfaction of the parties concerned, in thofe commercial cities.

The fame benefits will extend to the populous towns of Paifly, Greenock, Port Glafgow, and the whole Weftern divifion of Scotland, when this work fhall be completed. The inhabitants of both fides of the kingdom, hitherto eftranged to one another, will drop their local prejudices, and become as they ought to be, one people, trafficking and bartering with each other, for their mutual advantage.

2. *Navigation between the Atlantic and Lochfine.*

TO render the fouthern navigation ftill more complete, it will be neceffary to fhorten the paffage from the Atlantic to the Clyde; or, in other words, from the Hebrides and Weft Highlands, to Glafgow, Greenock, and other trading towns on that celebrated river. The navigation of the Highlands being greatly lengthened by head lands and other obftacles, which muft be carefully avoided, we cannot eftimate the voyage from Cape Wrath to Glafgow at lefs than 400 miles, or 800 miles outward and homeward. This is a bold undertaking for little open boats, badly conftructed, and ftill worfe provided; and if, to the great diftance, we confider the almoft inceffant gales, the numerous iflands, lee-fhores, rocks, fands, and currents, attending thefe voyages, we may pronounce them not only long and tedious, but extremely hazardous to the poor natives, whofe neceffities compel them to fuch defperate attempts. Nor are thefe the only difficulties which they have to encounter in their paffage to Glafgow. The wind which favoured their voyage to the Mull of Cantire, becomes, confequently, adverfe after having

ing doubled that cape; they must then furl the sail, and ply at the oars, through a heavy sea, up the Firth of Clyde, sometimes for several days, before they can reach the intended port. Having disposed of their small assortment of bark, skins, wool, and dried fish; they have, in their return, to combat the same round of difficulties, toil, and danger; the whole trip employing four men, from three to five weeks. This traffic, however insignificant, is suspended during the winter season; the navigation becomes then impracticable for open boats, and the people as hath been already observed, are shut out from all intercourse with the seats of industry, population and affluence. Such is the commerce and navigation of a people inhabiting the richest, and most improveable shores in the British dominions.

The herring fishery, though an object of great importance, not only to that country, but to the West-Indies, and other dependencies abroad, labours under the same difficulties in these western seas. We have observed, that the busses fitted out from the ports of the Clyde, must, in their outward and homeward voyages, steer round the Mull of Cantire; and, as all the hopes of the adventurers depend on a speedy fishery, and a quick sale, nothing can prove more discouraging to that national staple, than the hazard, the delay, the expence, and the uncertainty of this circumnavigation.

In a dark, tempestuous night of January 1782, two busses, loaded with herrings, were wrecked, in their homeward passage from Loch Broom, on coming round the peninsula of Cantire. Many lives were lost; and as the crew of every vessel have generally a concern in the venture, several families were at once deprived of husbands, fathers, and property. It would be endless to enumerate the many catastrophes which befall these industrious people, in navigating those narrow seas, during the winter hurricanes. The melancholy tales of widows and

and fatherlefs children have too long paffed unregarded, as matters of trivial moment; and mankind, generally bufied in felfifh purfuits, have never deigned to carry the tidings to a quarter which feels for diftrefs, and is ever difpofed to relieve it.

Another inconvenience attending this navigation remains to be mentioned. It hath already been obferved, that though the arrival of the herrings be certain, yet the particular lake or bay of their rendezvous remains doubtful, until difcovered by the fowls which attend the fhoals. Sometimes the herrings are difcovered in Lochfine, and other lochs on this fide of Cantire; at other times, in Loch Broom, or amidft the Hebride iflands, on the other fide. In either cafe, the people of the one fide muft fail round that peninfula, before they can avail themfelves of the fifhery on the oppofite fide, and every boat, however fmall, muft make a circuit of more than 100 miles, before fhe arrives at fhores which lie parallel to the place from whence fhe fet out. Therefore, when all thefe circumftances are combined, and duly confidered, the expediency of a fhorter navigation between the Atlantic and the Clyde, muft appear obvious to every obferver. It is a matter not only of national utility, but of moral obligation. It touches the feelings of humanity, and calls loudly for immediate redrefs.

A ftranger from China, France, or Holland, would imagine that a work of fuch importance to a commercial nation, prefented difficulties in the execution, which could not be removed at a lefs expence than feveral millions fterling; but, how great would his furprize be, when informed, that nature had almoft completed the bufinefs, leaving only an ifthmus of five miles between the two feas; that the furface was almoft level, and that the expence of joining thefe waters upon a large fcale, would amount to no more than 60,000l!

A notion

A notion had long prevailed in Scotland, that a cut might be made between Lochfine and the Atlantic, at a village called Tarbet, on the peninsula of Cantire, where the neck of land between those waters is only a mile in length. With a view to examine into the practicability of such a work, I sailed, many years ago, from Greenock to the Tarbet*; but perceiving that this place did not fully answer my expectations, I hired a boat to Loch Gilp, 14 miles northward, where, though till then unnoticed, nature seemed to invite the public attention, and by which above 20 miles of the circuitous navigation would be saved, more than by a cut at the Tarbet.

Being fully convinced of the great utility of the work, the facility with which it might be completed, and the preference to the proposed canal at the Tarbet, I ventured to broach the subject in public, and to explain the essential difference between these two situations. A survey having since been made of both places, by authority, and being favoured with a perusal of the report, I repaired thither in 1784, and again went over the grounds, with a more than ordinary attention to every object worthy of notice by land and water; from which, as well as former observations, I am enabled to communicate the following particulars, most of which are omitted in the report.

Loch Gilp Sept. 1784. A storm of wind and rain, affords an opportunity of observing the security of this loch in all kinds of weather. The Glasgow packet of 18 tons, rides with very little rolling at the distance of half a mile on the east side of the channel. Wind S. W. good anchoring ground. A small island lies about

* Tarbet in the Scottish language, signifies an isthmus, or narrow tract of land between two waters. This term is most frequent in the Highlands, where in some places two or more lakes are nearly united.

a mile

a mile from the head of the loch, where there is safe riding, and from 6 to 8 fathom water. After passing that island there is deep water to Greenock at the distance of above 30 miles, and no hidden rocks or impediments to navigation whatever. * No winds can hurt a vessel in this loch, providing she hath good anchors and cables, nor have there been any instances of vessels being wrecked here within the memory of man. Any danger to be apprehended is from easterly winds. The loch ebbs about half a mile from its head, where it begins to deepen. If a canal shall be made at this place, one wind, without any variation, † will carry a vessel from Cape Wrath to Greenock, Campbeltown, the shire of Air, and all the towns on the Clyde, where busses are fitted out for the fisheries. The packet sails sometimes from Loch Gilp to Greenock in 6 hours. By the Mull of Cantire, she would take upon an average, a whole week, owing to contrary winds; besides the dangers and accidents of this navigation from storms, and in time of war from privateers, which swarm in that narrow pass, while the frigate stationed in those seas, lies snug in Belfast Loch, Campbeltown Bay, or Loch Ryan.

Having finished my observations at Loch Gilp, I set out with an intelligent person of that neighbourhood for Loch Crinan, on the west side of the peninsula. "The ground rises almost imperceptibly to the height of 18 feet above the sea, and the whole is composed of the most favourable soil, neither too hard nor too soft. It is properly a level valley,

* In this passage there are many safe bays and creeks, where vessels may take shelter in bad weather, without going out of their course, as east Loch Tarbet, the Kyles of Bute, Loch Nidan, Loch Strevan, Rothsay Harbour, Helle Loch, and Loch Long, all of them having sufficient water for the largest ships, the ground clean, and no rocks except at the Tarbet.

† There is a bend at the Kyles of Bute, but so very short, that in less than an hour a vessel may get through it by the assistance of the tide.

partly plowed and partly in grass, environed by hills on the north and south. Nearly at the center of the valley a rivulet divides itself, by falling into two opposite directions; one part runs east into Loch Gilp, and the other part into Loch Crinan on the west. This is properly the point of partition. The rivulet is supplied by numerous rills from the high grounds on each side, a most favourable circumstance for the purposes of a canal.

The descent on the west side is more perceptible than the former, and here the mountains approach near to each other, but there is sufficient room for a canal, and a good public road. Loch Crinan now appears. It is an extensive body of water, and ebbs half a mile or more from its head.

The views are magnificent, and to a person unacquainted with maritime affairs, the bay appears to be land-locked by hills rising on every side; the whole forming a fine natural amphitheatre.

I surveyed a creek on the south side, said to have water for ships of the line, a fine bottom, and to be perfectly secured from all winds. Mr. M'Kenzie's report, though not favourable to this loch, is however, to be relied upon, in preference to all other accounts " Loch Crinan being open to the " west is not sufficiently sheltered for vessels in the " winter time, nor is it safe to ride long in it at " any time of the year. The ground, however, is " clean, and in some parts very good; and it may " be convenient on some occasions to run for this " bay, when the wind or tide is contrary, and a vessel " bound to the northward, cannot get to Carseg, or " to the small islands of Jura, where there is better " shelter. The best anchorage is between Ilan " Daveyn, and the rock which is always above " water, that lies about a quarter of a mile east- " ward of it. In moderate weather, a ship may " stop any where northward of Ilan Daveyn, about " two cables length from the island."

We

We ſhall only obſerve further on this head, that the propoſed canal would open a paſſage immediately from the Clyde to the Atlantic, the Hebrides, the whole region of the weſt Highlands, and the great Loch Linnhe; whence, as ſhall be mentioned hereafter, a communication may be opened to Inverneſs, the Murray Firth, and the eaſtern coaſt of the kingdom. It would alſo ſhorten the paſſage from Clyde to the Orkney iſlands, to the early herring fiſheries on the coaſt of Shetland, and all thoſe channels and ſeas which are the great receptacles of herrings, white fiſh, ſeals, and whales.

Thus the cutting 5 or 6 miles would anſwer every valuable purpoſe, in that diviſion of the kingdom, but more particularly to the Highlanders, who by finding themſelves brought nearer, by 100 miles, to Glaſgow, and its communications with other parts of the iſland, would gradually forget the grievances under which they have laboured. A voyage, which frequently takes 3 weeks, would by this eaſy paſſage, be performed in 3 or 4 days, in all ſeaſons of the year, whether in time of war or peace. By cutting off the peninſula of Cantire, the voyage from Glaſgow to the Hebrides would be intirely inland, and thereby ſcreened in a great meaſure from the dreadful tempeſts of the Atlantic.

The expence of a canal of 10 feet water, and 14 locks, is eſtimated by Mr. Watts the engineeer at 48,405l. but as large buſſes, being ſharp bottomed, will require when full loaded, 11 feet, and as it is propoſed to admit veſſels of 120 upon the herring fiſhery, I conceive that 12 feet will be no more than ſufficient for the purpoſes of fiſheries*. But there is another object of very conſiderable importance, though hitherto unnoticed, for which a deep water

* It may be found neceſſary to carry the cut about half a mile along the ſide of Loch-Gilp from its head, in order to get at once into deep water, and the ſame plan may be adopted at the Crinan, which will extend the whole to at leaſt 6 miles.

canal

canal at this place would be essencially useful. That is, the expedition, facility, and security by which troops and military baggage would be conveyed between the Highlands and the Clyde, where the troops take shipping for the places of their destination.

I am happy to hear that the expediency of this navigation is now generally admitted, and that persons of rank have it seriously in contemplation. It would be still more pleasing, were government to undertake the execution thereof, at the public expence. Highways, inland navigations, the forming or repairing of harbours, have, in all ages and countries, Great Britain excepted, been considered as public works, and consequently executed by the public. In this manner, Ireland, France, Denmark and the American states, are at present carrying on very extensive navigations*. England, whose revenue far exceeds that of Ireland, Denmark, and

* It appears by the journals of the Irish House of Commons, that between the years 1753 and 1767, a sum amounting to 717,944l. or 47,863l. annually was granted by the Parliament upon inland navigations and collieries, deepening rivers, cleansing, improving, and building harbours, forming roads, building churches, hospitals, bridges, and other public works; besides the grants and bounties in favour of the linen and other manufactures, to a considerable amount annually.

France, however, claims the honour of having nearly completed the greatest inland navigation in modern times. It was undertaken by Lewis XIV. and the states of Languedoc, to open a communication between the Atlantic and the Mediterranean; the length of the canal between Port de Cette, in the Mediterranean, and Thoulouse is 153 English miles; besides a river navigation from Thoulouse to Bourdeaux of more than 100 miles. The whole inland navigation above 250 English miles, between the sea ports. The perpendicular height of the point of partition is 630 English feet, above the Sea Lock. The expence 8,12,500l. This work is still incomplete on account of shoals in the river Garonne, below Tholouse, which in dry seasons greatly interrupt the vessels. The remedy by means of a canal is estimated at 45,750l.

The canal just completed in Denmark, opens a short passage from the British sea to the Baltic, by which a navigation of some hundred miles will be saved.

America united, leaves these great national objects to the local views of traders, and speculators who clog the national commerce with excessive tonnage demands in return for the original expenditure, and annual repairs. Thus the canals in England, works which should be conducted upon the boldest plans, are stinted in every particular, and executed imperfectly, of which various instances could be produced, now too late for any effectual remedy.

England, which for a century or upwards, hath been pretending to raise empires in both hemispheres, and to rule the ocean; whose drains in support of these schemes would cover the road from Land's End to the Pentland Firth, with waggons loaded with silver †, is penurious to an extreme, where she ought to be generous, like a profligate husband who squanders his substance abroad amongst ladies of easy virtue, to whose extravagance and despotic sway, he is completely resigned; while at home, he is both niggardly and unjust.

Every Englishman who hath studied the history of his country, will coincide with this representation of the national policy, since the revolution. And it should be the endeavour of the public, to put matters into a contrary direction. National munificence, extended to national purposes, and particularly commerce, navigation, and fisheries, may be considered as making provision for posterity, besides the immediate benefit flowing therefrom to the present age.

Of

† Several years ago, a calculation was made of the extent of road, which the then national debt of 75,000,000l. would cover, supposing each waggon to contain a quantity of silver sufficient for six horses to draw, and that the waggons should keep close to one another; when it appeared that the national debt, were it realized in silver, would cover the road from London to York, and 20 miles further, being 210 miles. The distance from Land's End

Of this nature are the objects principally recommended in these sheets; the improvement of the Highlands and the fisheries of that country, to which the proposed canal will be the key-stone.

I apprehend that many persons, some influenced by a disinterested patriotic zeal, and others by less honourable motives, will propose to execute this work by means of a subscription, to be refunded, agreeable to the usual method, by tonnage dues upon such craft as shall navigate the same. To prevent those persons, and the public, from being deceived, it is necessary that the matter be stated in its true light. When a canal is proposed to be executed upon this plan, the parties concerned have at least a strong probability, if not an absolute certainty, of being repaid at the rate of 5 to 7½, or 10 per cent. annually. At present, the public funds produce 5 per cent. or upwards, without any trouble whatever; which is equal to 7½ per cent. upon a given sum expended in the manner now proposed, supposing that the canal had a *probability* in its favour, of producing that amount. The lowest expence of the proposed canal, 12 feet deep, with 14 locks, will amount to 60,000 l. The tonnage to be raised on that capital to pay 7½ per cent, will be 4,500 l. annually, besides repairs, collecting the dues, and contingent expences, which may be stated at 500 l. annually; the whole, 5000 l. We are next to consider whether the tonnage of the canal will afford that annual sum.

The navigation in question is not general, but provincial; calculated chiefly for the benefit of a considerable body of indigent people, who, by means of this canal, and other public assistance, may be brought into the line of action; and, in process of

End to the northern extremity of Scotland, by the shortest road, may be 700 miles, and the expenditures of England in foreign parts, within these last 100 years, amount to 400,000,000 l. At home, during that period, she hath expended upon inland navigation, 0 l. 0 s. 0 d.

 time,

time, be able to procure a comfortable subsistence. Secondly, to facilitate the fisheries of those districts, by opening a short passage for the busses to and from the Clyde. Possibly 10 or 12 vessels from that river may also use this navigation annually, in their voyages to the Baltic, providing that the tonnage shall be moderate; but the sum arising from these will be so trifling, and so precarious, that it cannot be brought to account. Were a communication opened between Fort William and Inverness, some coasters or traders would also navigate this canal, which could not, however, afford much aid to the subscribers, and the prospect is distant. We must therefore recur to the former statement respecting the number of decked vessels, which, with every public encouragement, may be engaged in the western fisheries, These we stated at 500; which, at 10l. each, would repay the subscribers, providing that all the busses submitted to that exorbitant demand, which is very doubtful. In summer, and in apparently moderate weather, through the whole fishing season, many vessels, to avoid the tonnage, would prefer the passage by the Mull of Cantire; probably one half of the voyages would be thus performed *: if so, the subscribers would not receive 4 per cent. supposing the 10l. to be chearfully paid by the other half, and that this toll or tonnage should not prove a strong discouragement to the fisheries. To hold out allurements for extending that branch, and at the same time, to burden it with with an annual tribute of 5000l. would, in effect, defeat the laudable intention of the public. The fishing vessels generally return with half cargoes; frequently with one fourth, and sometimes in ballast.

* Merchants trading to the Baltic have already two channels for carrying on that commerce, viz. the long navigation by the Mull of Cantire, and the short passage by the great inland canal. If the proprietors of this latter navigation lower their tonnage, few or no vessels would go either by the Mull of Cantire, or by the Crinan navigation.

These

These facts being fully sustained, any demand beyond 40s. per vessel annually upon an average, would be oppressive and detrimental to the main object. This sum, and no more, might possibly be raised by the buss fleet, or 1000l. annually, supposing 500 vessels to be actually engaged in the fisheries.

It may be argued by the friends of a subscription-navigation, that the small craft would raise a large sum. But this argument ought to have no weight with humane minds. The craft which would navigate that canal are little Highland boats, passing to and from the Clyde, with cargoes seldom amounting to 20l. each trip; and money is of such value with these people, that, to save 5s. tonnage, they would risque the voyage by the Mull of Cantire, though, in so doing, many would perish. The arguments, which have been offered against cramping the fisheries, have double force, when applied to this petty trade; the tonnage upon boats, however small, would also protract the improvement of that infant colony.

Were the Highlands in a flourishing state, abounding in people and towns, beneficially employed in all the branches depending on the fisheries, a trifle might be raised upon their decked vessels; but these desirable objects are yet at a distance; and much remains to be performed, before it would be safe or politic to levy burdens upon these indigent people, and their insignificant traffic.

Upon the whole, the objects of an annual tonnage, instead of raising 5000l. cannot, with propriety, be calculated to raise above 1000l. which, after deducting the annual expenditures upon the canal, in repairs and attendance, leaves only 500l. to the subscribers, being less than 1 per cent. upon their capital.

But even this is too much to collect from a branch which already pays considerably to government.

 Seas,

Seas, rivers, and artificial navigations, leading to these distant people, shores, and fisheries, ought at least to be free. Upon this principle, every proposal of individuals should be rejected as incompatible with the cause of humanity, the general interests of the empire, and the success of that naval bulwark by which the remaining constituent parts may be retained. A draft upon the exchequer of Scotland for 60,000l. payable to Mr. Smeaton, or Mr. Whitworth, engineers, would at once settle the matter, and gratify the wishes of a whole kingdom.

Navigation between Inverness and Fort William.

A THIRD, or northern navigation, of very considerable utility, also claims the attention of the public. Geographers have usually described Scotland under two natural divisions; the countries lying south of the Forth, and those on the north side of that river. Such people, however, who have traversed the kingdom, must have perceived that Nature seems to point out three divisions, the south, the middle, and the north.

Between the sound of Mull on the west, and the Murray Firth on the east side of the kingdom, there is a level or chasm composed of land and water, which separates the mountains of the middle division, from those of the north, so completely, that, with the assistance of art, ships might pass between them, from sea to sea.

On the west side of this extensive valley is the Linnhe-Loch, penetrating from the sound of Mull, 24 miles * north-east, and so capacious, that ships of the line have been moored as high as Inverlochy, now known by the name of Fort William or Mary-

* The miles in the following calculations, are geographical miles, 60 to a degree; and which make 69½ English statute miles.

burg.

burg. This fine salt-water lake communicates with Loch Creran, Loch Leven, and Loch Eil; all of which are navigable for vessels of burden, to whom they afford a safe retreat, when the violent gusts of wind render the Linnhe navigation hazardous.

The fish peculiar to these waters are herrings, white fish, salmon, trout, and phinoes, supposed to be the young of what the fishermen call the great trout, some of them weighing 30 pounds. The timber is birch and pine.

The proposed line of communication from Fort-William to Inverness lies in an eastern direction, and is 53 miles in length. The first branch of which is the river Lochy, issuing from the loch of that name, at the distance of 7½ miles. It is a considerable river, very rapid, and hath a fall of 80 feet. Loch Lochy is a beautiful sheet of water, 10½ miles long; half a mile broad; 90 fathom where deepest, and never freezes. It abounds in salmon, trout, and other fish peculiar to fresh water lochs: the banks are shaded with natural woods.

At the distance of a mile on the north side of this lake is Loch Arkek, nearly of the same dimensions as the former, and whose banks are shaded with very extensive woods of fir.

Keeping due east in the line to Inverness, there is a space of 2 miles without any river; the soil gravel and earth. This may be called the canal of partition, being the highest ground in the whole extent of the valley between the two seas, and rises 22 feet above Loch Oich, to which it is joined on the east. Loch Oich is 4 miles long; a quarter of a mile wide; of sufficient depth for the purpose of navigation, and its surface is about 100 miles above high water at neap tides. Its banks, and some small islands, are beautified with woods. Here is also limestone sufficient for the supply of the whole country from sea to sea, as soon as the navigation shall be formed.

Near the head of Loch Nevish, on the western

ocean, facing the Isle of Skie, issues a rivulet called Joine Water; which, after a short course, falls into Loch Quich, 8 miles long; from thence the united waters keep a south-east direction of 12 or 15 miles, when they fall into Loch Garry, 6 miles long; 2 miles further, these auxiliary streams reach Loch Oich, from whence a river of the same name flows 5 miles eastward into Loch Ness; this river hath a fall of 55 feet, over a gravelly bottom, from 30 to 40 yards wide.

Lochness, the glory of the North Highlands*, is 22 miles long; from 1 to 2 miles broad; and from 5 to 140 fathoms deep. This loch hath some qualities peculiar to itself, some few waters excepted; it never freezes; and, in winter, it is covered with a steam or smoke, proportioned to the severity of the weather. It even softens the rigour of the air in that northern climate, and assists vegetation, particularly trees, which, on the south side, form one continued wood of small birch, ash, and oak. Its waters are also salubrious and extremely favourable to longevity. The fish are salmon, trout, pike, and eels. The surrounding woods and mountains of this loch, and through the whole tract which we have been describing, besides small cattle, sheep, and goats, are also frequented by stags, roes, harts, ptarmigans, grous, and black game; likewise the scarce bird called the capercally, or cock of the wood. The principal waters which supply this lake, exclusive of the Oich before-

* There is about 40 miles northward, in the county of Sutherland, a lake called Loch Shin, which winds beautifully, in a course of near 20 miles, amongst hills whose declivities to the edge of the loch are generally fringed with wood. The waters of this loch form a considerable river, which forces its way in a copious torrent through a glen darkened with over-hanging trees. In one place it forms a mighty cascade from side to side, and in rainy weather is heard at a great distance. This river, after winding through a romantic country, falls into the Firth of Dornoch, at the Ferry of Invershin, about 25 miles from the sea.

mentioned,

mentioned, flow from the western coast to Loch Glunny, and from thence through a valley of many miles, called Glen Morison, where they fall into Loch Ness, near Fort Augustus *.

From the eastern extremity of the lake issues the river Ness, gliding in a copious stream through a tract of 8 miles, to Inverness, where it falls into Loch Beaulie, a capacious salt-water lake, which communicates with the sea at a narrow strait called Ardersier, guarded by the modern Fort George. The river Ness runs upon gravel, 40 to 80 yards wide; its greatest depth 4 or 5 feet; the declivity of the surface 45 feet. The tide flows about 1 mile above the town; but, on account of floods, and other obstructions, the cheapest and most effectual navigations would be to make cuts along the sides of the rivers, which is found to be practicable.

The whole line of communication from the Sound of Mull to Inverness, comprises an extent of 82 miles, and is thus composed of land and water, viz.

Linnhe Loch † —	24	River Lochy —	7
Loch Lochy —	10	—— Oich —	5
—— Oich —	4	—— Ness —	8
—— Ness —	22		
	60		20

Land, from Loch Lochy to Loch Oich, the level 122 feet above high water at neap tides — — — } 2

* The garrison at Fort-Augustus are supplied with provisions and stores from Inverness, by means of a galley of 60 tons, which ornaments this fine sheet of water.

† Mr. Mackenzie, whom I have followed, makes this loch only 24 miles.

Lakes

Width of the canal 70 feet; depth 10; Length of the locks 90 feet; width 25.	Lakes	60
	Rivers	20
	Land	2
		82

The navigation ſaved in a voyage from Inverneſs to the Sound of Mull, above	200
Ditto, from Buchanneſs to ditto — —	127
Ditto, to veſſels keeping the outſide of the Orkneys, at ſeaſons when the Pentland Firth cannot be navigated — —	187

Veſſels of 9 feet water might paſs from Inverneſs to Fort-William in 3 days; ſmall craft much ſooner. The voyage by the Pentland Firth is upon an average 2 weeks, ſometimes 2 months.

The objects of this northern navigation are, for the moſt part, ſimilar to thoſe of the ſouth: but as the expence will be nearly in the proportion of three to one, viz the ſouthern canal 60,000 l. the northern ditto 164,000 l. beſides the value of grounds to be purchaſed, I ſhall attempt to ſtate the principal circumſtances relative to the latter, by which the reader will be able to form ſome concluſion upon the propriety or impropriety of the expenditure thereon.

The leading arguments in favour of the ſouthern canal are the improvement of the Weſt Highlands, and their fiſheries. In thoſe reſpects the ſame arguments are applicable to this on the north. If a new road or channel of communication be neceſſary on the ſouth ſide of the Grampian Mountains, another road is alſo neceſſary on the north ſide of that ridge; and nature, as before obſerved, hath done much towards this deſirable work. We have alſo, as auxiliary arguments, mentioned the benefits which the people of the Lowlands, inhabiting the ſouth-weſt parts of the kingdom, would derive from the canal at Crinan. It is ſtill more neceſſary to enforce this ſubject, reſpecting the people inhabiting the north-east side; who, far removed from the seat of government, Edinburgh, Glasgow, and other commercial marts, lie under the same inconveniencies, climate and soil excepted, as the Hebrides and western shore.

This district was considered of such importance in antient times, as to draw thither the fierce Danes and other warlike people, from the northern hive of Scandinavia; who, as appears from history, tradition, hieroglyphic pillars, urns, and other monuments, maintained a long and bloody struggle, in the hopes of a final establishment; which, however, they could not effect.

Leaving those ages of hostility, we shall attempt a review of these shores in their present half-improved state.

Inverness, capital of the north, a town of great antiquity, and occasionally the seat of kings, stands in the centre of a line of coast extending above 270 miles in length. The northern side reaches to Dungsbyhead, at the east entrance of the Pentland Firth, and from thence to Cape Wrath on the west. This district lies on the north side of the proposed communication with the west sea, and comprehends the counties of Ross, Sutherland, and Caithness, which compose the third natural division of the kingdom. It is entirely a Highland country; tho' along the east coast the inhabitants speak both languages promiscuously. The mountains of the West Highlands generally extend to the sea, which in many parts they over-hang in a bold magnificence. On the eastern side, nature hath been more indulgent. The district around Inverness is level and fertile; as also the whole coast of Rossshire to the distance of 20 miles from the sea, producing good crops of wheat, oats, and barley. After passing the Firth of Dornoch into Sutherland, the low country diminishes in breadth, and at the northern boundary of that county, the

mountains

mountains dip into the sea. From this pass, called the Ord of Caithness, the hills begin gradually to recede, and here the country is level and very improveable.

The chief produce of this division is grain, cattle, timber of various kinds, white marble and limestone. The river Ness is the great thoroughfare for salmon between the sea and Lochness. They are taken in cruives by a society of distant monopolizers, who farm the river, at a considerable rent annually, to the great prejudice of the natives, who are totally excluded from the benefit of this delicious Heaven-directed food. The waters of the Beaulie are still more valuable. To the fish peculiar to inland lakes, as salmon, here farmed also by monopolizers, are added the various riches of the ocean, particularly a small but well-flavoured species of herrings, which the inhabitants capture at pleasure, for home use, and sometimes for manure, being too small for curing. This species of the herring, salmon, and white fish, abound upon the whole line of coast we have been describing; but though the gentlemen of the north are both patriotic and great improvers, the generality of the peasants are miserably poor and wretched.

Were the proposed line of navigation opened to the great western fisheries, and to all the Hebride Isles, a new species of traffic and commercial intercourse would immediately arise; markets of reciprocal benefit would enliven both shores, and give employment to all those who prefer useful industry to indigence and idleness, of whom there are many thousands in this very remote district.

Nor is it the Highlands only, that requires the aid of a communication between the two seas. Due east from Inverness, the Murray Firth washes a coast of 105 miles to Buchanness, the eastern extremity of Aberdeenshire.

The

The climate along the banks of the Murray Firth is moist, and the soil excellent, as appears from the exports of grain to Glasgow, and the west Highlands. This country hath also many considerable woods, much iron ore, and some lead. The sea is bountiful in white fish and salmon, particularly the latter; which, being mostly farmed, are taken at the entrance of the rivers Findhorn, Lossie, Spey, and Devron, to the value of some thousand pounds annually. Besides the maritime districts on the Murray Firth, there are sundry extensive vallies which penetrate far into the back country, winding beautifully amidst lofty mountains, to whose heathy appearance, the verdant vallies form an agreeable contrast.

Each valley hath, as usual, its stream of water gliding through the center in numerous meanders; extremely beautiful, and often fringed with woods. The principal vallies are Strath-Spey, Strath-Avon, Strath-Devron, and Strath-Bogle, whose numerous inhabitants, aided by the patriotic exertions of the families of Gordon, Fife, Finlater, Grant, Forbes; and, in general, the whole gentry of these parts, are emerging from idleness, and bid fair, with further encouragement, to become valuable colonies, and useful members of the community.

But these shores and vallies, though thus abounding in people disposed for industry; and though amply supplied in the produce of land and water, labour under a natural misfortune, which no human efforts can remove. A ridge of hills, called the Grampian Mountains, forms an almost impassable chain from Loch Lomond to Aberdeen. This, nearly crossing the kingdom from sea to sea, cuts off the northern counties from all inland communications with the south and west, during the winter; nor do the narrow steep passes admit conveyance of goods, even in summer.

All mercantile intercourse, with the west and south-

ſouth-weſt parts of the kingdom, muſt therefore be carried round by the long, the tedious, and the very hazardous navigation of the Pentland Firth; and all veſſels paſſing to and from the herring and white fiſheries of the Hebrides, muſt alſo hazard the ſame navigation; though in winter, the ſeaſon of the large herrings, and moſt proper for curing, this paſſage is almoſt impracticable.

The ſame inconvenience attends the inhabitants of the Weſt Highlands, in procuring from the eaſt coaſt thoſe ſupplies of grain and meal which their native mountains do not afford in ſufficient plenty for half of the inhabitants, and which Ireland ſometimes denies them. Of theſe particulars, I was furniſhed with an affecting narrative by perſons principally engaged in this trade, for the ſupply of the Hebrides, as well as the main land.

Before ſufficient cargoes of grain can be threſhed out, or grinded into meal, the long nights, and almoſt inceſſant ſtorms of the winter, have commenced. In this ſeaſon, the merchant ſends his veſſel from the latitude of Mull, round Cape Wrath; from thence, along the coaſt of the Pentland Firth, amidſt contending elements, jarring currents, and rapid tides, where ſhe ſtruggles to paſs the ſtrait, or to get into ſome creek, where ſhe may elude the impending rocks, and all the dangers of a lee-ſhore, though from ſuch creek, if the wind blows ſtrong from the eaſtern points, ſhe cannot proceed with any degree of ſafety.

After paſſing the rapid ſtrait of 7 miles, between the mainland and the Orkneys, where ſpring tides run at the rate of 7 miles an hour, the veſſel ſees herſelf on the unprotected cold coaſt of Caithneſs, Sutherland, Roſs-ſhire, or the Murray Firth, where, if ſo fortunate as to make the deſtined creek or port, ſhe loads her cargo; and hath again to encounter the ſame train of difficulties in her return. The trip, outward and homeward, frequently employs plays three months; in the mean time, the unhappy people on the western ſhores are reduced to the greateſt diſtreſs.

At length, when the long-wiſhed-for veſſel appears on the coaſt, thoſe perſons who have been able to collect a few ſhillings, flock to the beach; when, to the unſpeakable diſappointment of the merchants and purchaſers, the meal is often ſo heated, by the length of the voyage, that no perſon can remain in the hold above three or four minutes without being ſuffocated. Frequently the meal is damaged by ſalt water, and found in lumps unfit for human uſe; but even in this ſtate, it is eagerly purchaſed by thoſe unhappy people, at a price enhanced by the extra expence of a long voyage. By the propoſed inland communication, the whole trip outward and homeward, would not, at a medium, require above 10 days, between the ſound of Mull and Findhorn, Portſoy, and other towns on the Murray Firth; beſides the ſafety of the veſſels, and the good condition of the cargoes.

Conſidering this voyage in a general view, its benefits will extend more or leſs to the whole ſouthern coaſt of Scotland, to Liverpool, Briſtol, and Ireland. Veſſels trading to the Baltic, and which cannot navigate the ſhallow canal between the Clyde and the Forth, might here find a ſafe paſſage during the greateſt part of the year. The facility of this conveyance to the army is alſo obvious. Here is a chain of modern fortreſſes, viz. Fort George at the eaſt end of the paſs, Fort Auguſtus in the centre, and Fort William on the weſt; which ſerve, particularly in time of war, as barracks and magazines, from whence detachments of the army may be ready to ſail on the ſhorteſt notice. By means of this navigation, therefore, a ſhort, ſafe, and commodious military intercourſe may be kept up between theſe detachments; and alſo between the two ſeas, upon the oppo-

ſite

sea sides of the island, which no enemy could annoy or interrupt.

Thus the three above-mentioned canals would open a circumnavigation, within the heart of the kingdom, to the unspeakable benefit of commerce and the fisheries. A vessel setting out from Inverness to Edinburgh on the east side of the Island, might return by Glasgow, the Hebrides, and other parts on the west side; and so, *vice versa*, as might seem most beneficial to the parties concerned. Inverness, which is well situated for commerce, would become the emporium of the north, a centrical port between the Atlantic and the east sea, supplying navigators in stores and provisions, giving employment to the industrious, and diffusing universal comfort amongst a people whose patience is completely exhausted.

This circumnavigation, amounting to about 500 miles, would include almost the whole trading part of Scotland: a circumstance which requires the most serious attention; and the more so, when we consider with what facility it might be accomplished, and the smallness of the expence, compared to the solid and permanent advantages to the Highlands in particular, and to the trade of these kingdoms in general, as will appear by the following statement:

Completing 6 miles of the canal between the Forth and Clyde, 7 feet water, by which vessels of 100 tons, built on a certain construction, would save near 500 miles, and elude privateers.	The money already advanced.
Cutting 2 miles of land, and deepening 20 miles of rivers, or rather, by making canals on the sides of these rivers 10 feet deep, between Fort William and Inverness, which would save near 200 miles.	£. 164,000

Cutting

Cutting 5 miles between Loch Crinan and Lochfine, 12 feet deep, which would save above 100 miles.	60,000
Expence not yet provided for —	£. 22[illegible],000

The accumulated loss sustained by the tedious and hazardous passage round the Pentland Firth, in delays, damages at sea, shipwrecks*, captures, extra freight and insurance, amounts, in one year only, to more than would complete the above works of general utility to commerce and navigation; and if to this we add the great object of relieving the distresses of 300,000 or 400,000 people; of bringing them forward into the line of action; and of opening new sources of commerce and wealth within our own island, it is matter of astonishment that these works have not been completed long ago.

Expediency of laying the Foundation of Towns in the West Highlands.—Plan of those Towns.—Estimates of the Expence.

THE necessity of bringing the Highlanders nearer to the Low Countries, by means of inland navigations, hath been stated, as the ground work in the proposed plan of national improvement. The facility by which that business may be completed hath also been explained; and no argument of any weight can be advanced against its being carried into execution. A requisition, founded on humanity, justice, and national expediency, cannot have many opponents. Happy would it be was this the only expence necessary to extend the fisheries,

* Numbers of people in the Orkney islands get a living by attending the shores in stormy weather, where they find the timbers, also casks, and other floating parts of the cargoes of vessels that have been broke to pieces on the rocks.

 and

and to eſtabliſh in thoſe parts a populous colony of induſtrious ſubjects. In a country where ſoil and climate have been ſo niggardly of their favours, ſome further expenditures are poſitively requiſite. The people ſhould be comfortably lodged, and accommodated with proviſions, firing, ſtores of ſalt, materials and utenſils for the herring and white fiſheries, independent of lairds, ſtewards, or intermediate jobbers. They ſhould enjoy, in the moſt ample manner, and in all poſſible caſes, the freedom and ſpirit of the Britiſh conſtitution. The idea of feudal ariſtocracy, and of feudal ſubordination ſhould be utterly extinguiſhed; and every man, of whatever degree or profeſſion, ſhould be maſter of his own time in all ſeaſons, whether at the height of the harveſt, or the fiſheries, without the interference of any ſuperior whatever. This implies the erection of towns at convenient diſtances, and in the moſt eligible ſituations, on thoſe extenſive ſhores; which towns ſhould be endued with all the privileges of royal boroughs, for the diſtribution of juſtice, as well as the conveniency of the inhabitants in whatever relates to trade, navigation, and fiſheries.

After having ſelected the particular lakes deſtined to become the ſcenes of population and buſineſs, it would be neceſſary to examine into the depth of water, the prevailing directions of the winds, and their effects; alſo the rivulets, woods, metals, ſoil, and whatever may be uſeful or requiſite in the foundation, advancement, and ſucceſs of the town. This previous enquiry into the beſt ſituations on each reſpective lake or bay, being a matter of conſiderable conſequence to the preſent age, as well as poſterity; and alſo to prevent bribery, jobbing, influence, connivance, partiality, or breach of truſt; a committee of diſintereſted perſons, having no connections in, or with the Highlands, might be appointed by government; and, to prevent miſtakes, the report, when completed, might be laid before parliament for their inſpection, by which means the proprietors of lands in the Highlands, and the public at large, would have a fair opportunity of canvaſſing the buſineſs, of pointing out errors, if any occurred, in the ſelection of the place or places, and where better ſituations might be found.

The report being agreed upon, either in its original ſtate or with amendments, an act of parliament would enable the committee to purchaſe certain lands thus approved of, ſufficient, not only for the erection of the buildings after ſpecified, accommodated with ſmall gardens and fields, but likewiſe for the future increaſe of the towns by individuals, independent of the original proprietors.

Every town would alſo require a territorial revenue of 300 pounds or upwards, for the ſupport of a clergyman, free-ſchool, a ſmall annuity to a reſident ſurgeon, a ſuperintendent of the fiſheries, and ſuch other purpoſes as the parliament ſhould deem expedient during the infancy of ſuch towns.

The price of lands, thus purchaſed, for the various purpoſes of building, accommodating, and endowing every reſpective town, may be eſtimated at 10,000l.

The buildings poſitively neceſſary at the firſt eſtabliſhment of the propoſed towns, are,

1. A key or breaſt for veſſels of 15 feet water or upwards.

2. A range of warehouſes for caſks, ſtaves, hoops, ſalt, nets, ſails, cordage, and other materials for the building of boats and decked veſſels; alſo for ſtoring fiſh, oil, grain, meal, ſkins, wool, flax, hemp, bark, timber, kelp, coals, and other bulky articles. The various apartments in theſe warehouſes

to be numbered and put under certain regulations *.

3. Sheds for persons employed in gutting, salting, and curing the herrings and white fish, and other purposes; also lofts where those persons may be sheltered at night from the inclemency of the weather †. It may occasionally happen, that the loch or bay,

* In 1776, Mr. Alexander, a merchant of Derry, for the convenience of carrying on the herring fishery in Loch Swilly, began to erect a set of buildings composed of the following denominations, viz. a complete salting house, consisting of a range of houses for all the operations, divided into four apartments, one of 20 feet by 18 as a store-room for coarse salt, which will contain from 150 to 200 tons; another room of the same dimensions for fine salt; a third, the same size, for receiving the herrings from the boats, and gutting them; and a fourth for a cooper's shop. All these apartments communicate with a second range, 80 by 18 feet, which is filled with vessels for striking the herrings, that is, putting them in salt 10 or 12 days; and this range communicates with a third, 80 by 14 feet, in which the herrings, being taken from the vessels above mentioned, are barrelled and finally cured for the shipping. Besides these, there is a dwelling house for the clerks, and other persons employed in that business, of 28 by 14 feet. All the buildings are of stone, lime, and slate, and proof against all weather. The finishing house contains the boats when not employed, and over it is a loft for the nets. Over the curing house is a capacious loft for empty barrels; over the cooper's shop are apartments for the workmen; and over the gutting house is a hoop store. These buildings cost 5 or 600l. They are a market where the country people sell their herrings, and where 100,000 may be lodged for the various operations of gutting, salting, and packing. The fishing season in this loch is from the middle of October to Christmas; the price paid by the merchant to the country boats is 4s. 6d. per 1000 of large herrings, 500 of which fill a barrel. The above-mentioned buildings might serve as a model to the proposed erections in Scotland, for which purpose an architect might examine them, and also converse with the proprietor respecting any improvements which could be made on the original plan.

† The gutting is performed by women and children, who, for the small pittance of three half-pence per barrel, travel to the fisheries from all parts of the country, and through all inclemencies of weather, carrying on their backs the infants, the meal, kettle, and other little matters, which the townless coasts do not afford. Their situation, while in this employ, during the winter season, without proper shelter, food and cloathing, reflect dishonour on the boasted humanity of Britons.

where

where a town is erected, will have no fishery, while the next loch shall be crowded with herrings and vessels. Every town should therefore be furnished with materials for erecting temporary sheds or tents, for the conveniency of persons employed in these fisheries upon shore.

4. A small market-place.

5. A corn mill.

6. A church; also a house, garden, and glebe for the minister, with proper offices.

7. A school-house, where reading, writing, the common rules of arithmetic, and practical navigation may be taught gratis.

8. A house and shop for an apothecary skilled also in surgery.

9. A house for a superintendent of the fisheries.

10. A public inn, with stabling, garden, and other conveniencies.

11. A piece of ground for a common, with the privilege of a stone quarry to the inhabitants, free of all charges or demands whatever.

12. There might possibly be some difficulty in procuring useful mechanics to settle in these remote parts, previous to the regular establishment of fisheries and commercial intercourse. Therefore, to encourage adventurers, as coopers, ship and house carpenters, net makers, blacksmiths, masons, &c. it would be necessary to build 15 or 20 dwelling houses, where these persons might live rent-free; each house to be accommodated with three small inclosures. 1. For a garden and offices. 2. For potatoes. 3. For the support of a cow. The tenure of these houses and fields might be for a given number of years; renewable at the discretion of government, if further indulgence should be thought necessary; and ultimately, upon the full establishment of a town and corporation, to become the property of such town, and to form a branch of its revenue.

Such indulgencies as theſe, with variety of fiſh at no expence; exemption from taxes and exciſes upon coals, ſalt, &c. liberty to ſell their herrings to veſſels upon the bounty, or others, at their own option; alſo to take, cure, and dry white fiſh, not as ſlaves, but as freemen; with ſmall annual bounties from government, and other particulars formerly ſtated, might contribute to draw thither uſeful workmen and fiſhers from every quarter, and give ſtability to all the valuable purpoſes propoſed by the public.

Conſidering the great plenty of materials for building, in theſe parts, as ſtone, lime, timber, ſlate, and the cheapneſs of workmanſhip; a village thus compoſed of ſmall neat houſes, might be raiſed by contract at no great expence. The whole, including the key or keys, ſtorehouſes, church, &c. might poſſibly be completed for 10,000l.; conſequently the founding of eight commodious ports, with all the conveniencies for extending the weſtern fiſheries, improving a coaſt of 250 miles, beſides the interior part, and three hundred iſlands, would coſt only — — 80,000

Endowing of ditto as ſtated above —	80,000
Expence of eight towns — —	160,000
Ditto of inland navigations for opening ſhort communications with the Highlands and the fiſheries, as ſtated in page 433 —	224,000
Total amount of the original expenditure	£.384,000

which would be repaid in a few years by the increaſe of trade, fiſhing, and navigation; beſides opening new markets for Engliſh manufactures, and the increaſe of revenue thereby.

In the firſt progreſs of theſe towns it would be eſſentially neceſſary to have a view to conveniency, health, cleanneſs and neatneſs. I have often obſerved and lamented the inattention to theſe objects in in Scotland, where they are made subservient to the private interest of individuals, whose influence hath too much weight with magistracy, some of the parties concerned being themselves magistrates, or related by marriage, or consanguinity, to those in office. To this is owing the medley of symmetry and irregularity, of width, and of narrowness, which we often perceive in the same street. To this is also owing that odious deformity, by stairs on the outside of the buildings; and the permitting avaricious persons to counteract the intentions of magistrates, with the view of extorting a price disproportioned to the real value of their property. "If you do not, says "Gripus, give me 500l. for my ground (intrin-"sically not worth 200) I will suffer the old "thatched house, kiln, or barn, to remain in the "middle of your fine new street, or I will build "upon the same." But these persons should be informed, that there is a house near Westminster Abbey, which hath a controlling power over the whole island, to whom, in the dernier resort, even the most obstinate extortioner must submit with shame, and considerable expence.

When towns are to be erected upon new foundations, the streets should be of considerable width, laid out in straight lines, crossing each other at right angles. The houses should be built, as nearly as possible, on the same model, and of the same height. A strict uniformity should also be observed in the colour of the stone, lime and slate; in the size and adjustment of the windows. A variation in any of these particulars destroys the beauty of the whole. The man therefore, who from want of taste, from avarice, or ill-natured obstinacy, remains inexorable to the intreaties of his fellow citizens, should be considered as a nuisance in society, and as such excluded for ever from holding any place of honour or profit, in the town where he resides.

To prevent such consequences in the towns proposed above, the committee appointed to superintend that business, should publish on copper-plate, the plan of each town, and oblige every builder to submit thereto, under the penalty of forfeiting the premises to the town or corporation where trespasses shall be committed *. But there are objects of still greater importance, to which the committee, in this stage of the business, should pay particular regard; first, the means of inducing strangers to build; and secondly, the means whereby these strangers and their families may be supported through a winter of six months continuance, and often longer.

Though it may be necessary for the encouragement of the first settlers in these wilds, not only to accommodate them with houses, but also offices, garden-ground and fields, rent free; those who arrive at later periods, having the benefit of society, and of necessary supplies, cannot expect to be indulged to the same extent as the first settlers; the bountiful aid of government will be gradually withdrawn, but not to cease until at least 200 houses shall be built, which may be considered as the second stage of the business. The place will then assume the appearance of a town, and port; men will also embark in various branches of trade and fisheries; magistrates will be appointed, and a regular policy established.

For the speedy and effectual accomplishment of this desirable event, a portion of ground equal to a quarter of an acre should be given in perpetuity, and without a quit rent, to every person, their heirs and executors, who shall erect a house thereon agreeable to the plan for the regulation of the buildings; provided also that the expenditure on each house

* From the scantiness of level ground on the Highland shores, and the necessity of preferring the best situations for navigation, however improper the coast or beach for the purpose of building, the regularity and symmetry recommended in the erection of towns cannot be put in practice in many parts of the Highlands.

shall

ſhall not be under 25l. excluſive of offices, wells, and other conveniences *.

The proſpect of comfortable lodgings, plentiful ſupplies of roots and vegetables, and principally the poſſeſſion of a freehold, increaſing in its value proportioned to the increaſe of trade, and the number of inhabitants, would induce numbers to cooperate with government in raiſing theſe towns, and to proſecute the fiſheries with unwearied perſeverance. A town compoſed of 200 freeholders, beſides labourers and other inferior claſſes of people, would, in the ſituations hereafter mentioned, ſoon become poſſeſſed of decked veſſels, wherries and boats; a place of traffic or market for all the varieties of fiſh peculiar to thoſe ſeas, for oil, kelp, ſalt, coals and timber; for grain, meal, cattle, ſheep, poultry, and other produce of the main land, and the contiguous iſland, where, to ſum up the whole, the inhabitants of the town, and country; the hardy fiſherman, the coaſter, and the merchant, would ſupply and be ſupplied, in the productions of ſea and land.

Speculators, and ſuperficial writers, may propoſe ſchemes for erecting towns upon eaſier terms to the public, and conſequently more flattering to government; but every plan that doth not hold out allurements ſuited to the expence and hazards of the firſt ſettlers, will deceive that public and thoſe adventurers. Such perſons do not take into the account the various circumſtances of ſoil, climate, proviſions, firing, and neighbourhood. The uncertainty of the herrings, and the heavy expences to the traders and fiſhers, whether ſucceſsful or otherwiſe; theſe and other particulars being omitted, through ignorance or deſign, the plauſible ſcheme may amuſe

* In Ireland, where many villages have been erected or re-built within theſe laſt 50 years, the loweſt expence of a cabbin, as it is called, is 25l. they riſe from that to 40l. the coſt of a good farm houſe.

the

the public, but like all other quackeries, it will not bear the teſt of cloſe inveſtigation.

The moſt eligible Situations for Towns in the Weſt Highlands.

THE Weſt Highlands being compoſed of a double coaſt, viz. the main land and the Hebride iſlands, the ſituations which can afford the moſt general benefit to both, claim the preference.

All ſenſible, diſintereſted perſons, who are acquainted with thoſe parts, will at once ſee the propriety of chooſing the coaſt of the main land for the ſeat of towns; becauſe, lying in the centre, between an extenſive back country upon the eaſt, and the Hebrides directly in front on the weſt, the benefits of the propoſed line of towns, thus judiciouſly placed, would pervade the whole internal diſtricts of the continent, to the diſtance of 40 or 50 miles; and, in the north Highlands, from ſea to ſea *. By means of theſe towns, the inhabitants of the hills, valleys, and glens, would be drawn from ſlothful inactivity to uſeful induſtry; the farmer would find a ready market for his grain, potatoes, cattle, ſheep, ſkins, wool, tallow, butter, eggs, hemp and flax; the weaver for his cloth; the ſpinſter for her yarn; young perſons for their knitted ſtockings; every art and profeſſion down to the broom maker, would derive immediate benefit from a communication with populous thriving market towns, thus eſtabliſhed along the coaſt; while theſe towns, thus ſupplied with country ware, would in return furniſh the farmer,

* From Inverneſs northward, the main diſtance between the eaſtern and weſtern ſhores doth not exceed 60 miles; but if we take the diſtance between the heads of ſome of the oppoſite lochs, as Loch Broom on the weſt, which is every where navigable, to Dingwall at the head of the Firth of Cromarty, the diſtance is only 24 miles; from Loch Broom to the head of the Firth of Dornoch, 30 miles; and from the head of Calva Bay on the weſt; to ditto, 35 miles.

grazier,

granier, mechanic and ſpinſter, with herrings and white fiſh, both freſh and cured. The latter of which would, with potatoes, prove a comfortable ſupport through the winter, when grain and meal often fail, and when ſupplies cannot be procured elſewhere *. The ſame effects would extend to the Hebride iſlands lying in the front of theſe towns, where

* Were the diſtreſſes of thoſe inland parts, for the want of grain during the winter, more generally known, that circumſtance would contribute to enforce the expediency of eſtabliſhing towns and markets on the propoſed plan without delay. The ſmall portion of half-ripened oats and barley which hath been ſecured from the autumnal rains, is immediately threſhed out for the uſe of the family, but chiefly to pay the rents at the then market price, which we ſhall ſtate at 15 ſhillings per boll. When the ſpring arrives, and no grain being left for ſeed, the farmer muſt raiſe money by every poſſible means, to purchaſe that article, ſometimes the individual grain, which he had ſold a few months before, and which was ſtored for the purpoſe of ſelling it to the farmers at an advanced price, proportioned to the ſcarcity of the article, when moſt wanted. His family alſo requires a freſh ſupply, which he buys at the ſame diſadvantage, and is thus kept from year to year, at the ſole mercy of a laird, ſteward, or jobber, for daily ſubſiſtence, at a price which he can ill afford to pay. This is the general ſtate of certain internal diſtricts, in what is called good ſeaſons; but, when the crops fail, through a long continuance of cold or wet weather, which generally happens every third or fourth year, the diſtreſs is beyond deſcription, of which the following circumſtance will convey ſome idea to thoſe who are unacquainted with the ſtate of that country. " In the year ———, ſays a gentleman, who then reſided " in the Highlands, a poor farmer from a diſtant part of the country " appeared at our gate with three ſmall horſes, imploring three bolls " of meal to ſave his family and ſome of his neighbours, who having " exhauſted their ſtock, had collected three guineas to purchaſe " grain or meal, on which errand he was commiſſioned. We " had a few bolls left, but our own people being in the ſame " ſituation with this man, I could afford him no relief, and adviſed him to proceed to Inverneſs, where grain, in ſcarce ſeaſons, " is imported by the merchants. The man went away greatly dejected, his horſes were reduced to ſkeletons, and very unfit for " the journey home, under a load. In a few days, this poor man " appeared again, to acquaint me that neither grain nor meal could " be had at Inverneſs, or elſewhere in that country; and that his family and neighbours were, by that time, looking out for his return with the means of their preſervation. The account of the " ſcarcity

where ſcarcity and famine carry off numbers annually. Theſe iſlands, though in general rugged, and incapable of agriculture, have many ſmall, well-inhabited valleys and ſtraths upon their ſhores and lakes. The produce is ſimilar to that of the main land; and alſo their wants. To this range of iſlands, containing 48,000 people, the propoſed towns would give immediate relief, beſides enabling them to extend the fiſheries, for which buſineſs all iſlanders are naturally adapted.

If theſe towns would diffuſe ſuch bleſſings amongſt the remote diſtricts, and iſlands, we may eaſily conceive the ſtill greater benefits to the centrical line and coaſt on which they ſhall be immediately placed. The object is great, humane and politic; immortal fame awaits thoſe in power who ſhall accompliſh it. The ſituations mentioned in the former editions, for the erection of towns, having been generally approved of, by mariners, fiſhers, traders, and natives of all degrees in life; I reſume the ſubject with conſiderable ſatisfaction, and ſhall add ſuch further particulars as may tend to elucidate the ſame to perſons in both kingdoms who are unacquainted with thoſe parts. The nautical information communicated to the public by that able and experienced navigator Mr. Mackenzie, being too expenſive for general ſale,

" ſcarcity at Inverneſs rendered my ſituation more embarraſſing " than before; our own people, and the poor, had a prior claim " to my attention; I poſitively refuſed that relief which muſt " have been given at the expence of others, in the ſame ſituation. " The poor man, having liſtened with impatience, and watery eyes, " to the dreadful words, repreſented in very moving terms, the " feelings and ſituation of his family and neighbours, ſhould he " return empty-handed," 'Give me, ſaid he, one boll, and you ' ſhall have the price of three bolls; here, Sir, are the three guineas, ' I muſt not go back without meal, otherwiſe we muſt all periſh, ' there is no remedy elſewhere.' " Unable to reſiſt the ſimple, " but genuine eloquence of the poor man, I ordered him a boll of " meal, with which, and his money, I deſired he would inſtantly " depart to his family; which order he immediately obeyed in " tranſports of joy and gratitude,"

I ſhall

I ſhall give his remarks verbatim, in turned commas, relative to the propoſed ſituations, that of Loch Gilp excepted.

1. The firſt town ſhould be at the propoſed canal between Lochfine and the Atlantic, in that diviſion of Argyleſhire called Knapdale.

"* Loch Crinan, being open to the weſt, is not " ſufficiently ſheltered for veſſels in the winter-" time; nor is it ſafe to ride long in it at any " time of the year. The ground, however, is " clean, and in ſome parts very good; and it " may be convenient, on ſome occaſions, to run " for this bay, when the wind or tide is contrary, and " a veſſel bound to the northward cannot get to " Carſeg, or to the ſmall iſlands of Jura, where there " is better ſhelter. The beſt anchorage is between " Ilan-Daveyn, and the rock, which is always above " water, that lies about a quarter of a mile eaſtward " of it. In moderate weather, a ſhip may ſtop any " where northward of Ilan-Daveyn, about two cables " length from the iſland."

This ſituation hath the advantage of a ſoil partly level, and tolerably fertile. Knapdale abounds in black cattle, ſheep, wood, and limeſtone. The cattle are driven to the Low Countries for ſale. The woods on the banks of Lochfine are uſed in forges, and burnt for charcoal on the ſpot, by an Engliſh company for the ſupply of their iron works, and other purpoſes. Eſdale, and other ſmall iſlands on the coaſt, are compoſed of ſlate, or nearly ſo, of which about 3,000,000 are tranſported annually to various parts of Great Britain, Europe, and America.

The tract around the head of Loch Crinan, on the Atlantic ſide of the peninſula, is both fertile and plea-

* Though the above extract was inſerted in the article of canals, it is repeated in this place for the conveniency of the reader. I follow this gentleman alſo, in dimenſions and diſtances, upon the weſt coaſt; where he differs very conſiderably from other authors and charts.

ſant;

ſant; an extenſive plain, from which the ſea hath ſeemingly receded, affords paſture for large herds of black cattle. The riſing grounds on the north and eaſt, aſſiſted by lime and ſea wreck, raiſe crops little inferior to the beſt tracts in the Lowlands.

Whoever viſits the church-yard of Kilmartin will conſider this diſtrict as having been the ſeat of numerous warriors, who are repreſented on the tomb-ſtones, in their armour; but it is affirmed by the inhabitants, that many of the ſtones, with the fineſt effigies and carvings, were brought from Icolmkill, the antient ſepulchre of kings and heroes. Many ſmall caſtles ſtill remain in this diſtrict, moſtly uninhabited, and ſome ruinous.

At the diſtance of 8 miles north-eaſt from Crinan is Loch Awe, an inland lake of great depth; its banks an intermixture of woods and arable ground. Its waters afford a plentiful ſupply of trout and ſalmon to the gentlemen of the neighbourhood.

On the weſt ſide of Knapdale lies the iſland of Jura, ſeparated from the main land by a narrow, but navigable channel, called the ſound of Jura. This iſland is 20 miles in length, from 5 to 7 in breadth, and hath the appearance of one continued mountain, compoſed of rock, and covered with heath. Formerly it contained 1200 inhabitants; but the number hath been lately reduced through famine and migration; yet their ſhores abound in fiſh, and, in 1784, the whole ſound of Jura, with the lakes on the main land, were crowded with herrings, which in a great meaſure were loſt to the inhabitants, from the want of caſks, ſalt, and capital. No herrings were cured, no buſſes appeared. The captures by the boats were laid, every morning, in heaps upon the beach, waiting for purchaſers. The country people flocked thither from all parts, ſome as far as Crief in Perthſhire, at the diſtance of 80 miles. Theſe poor people travelled night and day with little reſt or ſleep. Some had ſmall horſes with a hamper on each ſide; others, in more opulent circumſtances, were furniſhed with

little

little carts. At length, when the country was supplied, the fishery ceased, though the herrings had not left the coast. Some persons proposed to cart the herrings across the isthmus to Lochfine, from whence they could be conveyed by water to Greenock. Had there been a town or village in this district, with necessary materials for taking, salting, and packing, it is probable that 50,000l. might have been realized in a few weeks. This loss is the more to be regretted, as the herrings seldom fall upon that south coast in such quantities, as appeared between June and October *.

In all probability the same shoal, or a detachment from it, made a voyage to the Mull of Cantire, which having doubled, they crowded northward by the Firth of Clyde, and from thence entered Lochfine, where 500 vessels might have been loaded in a few weeks. Here the country people found encouragement for their industry, by means of the water communication from this loch to Greenock, Paisley, and Glasgow.

Lochfine, the largest of all the Scottish lakes, and often the resort of the herrings, when the waters with which it communicates are forsaken, merits a particular description.

The length of this lake from Skipnish Point northward, besides the windings, is 30 miles; its breadth from 1 to 7; but, if taken in its largest sense, from Campbeltown, it will be found to measure 54 miles. Its depth is still more extraordinary, being from 10 to 92 fathoms. The herrings sometimes croud in shoals to the very head of it, pursued by the larger fish, and attended by gulls and other voracious sea fowls, who skim incessantly upon the surface of the water, where booty can be had to reward their labour. White fish are so plentiful, that large haddocks

* Except the mackarel, nothing can exceed the brilliancy of the herring immediately after they are taken. At this time they afford delicious eating after being nitched and broiled; and their flesh is perfectly white.

are

are sold at Inverary for 6d. per dozen; small cod, at nearly the same price; turbot, skate, and whitings, almost for nothing. Those however, who carry their fresh fish to Greenock, get a good price.

The great depth of water affords ample scope for those monstrous fish, the whales; two of whom, attended with lesser fish of that species, and also thousands of sea-gulls, frequented this loch during great part of the winter 1784; brought thither, probably, by the before mentioned shoal of herrings, and from whose long sojourning in that narrow water, the inhabitants prognosticated a good fishery during the following season. The whales were of the largest size, and the smaller fish, possibly grampusses, above 20 feet long. It is by the movements of these fish, and the birds, that the country boats know where to set their nets in the fishing season. Such are the natural advantages of the proposed pass between the trading, and the uncultivated divisions of the kingdom. Having Lochfine on the east, and the ocean on the west, it enjoys every possible advantage for the fisheries. Situated amidst the shoals of herrings which occasionally visit that lake, and the Firth of Clyde, the inhabitants, completely furnished with boats, and decked vessels, salt and casks, would be ready on the first approach of the fish, and in all kinds of weather, to sink their nets, and even to attempt the floating fishery; thereby gaining, almost at their doors, the means of commerce and wealth. Or should the herrings appear on the west side of the peninsula, the people, by means of the canal *, would soon arrive at the fortunate lake or bay. Their

* I have not been able to form a positive conclusion respecting the comparative natural advantages and disadvantages of the two opposite bays at the extremities of this pass, for the purpose of establishing the proposed town or market; I shall only therefore state a few remarks which seem to give Loch Gilp the preference. Around

Their local ſituation and ſuperior opulence would alſo enable them to embark in the white fiſheries with boats and veſſels, better manned and provided than thoſe which the indigent natives uſe at preſent. This place would likewiſe become the great reſort and thoroughfare of mankind, a centrical mart to which the Highlanders from all the northern parts of the main land, and the numerous iſlands facing that coaſt, would bring the produce of their country and ſeas, as to a ready market; or ſhould that fail, they would find themſelves within two tides of Greenock upon the Clyde, of itſelf a conſiderable mercantile town, but ſtill more important from its being the chief port of Glaſgow, a city well known in the commercial world. On the other hand, the people of the Lowlands would reſort to this Highland mart, to ſell or barter their various manufactures; and even the Engliſh riders, who in all ſeaſons, and in all kinds of weather, pay their reſpects to every town in Scotland, would find their way to the banks of Lochfine, with their ſamples from London, Coventry, Birmingham, Mancheſter, Sheffield, Leeds, Wakefield, Kendal, and other induſtrious towns of that induſtrious kingdom *.

Upon

Around this bay the ſoil is good, and the communication with the Clyde eaſy and expeditious, without the trouble of navigating the canal. Loch Gilp is likewiſe a ſtage on the main road from Inverary to Campbeltown, and Ireland. A road is alſo forming, at the expence of the gentlemen of the county, from this place to Oban, and the whole north-weſt coaſt of Argyleſhire.

* Thirty of theſe riders are ſometimes in Glaſgow at the ſame time. They live well at the inns, where they ſpend freely, and treat their cuſtomers like gentlemen. They have often reaſon to complain of the ſcarcity of caſh, and the poverty of the people. Were the meaſures recommended in theſe ſheets completely adopted, and vigorouſly proſecuted, theſe complaints would ceaſe. The Engliſh traders, inſtead of hundreds, would take thouſands, and better paid. Many traders are their own riders. They behold, with their own eyes, the integrity of their cuſtomers, and the difficulty which theſe people find in attempting to

diſcharge

Upon the whole, this opening or paſs to the *terra incognita* of the Britiſh dominions, accommodated alſo with a place of general traffic, would be the key to thoſe numerous ſhores, lakes and iſlands, whoſe hoſpitable and virtuous natives have been left to the mercy of boiſterous elements and unpropitious ſeaſons, to languiſh and to periſh through neglect, famine and deſpair. This therefore becomes the firſt object of attention in the improvement of theſe weſtern coaſts; the ground-work of the whole arrangement, worthy the immediate attention of the legiſlature, and calling ſtrongly upon the feelings of every liberal humane mind in both kingdoms.

2. Oban: The diſtrict lying north of this place is called Nether and Mid-Lorn. It is almoſt environed with water, viz. The ocean on the weſt, Loch Etive on the north, and Lochfine on the eaſt. The coaſt is every where indented with ſounds, lochs, bays and creeks, as Loch Craigniſh, abounding in ſmall iſlands; Loch Melfort, Loch Fechan, the ſound of Kerrera, Oban bay, and the beautiful Loch Etive; whereon ſtands the antient royal caſtle of Dunſtaffnage. On the banks of theſe waters are many tracts of good arable ground, and much wood. The coaſt is almoſt covered with inhabited ſmall iſlands, as Scarba, Lung, Torſa, Eſdale, Seil, and Kerrera. Thoſe iſlands, and ſome part of the oppoſite coaſt, afford inexhauſtible quarries of excellent ſlate. Some of them, aſſiſted by limeſtone and ſea-wreck, produce good crops; but neither the moſt

diſcharge a moiety of their debts. This, the Engliſh trader laments, while, from his confidence in the people, he ſolicits freſh orders. "I would ſooner," ſays he, "trade with my Scotch "friends to the extent of three thouſand pounds annually, than "with America or the Weſt Indies, for double that ſum. Here "my money is generally ſafe, my cuſtomers are within the reach "of an annual journey; if they cannot diſcharge the old ſcore, "they do as far as their abilities enable them. If they were in "better circumſtances, my claims would be better paid."

fertile

fertile tracts, nor the most favourable seasons in the Highlands, furnish sufficient supplies of grain for the inhabitants.

The coast of Lorn, hitherto unfrequented by travellers, is now laid open by means of a road generously carrying on at the expence of the country gentlemen.

This medley of land and water, of heathy mountains, naked rocks, and sloping fields; of little islands, bays, creeks, head-lands, and narrow channels, overlooked by the lofty mountains of Jura and Mull, * rising majestically from the Western Ocean, forms a landscape too complicated for prose description, but which may furnish the bard of some future period, with rich materials for the flights of his imagination †.

Towards

* The lofty mountains of Jura rise in the form of a sugar-loaf, and are called the paps of Jura. The highest is nearly 3000 feet, and commands a most extensive prospect of the Hebrides, the north of Ireland, and the firth of Clyde. The people of this island are remarkable for longevity, and are subject to few distempers, except those which arise from want of nourishment.

† In this division is the gulph or whirlpool of Corryvrekan, which is thus described by Mr. Mackenzie:—"Corryvrekan is a violent breaking sea and whirlpool, formed between the islands Jura and Scarba, which will wash over any ship's deck, and be apt to sink her if the hatches are open. The whirlpool is occasioned chiefly by an excessive rapid tide, which runs over a high steep rock, which lies on the north side of the sound, near the west point of Scarba. The rock tapers almost to a point at the top; over which the least water found was 16 fathoms: about 25 fathoms from it, on the east and west sides, the water is 36 fathoms deep; and 50 fathoms from it, the depth is 47 and 50 fathoms; 50 fathoms from it, north-west, the water is 83 fathoms deep; and 200 fathoms from it, south-west, the depth is 91 fathoms; so that this rock must be near 100 fathoms perpendicular, and its top 16 fathoms below the surface of the sea. At this rock the stream is so excessively rapid, and the sea swells and breaks so violently, even in the calmest weather, that it is impossible to measure the greatest celerity of the stream; but it does not seem to be less than 12 or 14 miles an hour. The principal stream of flood enters this sound from the eastward, and runs out towards the north west, forming an eddy about 2 miles long on the west end of Scarba. During

The

Towards the northern extremity of Mid Lorn, is the beautiful sound of Kerrera, and Oban bay, destined by nature for a place of trade. " In the " sound of Kerrera, by some called the Horse-shoe, " from a small creek in Kerrera, which is so named " there, is very good anchorage for ships and ves- " sels of any size; and it is a convenient place for " vessels that are bound either northward or south- " ward. The best parts to ride in are in the bay of

the time that the stream of flood runs westward through the middle of this sound, there is a counter stream that runs eastward, close along the shore of Scarba; and at a small point of that island, opposite to the whirlpools, is reflected southward toward them; and by its oblique direction, contributes to increase their egration, and the rage of the waves. This counter-stream seemed to run about 5 or 6 miles an hour; for a boat with 6 oars, in a calm day, could not stem it. The sea here continues to break, during ebb-tide, as well as with flood, but not so violently as with the flood. The sea rages, and forms itself into whirlpools on the Jura side of the sound likewise, both with ebb and flood; but the waves do not swell to such a height as in the part called the *gulph*, on the Scarba-side. During slack-water, which continues about half an hour with spring tide, and a whole hour with neap tide, the sea in this sound is as smooth as in other neighbouring parts. The stream of flood and ebb sets in on the Jura side, half an hour sooner than on the Scarba side.

If a vessel happens to be becalmed near the east entry of this sound, with flood and spring tide, if there is not a brisk breeze of wind, it will be in vain to get past Corryvrekan, either by sailing or towing: the most prudent way seems to be, to secure the hatches, and every thing that is loose on deck, and to endeavour by the sails and helm, to steer the vessel right through the middle of the sound, so as the tide may carry her between the most violent breakers, which lie on each side. If the tide shall happen to carry her very near the Jura side, it will be best not to attempt to get clear of it altogether, but to keep so near to it as that the tide may carry her between the eastmost small island and Jura; by which means, if the wind is any thing favourable, she may be brought into a small bay in Jura, opposite to the little island, where she may ride on clean ground, and pretty well sheltered, till the tide becomes favourable. To avoid being carried through Corryvrekan, when coming from the south with flood-tide, keep near Rilantra island, and then a moderate breeze of wind will be sufficient to carry the vessel past the sound of Scarba: or the tide alone will do it, except when it is about an hour before high water.

4 " Oban;

" Oban; and opposite to Oban, near Kerrera; and " between the ferry house of Kerrera and Ardna-" chroik, nearest the latter, on 8 or 10 fathoms, " without going within the bay, for it shallows fast " near that shore."

Oban bay is defended from westerly and southerly winds by the isle of Kerrera, which, at a small distance, stretches directly across it; on the east it is completely sheltered by the high lands of the continent. It is however open to north-west winds, which sometimes force in heavy seas by a narrow channel at the termination of Kerrera. Oban Bay hath from 11 to 26 fathoms water; a depth somewhat inconvenient for such vessels as resort thither. * Oban lies in the tract of fishing vessels and coasters passing to and from the North Highlands; and being situated near the entrance of the great Loch Linnhe, it may be considered as the western port of the proposed navigation between the Atlantic and Inverness. It lies also at the south entrance of the sound of Mull, a capacious channel, which separates that great island from the continent. The islands on the south, to which Oban is the port, have already been mentioned.

In front and on the north are Kerrera, Lismore, and Mull. Kerrera is a pleasant improveable island, 3 miles in length. Lismore is above 7 miles in length; and being composed of limestone, is considered as the granary of that coast. Mull is 25 miles in length, and in some parts nearly the same in breadth. It is in general a rugged barren country, incapable of supplying its inhabitants in grain, for which it chiefly depends upon the port of Oban, as doth the whole coast and islands of this district, Lismore excepted.

Some years ago, the convenient situation of Oban

* Which afforded ample scope for two young whales, who in August 1784, followed the herrings into this bay and remained several days, playing upon the surface.

for the relief of the people, and the various purpoſes of navigation, commerce and fiſheries, being repreſented to government, a cuſtom-houſe was built at the head of the bay, but neither key, wharf, nor ſtorehouſe. The want of a key was found ſo very inconvenient, that the collector and comptroller of the place, expended out of their pitiful ſalary, about 20l. in running out a little dike, to which a ſmall veſſel may lay her ſide, and this is the port of Oban. The town conſiſts of two or three ſlated houſes, viz. the cuſtom-houſe, and the inn; alſo a few huts built in the Highland ſtyle.

Fortunately the pariſh church is within 4 miles; a ſhort ſtep for a Sunday mornings exerciſe, compared to 20 miles, the medium diſtance inother parts.

Two merchants reſide at Oban, the landlord of the inn and his brother; who jointly carry on the whole trade of the place. They ſupply the continent and iſlands with meal from the eaſt coaſt, by the Pentland firth; and with other neceſſaries, from Glaſgow, by the mull of Cantire. They have alſo a concern in the remaining herring buſs fiſhery beforementioned; and here I ſaw the crew of a veſſel go through a cloſe examination reſpecting their age, reſidence, &c. at the cuſtom-houſe, on their clearing out for Loch Broom. They were in general ſhort, but ſtout young men, and ſeemed to be in good ſpirits; they loved Rodney with all their hearts, and did not fear the Monſieurs and the Dons; no, nor the Mynheers neither, ſhould they all three come athwart the Britiſh line,

3. Loch Sunart. Northward of Oban lies Loch Etive, a narrow inlet of conſiderable length; Loch Crerin, and the Linnhe Loch, whoſe waters almoſt environ Upper Lorn, a country abounding in picturesque views.

On the north ſide of the Linnhe Loch is the laſt diſtrict of Argyleſhire, called Morven *, environed

* The native country of Fingal, the Caledonian monarch, of whoſe exploits the Highlands abound in traditionary ſongs, and wonderful ſtories.

alſo

alſo by water; and on the weſt lies the main length of the iſland of Mull, ſeparated from the continent by the ſound of Mull, a noble and ſafe channel, 11 miles in length, ½ to 1½ in breadth, and accommodated with ſeveral excellent bays, particularly Tobirmoire bay, an extenſive circuitous baſon, on the Mull ſide, where in 1588, the Florida, one of the largeſt ſhips of the Spaniſh armada, was blown up by Mr. Smollet of Dumbarton. Several attempts have been made to recover the ſuppoſed treaſure on board, though at the depth of 60 feet. Pieces of gold and ſilver, beads, pins, toys, and ſome fine braſs cannon, have been recovered, but not ſufficient to defray the expence.

At the north entrance of the ſound of Mull, on the continent, is Loch Sunart, "a long arm of the "ſea, reſembling a river, and very little ſtream of "tide in it. It is quite well ſheltered, the ground "almoſt all of it clean and good, and capable of "ſeveral hundred ſail of the largeſt ſhips. The "greateſt inconveniency of this harbour is, the nar-"rowneſs of the entrance, which is little more than "a cable's length wide in the beſt channel. Small "veſſels, to ride in a conſiderable depth, muſt lay "one anchor on ſhore, except at the head of the "loch; but large ſhips may anchor almoſt any "where above a cable's length from the ſhore.

"Kyleſnacon, on the ſouth ſide of the iſland Oro-"ſay, is an extraordinary good place to ride in, "being well ſheltered, the ground good, and the "depth ſufficient for any ſhips. The bight on the "eaſt ſide of this iſland is alſo good anchorage, "about a cable's length from the ſhore.

"Between the two largeſt iſlands off Camiſeen, "there is good anchorage on 7 or 8 fathoms water. "Alſo on the weſt ſide of the point and iſland, ſouth-"eaſtward of Camiſeen."

Loch Sunart penetrates above 12 miles into the

country of Morven; abounds in ſmall iſles, and is navigable for large ſhips the whole way.

Its ſituation, at the north entrance of the ſound of Mull, facing Tobirmoire bay, points out the utility of an eſtabliſhment at this place, which would enliven an extenſive diſtrict on the continent, and the northern part of Mull. The diviſion of Morven, called Ardnamurchan, is in general a level corn country, and very populous. That excellent, but unfortunate gentleman, Sir William Murray, perceiving the abundance of lead ore upon the banks of Loch Sunart, began and completed the expenſive operations of mining, in which ſome hundred people have been employed at Strontian. But the glory of Loch Sunart is its woody banks, occupying a ſurface of 10,000 acres, and affording a never-failing ſource of wealth to the proprietors.

4. Loch Urn. The northern extremity of the ſound of Mull is formed by the point or cape of Ardnamurchan, the moſt weſterly land of the continent; and here leaving Argyleſhire *, and the Campbells, Macleans, and Macneils, we enter Inverneſsſhire, the reſidence of the Macdonalds, Macleods, Camerons and Fraziers. This ſhire, with Roſs and Sunderland, extends from ſea to ſea, thereby enjoying a double fiſhery, of which the weſt coaſt is the moſt conſiderable.

After doubling Ardnamurchan, the firſt inlet is called Loch Moydart, which receives the waters of Loch Shiell, a narrow inland lake, which ſtretches in the direction of Fort William, but its communication with Loch Moydart is not navigable, and nature hath formed a barrier againſt any paſſage by this channel from Fort William and the weſt ſea. Paſſing Loch Hallyort, Loch Morrer, Loch Neviſh,

* The length of Argyleſhire from the point of Ardnamurchan to the Mull of Cantire is 114 miles; the medium breadth from 30 to 40 miles, except the peninſula of Cantire, which is from 5 to 9 miles. To this great extent of territory may be added Illa, Jura, Mull, Tirey, Coll, and a number of leſſer iſlands.

and

and various bays of inferior dimensions, we arrive at Loch Urn "in Glenelk, a large well-sheltered arm "of the sea, of easy access, the ground good, and "capable of receiving a numerous fleet of the largest "ships. They may anchor any where from Kaser to "Barisdale, only avoiding a spring-tide rock on the "north side, which is a little eastward of Arnisdale.

"Small vessels may ride in a moderate depth in "the bay of Arnisdale, between the rock off the "east point and the shore, on 9 or 10 fathom water. "Opposite this loch is Lochindaal, a small bay in "Sky, where ships of any burden may ride safe, par- "ticularly on the south-west side, under shelter of "the peninsula. Go not further up this bay."

The advantages to navigation from two opposite bays, one on the continent, 5 miles in length, and the other on an island, need not be enumerated, and this circumstance, as well as the excellency of Loch Urn for shipping and the herring fisheries, gives it a preferable claim to become the mart of this double coast.

The back country falls off in natural produce, as doth the whole coast from Argyleshire to the Pentland Firth; but the sea hath made ample amends. Where corn fails, fish abound. The shoals of herrings appear upon the more fertile coast of Argyleshire once in an age; but along the sterile shores of the north, they crowd to the furthest extremity of the lochs, unless when the north-east winds keep them out at sea. Of these shoals, Loch Urn hath occasionally a good share *.

Opposite

* Mr. Pennant thus describes Loch Urn, which curiosity led him to explore in a boat.—After a struggle of 5 or 4 miles, with wind and tide adverse, we put into Loch Urn, on the Inverness coast, and anchored near a little isle on the south side, 4 miles within the mouth land on the north side, 3 miles distant from our ship, and visited Mr. Macleod, of Arnisdale. I shall never forget the hospitality of the house: before I could utter a denial, three glasses of rum, cordialized with jelly of bilberries, were poured into me by the irresistible hand of good madam Macleod. Messrs. Lightfoot

Opposite this Loch, at the distance of 2 miles, is the isle of Sky, 54 miles in length, equal in dimensions to Cheshire, and containing 15,000 inhabitants.

Though the island is, upon the whole, one continued mass of heath and mountains, it exports 3 or 4000 black cattle annually, and hath some spots of fertility, particularly the district of Strath, which lies contiguous to Loch Urn. To this great island therefore the proposed market town will be essentially beneficial, as well as to the lesser islands of Canay, Rum, Scalpa, Rasay and Rona. Loch Urn is also in the neighbourhood of Bernera, the usual pass between the continent and Sky, furnished with barracks sufficient to lodge 200 men, and from

Lightfoot and Stuart sallied out in high spirits to botanise; I descended to my boat, to make the voyage of the lake.

Steer south-east. After a small space the water widens into a large bay, bending to the south, which bears the name of Barrisdale; turn suddenly to the east, and pass through a very narrow strait, with several little isles on the outside, the water of a great depth, and the tide violent. For 4 miles before us the loch was straight, but of an oval form, then suddenly contracts a second time. Beyond that was another reach, and an instaneous and agreeable view of a great fleet of busses (August 6) and all the busy apparatus of the herring fishery; an unexpected sight at the distance of thirteen miles from the sea. A little further the loch has a very narrow inlet to a third reach, this strait is so shallow as to be fordable at the ebb of spring tides; yet has within, the depth of ten and seventeen fathom: the length is about a mile; the breadth a quarter. About seven years ago it was so filled with herrings, that had crowded in, that the boats could not force their way, and thousands lay dead on the ebb.

The scenery that surrounds the whole of this lake, has an alpine wildness and magnificence, the hills of an enormous height, and for the most part cloathed with extensive forests of oak and birch, often to the very summits. In many places are extensive tracts of open space, verdant, and only varied with a few trees scattered over them: amidst the thickest woods aspire vast grey rocks, a noble contrast! nor are the lofty headlands a less embellishment; for through the trees that wave on their summit, is an awful sight of sky, and spiring summits of vast mountains.

On the south side, or the country of Knodyart, are vast numbers of pines, scattered among the other trees, and multitudes of young ones springing up.

whence

whence there are military roads to Inverneſs, Edinburgh, and Glaſgow *.

3. GARELOCH. From the north end of Mull in latitude 56-50, to Cape Wrath, in latitude 58-44, the Long Iſland lies parallel to the continent, at the diſtance of 25 to 60 miles weſtward. The intervening channel is divided into two parts by the iſle of Sky, which ſtretches acroſs in a north-weſt direction, till it reaches within 17 miles of the Long Iſland. This channel, where contracted, is called the *Minch*, and is the great thoroughfare of European ſhipping to and from the north ſeas. Through this paſs alſo, the ſhoals of herrings proceed in their ſouthern migration, often filling the lochs of both iſlands, though of little uſe to the inhabitants, from the want of ſalt and other neceſſaries.

On the eaſt ſide of Sky, indulgent nature hath alſo left a channel between that iſland and the continent, of ſufficient depth for ſhips of any burden, but chiefly navigated by herring buſſes and ſmall craft. It commences at the mouth of Loch Urn, is 10 miles

* The miſerable ſtate of the people in this neighbourhood, as repreſented by doctor Johnſon, affords an unanſwerable argument in favour of the propoſed town. Here the doctor experienced the hard fate of all travellers who are under the neceſſity of putting up at the inns of theſe neglected regions. Having travelled from Fort Auguſtus through an almoſt uninhabited tract of near 50 miles, he was told at Glenelg, that on the ſea ſide he would come to a houſe of lime, ſlate, and glaſs. This image of magnificence raiſed his expectations; at laſt he arrived at the inn weary and peeviſh, and began to enquire for proviſions and beds. Of the proviſions the negative bill of fare was very copious. Here was no meat, no milk, no bread, no eggs, no wine. He did not expreſs much ſatisfaction. Here, however, he was to ſtay. A new diſappointment awaited him. He goes to examine his lodging. Out of one of the beds, on which he was to repoſe himſelf, ſtarted up, at his entrance, a man black as a cyclops from the forge. Sleep, however, was neceſſary. A faithful guide from Inverneſs at laſt found ſome hay, which the inn could not ſupply. He directed the Highlander to bring a bundle of it into the room, and ſlept upon it in his riding coat. Mr. Boſwell being more delicate, laid himſelf ſheets, with hay over and under him, and lay in linen like a gentleman.

in

in length, and in one place a quarter of a mile only in breadth, where droves of horſes and black cattle are ſwam over from Sky to the continent for ſale. The horſes are puſhed off a rock into the ſea, and conducted over, 4 at a time, by a little boat and two men, having a pair of horſes on each ſide, held with halters. The black cattle are ſwam over in droves from 6 to 10 or 12 at a time, tied with ropes faſtened from the horn of one to its tail, and ſo to the next; the firſt being faſtened to the pilot boat. Through this paſs alſo, the herrings, in certain winds, penetrate to the ſouth, when of courſe every opening is filled. Spring tides run here at the rate of 7 miles an hour, and the channel abounds in ſafe bays, generally ornamented with the caſtles or ſeats of the proprietors of theſe ſhores. Near the north end of the channel, we enter Roſsſhire, poſſeſſed chiefly by the Mackenzies, and Monroes. The coaſt, after paſſing the ſound of Sky, is one continued line of bays and lochs, as Loch Duich, Loch Carran, Loch Kiſſerne, Loch Toſcaik, Applecroſs bay, where the main expanſe of the channel again opens to view, having the continent on the eaſt, Sky on the ſouth, the Long Iſland on the weſt, and the main ocean on the north. It contains a ſurface, of 55 miles in length, by 40 upon a medium in width, unincumbered with rocks or ſhallows, abounding in fiſhing banks, its ſhores on every ſide deeply indented with lakes, ſome of them extending above 10 miles within land, and all of them the occaſional reſort of herrings in boundleſs numbers, and of excellent quality; beſides white fiſh, flat fiſh, ſalmon, trout, and ſhell fiſh. To theſe favourable circumſtances, is to be added the contiguity of theſe inhabitants to the great north-ſea white fiſheries, from which much wealth may be realized, were the people accommodated with ſtores, proviſions, and fiſhing materials.

Such are the local and maritime advantages of this northern

northern corner, and if we alſo take into the account the number of people around theſe lochs, their promptitude, and natural fitneſs for fiſheries, whether by boats or decked veſſels; the diſpoſition of the gentlemen for affording them every encouragement and relief, as far as their abilities will admit; a ſeaſonable effort on the part of government, in favour of this diſtrict, will enſure the moſt ſubſtantial benefits to the Britiſh kingdoms, in ſtrengthening their navy, extending their exports, and introducing their manufactures amongſt a numerous people hitherto known only by name to the empire. To this channel, or more properly this capacious bay *, itſelf a fiſhing ground, environed alſo with more than 50 openings,

* Though each loch, bay, ſound or creek, however ſmall, hath a name, yet this large body of water, and its fiſheries, have no particular appellation, being promiſcuouſly called the Loch Broom, or the Hebride fiſheries. We have an Engliſh channel, an Iriſh channel, and a Saint George's channel, but no Scottiſh channel; and as this ſea lies immediately within that kingdom, I had reſolved to propoſe that it ſhould hereafter be diſtinguiſhed by that name, upon charts and maps. Contemplating afterwards, the beneficent diſpoſition of his preſent majeſty towards all his ſubjects, without diſtinction or partiality; his confidence in a people who had long been kept at a diſtance from the throne; the ſtill further indulgencies propoſed in favour of their country, the proſpect of ſucceſs, and the happy change which is likely to be effected thereby during his majeſty's reign, I wiſh to perpetuate the remembrance of that reign and thoſe events, throughout the Highlands, by honouring them with the title of KING GEORGE'S CHANNEL, and this, in the name of all Highlanders of whatever rank or deſcription. And it being the ſociable practice of Highlanders in all ages, to ſeal, ratify, and waſh down every contract or bargain, in good old [illegible], let every loyal patriot pay a due regard to the following ſentiments:

The King and Royal Family.

May the ſpirit of the Engliſh conſtitution reach every glen, ſtrath, and ſhore of the Highlands, with the Hebrides alſo.

The Land of Cakes.

May the Improvement of the Highlands and Fiſheries engage the attention of King and Parliament.

Short communications with the Clyde and the Murray Frith, free of tonnage dues.

The

openings, the great receptacles of fiſh, and contiguous to thoſe inexhauſtible ſources which a ſurrounding ocean affords, the attention of the public ſhould be particularly directed.

On the Long Iſland at Stronaway, one of the fineſt bays in Europe, no effectual eſtabliſhment hath yet been made, though for a time the reſidence of Dutchmen, and greatly encouraged by the late Earl of Seaforth and his ſucceſſor.

The trifling progreſs of this place, in a courſe of two centuries, affords a freſh proof that public munificence well applied, and that only, can effectually accompliſh the great object of improving thoſe remote ſeas and lakes, and of bringing their valuable productions into the general line of Britiſh commerce.

After leaving Applecroſs bay, and its well-cultivated populous ſhores, the great Loch Torridon preſents itſelf; " a long arm of the ſea, of eaſy acceſs, " well ſheltered, and almoſt all of it good holding-" ground. Several hundreds of the largeſt ſhips may " ride in it in ſafety in all weathers."

Almoſt adjoining to Loch Torridon is Gareloch, or as it is called by the natives Loch Gareloch, " a large bay, ſheltered almoſt on all ſides, with " clean ground in all parts of it, and good holding-" ground in the principal anchoring place, and ca-" pable of a fleet of the largeſt ſhips. There are " no rocks or ſhoals to be feared either in it or near

The ſpeedy erection of Royal Boroughs on the weſt coaſt, where the induſtrious may buy and ſell, not as ſlaves, but as freemen.
The friends of the fiſheries of Great Britain.
May all unneceſſary reſtraints be aboliſhed.
No ſalt duties, or cuſtom-houſe fees.
Liberal bounties to buſſes and boats.
Ready markets in Europe and the Weſt Indies.
The wooden bulwarks of Great Britain.
Prince Henry, and the tars of Old England.
May every hardy fiſherman be ready to ſerve his king and country, when called upon in a juſt cauſe.

" it.

"is. Ships may ride in any part of this loch, when "it does not blow hard from the west or south-"west, particularly on the east side of Island Longa. "The best part in winter is any where between "Island Horisdale and Flowerdale, on from 9 to 20 "fathoms water. Small vessels may anchor in win-"ter on the west side of Island Horisdale, on the "south-east side of the rock in the sound which is "always above water."

This noble bay extends near 4 miles within land, by 2 in breadth. Its shores are populous, containing 3000 inhabitants, who are alternately engaged in the herring and white fisheries,* yet these poor people bleed their cattle in the spring and fall, which they preserve to be eaten cold; a species of food very general in the Highlands, from the want of grain. In Buchanan's time they eat both the blood and the meat, raw.

The inhabitants of this place preserve their potatoes by drying them in kilns.

Gareloch is surrounded by little inland lakes and rivulets, containing salmon and trout. The edges of the waters are generally covered with timber or

* Herrings, says Mr. Pennant, offer themselves in shoals from June to January; cod fish abound on the great Sand Bank, one corner of which reaches to this bay, and is supposed to extend as far as Cape Wrath; and south, as low as Rona, off Sky, with various branches, all swarming with cod and ling. The fishery is carried on with long lines, begins in February, and ends in April. The annual capture is uncertain, from 5 to 27,000. The natives at present labour under some oppressions, which might be easily removed, to the great advancement of this commerce. At present the fish are sold to some merchants from Campbeltown, who contract for them at two-pence farthing a-piece, after being cured and dried in the sun. The merchants take only those that measure 18 inches from the gills to the setting on of the tail; and oblige the people to let them have two for one of all that are beneath that length. The fish are sent to Bilboa: Ling has also been sent there, but was rejected by the Spaniards. This trade is far from being pushed to its full extent; is monopolized, and the poor fishers obliged to sell their fish at half the price to those who sell it to the merchants.

grain.

grain. The ſame kind of waters extend as far as Loch Broom.

6. Loch Ewe. "This is a large well-ſheltered "bay, of eaſy acceſs, a moderate depth of water, "good ground for the moſt part, and where fleets of "the largeſt ſhips may ride in ſafety at all times. "The beſt places to ride in are, on the eaſt ſide of "iſland Ewe; and in the bay of Tunag, on the "eaſt ſide of the bay, off Inveraſpadale, and off "Pluckart, near the head of the loch."

This capacious bay penetrates 6 miles into the country, where it receives, through a narrow paſſage, the waters of Loch Maree, a beautiful freſh-water lake, 12 miles in length, in one part 5 miles in breadth, of great depth, and abounding in ſalmon, char and trout. Of the trout is found the ſpecies which weighs from 25 to 30 pounds. The banks and head-lands of this lake are, as uſual, fringed with woods.

The narrow ſtrait through which the waters of Loch Maree paſs into the bay, is the centrical ſtation between Inverneſs on the eaſt, and Stronaway in the Long Iſland on the weſt, communicating with the former by a military road, with the latter by a government packet, which ſails from port Ewe every ſecond Monday, and hath a commodious cabin. This is the laſt thoroughfare between the two ſeas in Scotland, on which account, as well as its ſituation for the freſh and ſalt water fiſheries, its populous ſhores, and the ſecurity of its bay for ſhipping of all dimenſions, it hath a claim to public attention.

7. Loch Broom. "This is a large and ſafe arm "of the ſea, capable of containing hundreds of the "largeſt ſhips; and no rocks or ſhoals within it, "but one ledge on the eaſt ſide of Ulapoole, which "extends above a cable's length from the ſhore, "and is avoided by keeping one third from the "Ulapoole ſide. The beſt places in this loch to "anchor in are, in Ulapoole bay, on 14 or 15 fa-

"thoms

"thoms water, above a cable's length from the "shore, and any where above Logie point, on from "13 to 24 fathoms."

"Loch Kenard is a harbour on the east side of "Island Martin, about a mile northward of the "mouth of Loch Broom, in which vessels may ride "very safe on 4 or 5 fathoms water, good ground, "and well sheltered."

The entrance to this celebrated lake forms a capacious bay, 5 miles in length, and from 7 to 10 in width.

Loch Broom extends 7 miles further into the country, is from ½ to 3 in width, and of great depth. This lake on the west, and the firth of Cromarty on the east, approach so near each other, that the distance in a direct line, between the salt water on each side, does not exceed 25 miles. The produce of the country around Loch Broom is cattle, which are generally purchased by graziers from Yorkshire; also timber, mountains of marble * and limestone.

* As the north of Scotland abounds in marble of curious colours and qualities, it may be proper to employ certain qualified persons to examine into the different veins, and make a report of their observations to government. The expediency and utility of such information will appear from the following account of this manufacture in Ireland, delivered in the manner of a journal. Having, says the author, observed every thing remarkable in Kilkenny, we paid attention to its environs, and among other places visited the marble mills, the finest piece of mechanism our eyes ever beheld. I think the inventor, Mr. Collis, ought to have his statue cut by the chisel of a Praxiteles. This admirable invention is situated a small mile below the town, upon the river Nore, in a delightful bottom, the passage to it through a pleasant grove. This engine, or rather the different engines, do their marvellous work by the help of the river, and are so wonderfully contrived, that they saw, bore and polish at the same time. I am concerned that I have not judgment enough to describe it fully as it deserves; had I not seen any thing worthy of notice in this kingdom, but this one, I should think all my labours fully paid. Near the mill are apartments called warehouses, where you may see such a diversity of chimney-pieces, cisterns, buffets, vases, punch-bowls, mugs of different dimensions,

limestone. The rivers and fresh water lakes communicating with Loch Broom, abound in salmon, trout and char. The shores are populous, but the people are discontented, and strongly disposed to emigrate. On these accounts, Loch Broom appears to be a proper station for a town or village, and still more so when we consider it in a commercial light.

This lake is not only the greatest resort of herrings in Britain (the Shetland isles excepted) but the fish have the reputation of being the richest, and most delicious of any that have been taken in the western seas *. Loch Broom hath therefore been the

sions, frames for looking-glasses, pictures, &c. that they would employ the eye the longest day, and yet find something to admire. The marble quarry that this precious work is formed from, is not above 200 yards from the mill that does all these wonders; and though it is not variegated like the Italian, I am told it is full as durable, and bears as fine a polish as any brought from Italy. Though the stone in this quarry sometimes might weigh several ton, yet the method the contriver has used to lift them, draw them out, and convey them to the mill, without any other than manual operation, adds still more to the surprize. I am informed this ingenious gentleman sends yearly several ship-loads to England. Several, I am informed, have been to examine this artful wonder, (for it is open to all) but I cannot hear that any one has attempted to imitate the machinery. It is perpetually at work, like a ship at sea, by night as well as by day, and requires little attendance.

* From Orfordness, says Sir William Monson, the herrings direct their course to the North Foreland in Kent, where they furnish both the English and French shores with so many as are taken by both nations, though they be both shotten, and of the worst kind.

An easterly wind carries them the length of our channel, till they arrive at the Land's End in Cornwall; from thence they divide themselves like a fleet of ships that should be directed by a general. Some go through St. George's channel, betwixt England and Ireland; others to the westward of Ireland, till they arrive at the islands of Hebrides, the place of rendezvous; and we may suppose they are at home, by the strength and goodness they find in that place; for though they run the length of our channel lean and sick, yet as soon as they repair to those islands, they become the largest, the fairest, and the best herrings in the world; and here they are taken in loughs and harbours, as I have said, and valued at 40s. the last above others.

chief

chief ſcene of the weſtern fiſhery for many ages, and is at preſent the moſt uſual rendezvous of the buſſes from the Clyde, though much diſcouraged by the dangers of a long navigation, which, as hath already been obſerved, might be ſhortened with great facility. Loch Broom hath alſo ſuſtained a temporary misfortune during theſe laſt 7 years, owing, it is conjectured, to the unuſual prevalence of eaſterly and north-eaſterly winds, which force the herrings by another channel, in their migrations ſouthward.

Near this lake is little Loch Broom, 3½ miles in length, half a mile in breadth, and very deep; where alſo the herrings crowd to the fartheſt extremity *.

8. From

* This character of the Loch Broom herrings is thus corroborated by Mr. Pennant, who ate them on the ſpot.—Found in our harbour ſome buſſes, juſt anchored, (July 28) in expectation of finding the ſhoals of herrings uſually here at this ſeaſon; but at preſent were diſappointed: a few were taken, ſufficient to convince us of their ſuperiority in goodneſs over thoſe of the ſouth: they were not larger, but as they had not waſted themſelves by being in roe, their backs, and the part next to the tail, were double the thickneſs of the others, and the meat rich beyond expreſſion. It is here proper to remark, that as Mr. Pennant ſpeaks of the ſummer herrings, and Sir William Monſon of the winter herrings, they are both right, though they differ in their deſcription of the ſize; the early herrings are ſmall on their firſt arrival, but they gradually increaſe in ſize, and about December they are very large.

The pariſh of Loch Broom, adds Mr. Pennant, is one of the largeſt on the main land of Scotland, being 36 miles long, and 20 broad. It has in it 7 places of worſhip, but is deſtitute of a parochial ſchool. None of the people, except the gentry, underſtand Engliſh. Diſpirited, and driven to deſpair by bad management, crowds were now paſſing, emaciated with hunger, to the eaſtern coaſt, on the report of a ſhip being there loaded with meal. Numbers of the miſerables of this country were now (1774) migrating: they wandered in a ſtate of deſperation; too poor to pay, they madly ſell themſelves for their paſſage, preferring a temporary bondage in a ſtrange land, to ſtarving for life in their native ſoil.

Before I leave this bay, continues Mr. Pennant, it muſt be obſerved, that there are here, as in moſt of the lochs, a few, a very

few,

8. From Loch Broom to Cape Wrath, the lakes diminiſh in ſize, though not in number, and the coaſt is leſs populous. It is a country little known, being cut off, by ſtupendous ridges of mountains, from any intercourſe with mankind, and is the leaſt productive to individuals or the ſtate, in the Britiſh kingdoms. Lying, however, ſo favourably for the north-weſt fiſheries, and in the track of ſhipping to and from the weſt coaſt of England and Ireland, and the Baltic, a harbour towards Cape Wrath would prove a moſt deſirable ſhelter amidſt the hazardous navigation, and frequent hurricanes on that northern ſhore. The diſtance from Loch Broom to this Cape is nearly 50 miles; the channel, hitherto protected in ſome meaſure by the Long Iſland, now opens to the main ocean, which rages from the north and weſt with inconceivable fury, and where the devoted veſſel ſtruggles, often in vain, to gain ſome creek or bay, amidſt almoſt uninhabited wilds, covered with eternal ſnow.

few, of the natives who poſſeſs a boat and nets; and fiſh in order to ſell the capture to the buſſes: the utmoſt theſe poor people can attain to, are the boat and nets; they are too indigent to become maſters of barrels, or of ſalt, to the great loſs of the public, as well as of themſelves. Were magazines of ſalt eſtabliſhed in theſe diſtant parts; was encouragement given to theſe diſtant Britons, ſo that they might be enabled, by degrees, to furniſh themſelves with the requiſites for fiſhing, they would ſoon form themſelves into ſeamen, by the courſe of life they muſt apply themſelves to; the buſſes would be certain of finding a ready market of fiſh, ready cured; the natives taught induſtry, which would be quickened by the profits made by the commodity, which they might afford cheaper, as taken at their very doors, without the wear and tear of diſtant voyages, as in the preſent caſe.

A bounty on theſe home captures would ſtimulate the people to induſtry; would drive from their minds the thoughts of migration; and would never leſſen the number of ſeamen, as it would be an incitement for more adventurers to fit out decked veſſels; becauſe they would have a double chance of freight, from their own captures, and from thoſe of the reſidents, who might form a ſtock from ſhoals of fiſh, which often eſcape while the former are windbound, and wandering from loch to loch.

In

In the selection of a station for the preservation of many lives, and the safety of much property, Mr. Mackenzie is our surest, and almost only guide. He points out Loch Laxford as "a capacious very fine "harbour, where there is nothing to fear coming in, "but what is always above water, except one half "tide rock, about a cable's length west from Dunskere; the ground and shelter are good; and the "depth moderate for ships of all sizes."

This loch lies in Sutherland, a country inhabited chiefly by a hardy race of that name, brave in war, and ever ready to turn out in defence of our island.

Of the North Coast from Cape Wrath to Dungsbay-Head.

LOCH LAXFORD lies within 15 miles of Cape Wrath, which having doubled, we leave the Hebrides, and what is called the North-west Highlands, and launch upon a coast facing the northern ocean, considered by mariners, as the most dangerous and difficult navigation in these kingdoms. To the dark fogs, and frequent hurricanes of the north seas, are added the whirlpools, counter tides, and violent currents of the Pentland firth, occasioned by the weight of the ocean falling upon the narrow channel which separates the continent from the Orkney islands. The rapidity of these currents, at certain periods of the tide, often baffle all the efforts of the most skilful seamen, to prevent vessels from being driven against the rocks or shores on either side of this tremendous passage. The navigation is equally hazardous in calm, as in stormy weather; because, in a dead calm, the ship, not being under the government of the helm, is hurried on, with irresistible velocity, to whatever direction the current leads, whether towards the impending rock, the sandy beach, or the open sea. On the other hand, should a vessel be driven into the firth, by the violence of a tempest, in the dark winter's night, her situation is dreadful beyond description. Such is the force of the winds and waves, that stones of considerable size are torn from the cliffs, and heaved over the high rocks, into the adjoining field *.

Notwithstanding these obstructions to the navigation from Ireland, Bristol, Liverpool, and the whole western coast of Great Britain, to the Baltic, nothing hath been done to assist that navigation, and to lessen the frequent disasters which every succeeding winter brings upon those who are engaged in it. Here are no towns, harbours, lighthouses, dockyards, or carpenters for the repairing of damages. The unfortunate vessel, though reduced to the greatest distress, must proceed to the Baltic or the Irish channel, before she can receive the smallest repair. A coast of near 400 miles, from Ireland to the Orkneys, could not, in the greatest emergency, furnish a sail, a

* The caverns formed by the violence of the ocean upon these shores, excite the admiration of every curious traveller. Some of them reach so far under ground, that no person dares venture to the extremity. They are the resort of seals, sea-dogs, and fowl; the former of which, the natives, at the risk of their lives, turn to good account. These bold men enter the caverns in boats, and having lighted their torches, make a loud noise, which brings down the animals in a confused body, with frightful shrieks and cries. They pass out of the cave in such numbers, that the men are obliged to give way until the torrent hath spent itself, when they fall upon the stragglers, whom they knock on the head with clubs. Some of these caverns have openings through the roof like the chimneys of cabbins; through which openings, though at a considerable distance from the entrance on the beach, the roaring of the sea is heard like thunder, and sometimes the foaming spray is perceived by those who have courage to approach the verge.

In the parish of Far, there is a small head-land composed of solid rock, into which the sea enters by one of the most curious natural arches in the world, and hath formed a magnificent vault, through which a boat may navigate to the extent of 200 feet from the entrance. Writers conversant in natural history have not been able to account for this extraordinary effect of the sea in thus boring a rock, as if done with instruments, of such considerable extent.

cable,

cable, or an anchor. These considerations serve to enforce the expediency of two harbours on this northern front of our island; one near Cape Wrath, on the west, and the other within Dungsbay-head on the east.

Nor is the relief of the natives, and the improvement of the country, a matter of less importance. Here is a coast, extending near 70 miles in length, abounding in white-fish, seals, oysters, and other shell-fish. Its rivers are more copious than those on the east and west sides of that district. They issue from inland lakes, as Loch Loyal, Loch Navern, and are the channels by which salmon pass, to and from, in considerable quantities, though little benefit hath been derived from these fisheries in modern times, owing to the neglected state of the country, and the absence of the proprietors.

The country lying upon the coast is more fruitful than might be expected from its northern situation; it is highly improveable, and abounds in limestone, marle, and iron stone. The county of Caithness, the residence of the Sinclairs, exports, in good years, from 30,000 to 40,000 bolls of grain; but it often happens otherwise, when the inhabitants experience a scarcity bordering upon famine. The numerous remains of Pictish houses, Scottish castles, and other buildings upon the north and east side of this district, seem to indicate a greater degree of population in former times. Its importance is further confirmed by the Danish historian Torfaeus, in his account of the attempts made by that people to obtain a settlement in these parts, and the able defence maintained by the natives, through a series of ages, till at last the Danes, tired out with fruitless expeditions, bade a final adieu to that country, and its warlike inhabitants. Of the many bays along this coast, that of Loch Eribole claims the preference, being one of the finest roads for shipping in the kingdom, and so capacious, that ships of the line may enter at low water,

 and

and find good anchorage in the south-east part of the bay *.

" Above the island Chorie, there is good anchorage for any number of ships on 12 and 14 fathom " water. It is proper in case of flans of wind blowing down from the mountains, to lie at some distance from the island, so as to be able to clear it. " When ships have advanced so far as to be off two " rivulets that run down from a hill on the west side " of the loch, that is the proper place to drop anchor. In the south side of Rispan bay, at the entrance of the loch, a few ships may lie safely."

This fine bay lies in that part of Sutherland called Strathnaver, a county destitute of every necessary for navigation, or the fisheries. Its situation near Cape Wrath, renders it still more worthy of public consideration, as a place where the unfortunate and distressed mariners might be supplied with stores, provisions, or materials for enabling them to complete their voyages.

Proceeding eastward, we come to Loch Tongue, where, " between the two Rabbit islands, ships may " anchor in 4, 5, or 6 fathom water, land-locked " by Island Roan: at about a cable's length south of " this there is a bank of sand. On the south-east " side of Island Comb, there is a small creek, where " a few ships may lie safely in 8 or 9 fathoms water. " Behind Torrisdale head, on the west end of the " land, ships enter with the flood, and lie safely." †

" Scrabster

* Mr. Mackenzie did not survey this and the eastern coast; the nautical descriptions of the former, marked with inverted commas, are copied from a chart of this coast, drawn at the desire of the philosophical society at Edinburgh,

† Near the shore, on the levelest part of the firth, there formerly was a sea-port town, the public mart of Strathnaver. The firth, indeed, with the islands, forms a charming harbour. It had almost ceased to be remembered, that there ever was a town there But on the 27th of July 1751, a very heavy cloud of rain fell on the adjacent mountains: the showers were peculiarly violent, and their force impetuous. These congregated waters rushing

"Scrabster road is a very good harbour, where "ships of any burden may ride out any storm, upon "6, 7, or 8 fathoms water. The anchoring ground "is good; and besides, for the better securing of "ships, there are two iron rings fixed to the rocks on "the shore." These two rings are the only aid to shipping between Ireland and the Baltic. Here also stands the antient town of Thurso, at the mouth of the river of the same name; but though a place of some exports in grain, meal, salmon, herrings, and white fish, the vessels unaccommodated with a harbour or key, except the two rings above mentioned, are obliged to go up with a spring-tide into the channel of the river, where they lie to for loading and unloading, along its banks. This being the only town upon the coast of Scotland since we left Campbeltown at the distance of more than 300 miles, being also at the west entrance of the narrow strait between the continent and the Orkney islands, so fatal to navigation, the utility of a key or harbour is obvious.

This place seems to have been the capital of the northern coast, the residence of the earls of Caithness and Sunderland, who, says Torfaeus, were first raised to that dignity by a charter from Malcolm II. in 1030; the same author mentions a count of Thurso, in 1136, when the place was considerable and populous. Thurso was likewise the residence of the bishops of Caithness. Its neighbourhood abounds in ruinous castles, rude obelisks, cairns, and other remains of antiquity. The coast is fertile, the sea and rivers are rich, particularly the river Thurso, which flows from a small inland lake called Lochmore, abounding

rushing in a thousand torrents down the hills, assembled in the deep-worn channel of the dale, and, foaming through with their whole united force, swept an extensive bank of sand to the sea. On its removal, the ruins of the town were discovered; whole ranges of buildings appeared, which had lain from time immemorial beneath the sand.

ing in ſalmon, and gives employment to 60 nets, which are ſhot every night, and frequently fiſh are found in each of them. This water, not being farmed to ſtrangers, is of courſe a common bleſſing to the whole neighbourhood. But the great fiſhery is at Thurſo, where the river falls into the ſea; and, if report be true, 2500 ſalmon have been taken in one tide, within the memory of man.

Leaving Thurſo, we paſs Dunnet-head, the moſt northern land of Britain, with a tremendous tide on the point of it; and here commences the narrow ſtrait of 6 miles between the main land and the Orkney iſlands, called the Pentland or Pictland firth; ſo named from the Picts, who inhabited the eaſt ſide of the kingdom, while the Scots poſſeſſed the more rugged parts on the weſt ſide. This ſtrait is the great thoroughfare of ſhipping between the eaſtern and weſtern ſeas, the terror of the boldeſt mariners, and the grave of thouſands; where the winter's ſtorms afford many natives, on the oppoſite ſhores, a better livelihood than they could obtain by fiſhing or huſbandry. They ſearch from place to place, and from one cavern to another, in the hopes of finding timber, caſks, and other floating articles of the wrecked veſſels, of whom 6 or 8 are thus ſacrificed ſometimes in one night.

The navigation of this paſs is rendered more dangerous by the iſland of Stroma, and two rocks called the Skerries, lying near the middle of it. Stroma is noted for its natural mummies, being the entire uncorrupted bodies of perſons who had been dead above half a century; light, flexible in their limbs, of a duſky colour, and on whoſe bellies the boys beat like a drum. The coffins are laid on ſtools above ground, in a vault, which being open on the ſea edge, and the rapid tides of the Pentland firth running by it, there is ſuch a conſtant ſaltiſh air as hath thus converted the bodies into mummies.

We now arrive at the eaſtern extremity of the firth

firth called Dungſbay-head, but better known by the name of Johnny Groat's, from a family of the name of Groat, who formerly reſided here, and to whom the village and ferry belonged. Notwithſtanding the tremendous conteſt between the currents and contrary tides at this place, there is no ferrying veſſel to the Orkneys, beyond the ſize of a ſmall open boat. The diſtance from this northern extremity of our iſland is, by the ſhorteſt poſt roads, to

			Miles.
Edinburgh,	—	—	273
Glaſgow,	—	—	280
Mull of Galloway,	—	—	385
London,	—	—	651
Land's End,	—	—	831

But the aſtronomical length of the iſland, in a direct line, does not much exceed 600 miles.

After travelling northward to Cape Wrath, and from thence eaſtward to Dungſbay-head, we now paſs that famous cape, and take a ſouthern courſe along the coaſt of the Britiſh ſea *, which preſents a line of 80 miles in length, without a harbour, and ſcarcely a town that merits notice. It hath all the advantages of the fiſheries which have ſo often been deſcribed, though in a leſs degree than thoſe on the weſtern coaſt. It is commodiouſly ſituated for commerce, and the people are remarkably induſtrious. The only place that hath the appearance of a port, is Wick, a ſmall, but antient borough town, ſituated at the mouth of the river Wick, which forms a tide

* Styled in foreign maps, the *German Ocean*, but with great impropriety, as it barely touches that empire; whereas, it waſhes the whole eaſtern ſhore of Great Britain, from the Pentland firth to the ſtraits of Dover. Neither hath it any claim to the appellation of *ocean*, which implies a great body of water, without any intire ſeparation of its parts by land, as the Atlantic, and the Pacific ocean. A ſea being a ſmaller collection of water, confined between lands; but, communicating with the ocean, juſtifies the deviation which I have made from the uſual cuſtom, reſpecting the name of what ought properly to be called, *The Britiſh Sea*.

tide-harbour for a few veſſels of ſmall burden, and might be improved. But at the diſtance of 3 miles north is Sinclair bay, a capacious road, with good anchorage for ſhipping of any ſize. As this bay lies directly on the eaſt entrance of the Pentland firth, as Thurſo does on that of the weſt, the expediency of a harbour on the former muſt appear obvious to any perſon who chooſes to conſider the ſubject, and who wiſhes to aſſiſt the diſtreſſed mariner, and promote the commerce of his country. Of ſtill greater importance will this place appear, when it is known, that from Wick to the firth of Cromarty, a diſtance of 60 miles, the ſhore is bold, rocky, and utterly inadmiſſible to ſea-veſſels of any ſize, the waters of Dornoch excepted, which, however, are of no great utility to navigation, by reaſon of ſhallows and quick-ſands. Neither can the firth of Cromarty*, though one of the fineſt harbours in the world, be conſidered as an aſylum to ſhips in diſtreſs, becauſe it lies out of the general track of navigation. The ſame obſervation is applicable to the harbour of Inverneſs, which lies ſtill further from the courſe of ſhipping. The coaſt along the Murray firth, though more commodiouſly ſituated, is, however, deſtitute of good harbours; conſequently, a ſhip paſſing from one ſide of Great Britain to the other, by the Pentland firth, cannot be accommodated with the ſmal-

* Twenty-two miles in length, in ſome parts 4 in breadth, the entrance narrow and bold, being formed by two lofty rocks, which project into the ſea, till they approach within a mile of each other, and therefore defend the fine bay from winds and ſtorms. Theſe rocks thus approaching each other, and having alſo a ſimilar appearance, are called by the natives, *The Sootors of Cromarty*, which, in the Scottiſh language, means *wooers, or lovers*.

At a ſmall diſtance from the entrance of the firth, is Cromarty; a place riſing into ſome conſequence, through the liberality and unwearied zeal of Mr. Roſs above mentioned. At the head of the firth ſtands Dingwall, the capital of the county, a poor ruinous place, chiefly compoſed of hovels, though its ſituation is delightful, the country fertile, and the waters, both ſalt and freſh, abound in fiſh.

 leſt

left assistance between Peterhead and Belfast loch, a voyage of 500 miles. As the same inconvenience attends the Baltic and east country trade in general, it is unnecessary to speak further on the subject. We shall therefore conclude this survey of the maritime parts of the Highlands, by observing, that the money expended in improving that country, will, at the same time, preserve the property of the merchants, save the lives of the mariners, promote the commerce, and facilitate the navigation of all the three kingdoms.

	Miles.
Astronomical distance from Cape Wrath to Dungsbay-head —	70
Ditto, from Dungsbay-head to Inverness	90
	160

without a harbour; and what is equally extraordinary, for the most part without a good carriage-road. The rivers are numerous; many of them large; but instead of convenient bridges, the traveller must either ferry or ford these waters, however dangerous to men and horse, in the rainy seasons, when the accumulated waters of far distant mountains rush towards the sea with furious impetuosity. The boats appropriated for these ferries are generally old and rotten; neither can horses get in or out without the risque of being lamed, owing to the great height of the banks, and their want of slips.

These inconveniencies are extremely prejudicial to the country, by preventing strangers from extending their journeys beyond Inverness, and of gratifying their curiosity in viewing the lofty promontories*, cliffs,

* The southern entrance to Caithness is formed by a ridge of mountains which penetrate directly into the sea; and thus leaving no opening or intermediate space for a road, the traveller must mount the promontory, called the ord of Caithness, before he can arrive in that country. He is, however, well rewarded for the

cliffs, and caſcades; the immenſe caves, the reſort of ſeals and ſea-fowls; the diſtant views of the Orkney iſlands on the north, and of the coaſt of the Murray firth on the ſouth, bounded, at the diſtance of 5 to 10 miles from the ſea, by that mighty natural rampart the Grampian mountains, which cloſes the horizon from eaſt to weſt.

The want of good roads and bridges proves an inſurmountable impediment to the improvement of the country, particularly in agriculture; keeps the natives at a diſtance from each other, in a ſtate of nature, and the moſt abject poverty.

The proprietors of lands are great improvers of their reſpective eſtates, as far as their finances and the natural ſtate of the country will admit; among whom George Roſs eſquire, of Cromarty, hath particularly diſtinguiſhed himſelf; but it cannot be ſuppoſed, that the few gentlemen who poſſeſs thoſe heathy mountains will involve themſelves, their families, and poſterity in debts, by extending their expenditures to the making roads, building bridges, harbours, and other objects of a public nature, which in juſtice ought to be done in time of peace by the military ſtationed in theſe parts.

As this country, from the cauſes above mentioned, as well as its remote ſituation, hath been leſs expoſed to the ravages of Oliver Cromwell, and other deſolating invaders, it contains many remains of antiquity; the works of the Druids, Picts, Scots, Danes,

the fatigue of his journey; in the grandeur of the proſpects on every ſide by land and ſea, while immediately underneath, he perceives the ſeals floating on the waves, accompanied by ſea-fowl, which ſwim among them with great ſecurity, and whoſe territorial reſidence is in the caverns, which nature hath formed for them on the ſides of the ord next the ſea. The reader will be able to conceive ſome idea of the extent of the diſtant views, when informed that the deſcent on the north ſide is 4 miles, and probably the perpendicular height is above half a mile.

The diſtance betwixt this cape and Forres, a town on the Murray firth, is 45 miles in a ſtraight line acroſs the ſea; from whence I have ſeen the cape diſtinctly at midnight, in the month of June, appearing like a dark cloud, overhanging the ocean.

 and

and Norwegians; though, of late, the gentry, with an indifference for those objects, so peculiar to the modern Scots, have permitted several buildings to be erased by their tenants, by which they gain a little ground, and have the benefit of the stones.

Some of these works have been explored and described by the antiquaries of the last and present century, particularly the reverend Mr. Cordiner at Banff, who hath also the merit of bringing to light many curious remains which have lain for centuries in obscurity, or have been imperfectly described by others who had no opportunities of seeing them. They are almost the only guides now existing respecting the ages which preceded the use of letters in that country, and by which we may be able to trace and bring down some sketches of remote ages to the period, when the national events were recorded in writing.

Of the Coast of the Murray Firth from Inverness to Kinnaird's Head.

Leaving the Highlands, at Inverness, we now enter a pleasant low country of near 100 miles in extent, having the Murray firth on the north, and for the most part, the Grampian mountains on the south, between which boundaries the width is from 5 to 10 miles.

Thus having the sea breezes on one side, and the lofty ridge of mountains on the other, the climate is much warmer than might be imagined between the 57th and 58th degrees. The crops are generally good, and nearly as early as in Middlesex. On these accounts, grain and meal form a principal part of the exports, not from the thinness of the people, who are extremely numerous on this coast, but from their poverty, and the necessity of selling their grain and cattle, wherewith to pay the rent.

Thus situated in a fertile country, watered by copious streams, abounding in salmon, and washed by a rich a rich ocean, this coaſt may, with ſome public aid, recover its former ſplendour, and even ſurpaſs the moſt flouriſhing periods of the middle ages. This conjecture is partly grounded on the public-ſpirited exertions of the nobility and gentry upon that ſhore, who during theſe laſt 40 years have performed wonders for the benefit of navigation and manufactures, particularly in the articles of linen, lawns, nappery, ſtockings, thread, linen-yarn, and bleaching. Theſe gentlemen have alſo expended conſiderable ſums in repairing or extending the numerous, but ſmall harbours of the coaſt, in raiſing more commodious houſes for their own reſidence, and that of their tenants. Every encouragement is given to the raiſing of clean-looking healthy villages, upon regular plans, and with good materials.

The families to whom Great Britain in general, and this diſtrict in particular, owe ſuch obligations, are thoſe of the duke of Gordon, the earls of Fiſe, Aberdeen, and Finlater, the Grants, Forbeſes and Fraziers; families of great antiquity in the Scottiſh annals, and famous for their heroic bravery againſt the never-ceaſing invaſions of the Danes, of which the encampments, tumuli, urns, and other appearances upon the coaſt are convincing evidences.

This diſtrict contains a ſmall portion of Inverneſsſhire; the whole of Nairnſhire, Murrayſhire, Banffſhire, and the north-eaſt diſtrict of Aberdeenſhire.

Inverneſs, the capital of the county, and the whole northern diviſion, beyond the Grampian mountains, is a handſome town, pleaſantly ſituated on a plain, and almoſt ſurrounded by water. It contains 7000 inhabitants, who ſpeak the Erſe and Engliſh promiſcuouſly. On an eminence near the town are the remains of a caſtle, where, according to ſome hiſtorians, the famous Macbeth murdered Duncan his royal gueſt.

Two miles from Inverneſs is Culloden moor, where on the 16th day of April, 1746, the rebel army, conſiſting of 5000 men, were totally defeated by by the duke of Cumberland, which gave the finishing blow to the hopes of the abdicated family, upon the throne of these kingdoms. From this place the pretender fled immediately, and almost alone, to the wild recesses of the West Highlands, where he wandered for several months, till a French ship of war conveyed him to that kingdom.

At the distance of 5 miles from Inverness we enter the small county of Nairn, whose inconsiderable capital of the same name had a small harbour, now choaked up with sand. Near this place is Calder, or as Shakespear calls it, Cawdor castle, from whence Macbeth derived his second title, *Thane of Cawdor*. Its walls are of great thickness, arched on the top with stone, and surrounded with battlements. A fragment of the draw-bridge still remains.

Leaving Nairn we enter the road where Macbeth met the three wayward sisters, and a little farther, at the distance of 11 miles from Nairn, we arrive at the small, neat town of Forres, in Murrayshire, pleasantly situated near the river Findorn, and remarkable for one of the finest hieroglyphic pillars now in existence. It hath been the subject of many able pens, but totally overlooked by doctor Johnson, who says, "at Forres we found good accommodation, but nothing worthy of particular remark."

"Your instructions, says Mr. Cordiner, in a letter to Mr. Pennant, with respect to the pillar at Forres, made it an object that demanded my best attention, knowing that it far surpassed, in magnificence and grandeur, the other obelisks in Scotland, and was said to be the most stately monument of the Gothic kind to be seen in Europe; you may rely on the fidelity of the drawing, and I made the following remarks.

"That in the first division, underneath the Gothic ornaments at the top, are 9 horses with their riders, marching forth in order: in the next, is a line of warriors on foot, brandishing their weapons, and appear to be ſhouting for the battle. The import of the attitudes in the third diviſion very dubious, their expreſſion indefinite.

"The figures which form a ſquare in the middle of the column, are pretty complex, but diſtinct; four ſerjeants, with their halberts, guard a company, under which are placed ſeveral human heads, which have belonged to the dead bodies piled up at the left of the diviſion: one appears in the character of executioner ſevering the head from another body; behind him are three trumpeters ſounding their trumpets; and before him two pair of combatants fighting with ſword and target.

"A troop of horſe next appears, put to flight by infantry, whoſe firſt line have bows and arrows; the three following, ſwords and targets. In the lowermoſt diviſion now viſible, the horſes ſeem to be ſeized by the victorious party, their riders beheaded, and the head of their chief hung in chains, or placed in a frame; the others being thrown together beſide the dead bodies, under an arched cover.

"The greateſt part of the other ſide of the obeliſk, occupied by a ſumptuous croſs, is covered over with an uniform figure, elaborately raiſed, and interwoven with great mathematical exactneſs; of this, on account of its ſingularity, there is given a repreſentation at the foot of the column. Under the croſs are two auguſt perſonages, with ſome attendants, much obliterated, but evidently in an attitude of reconciliation; and if the monument was erected in memory of the peace concluded between Malcolm and Canute, * upon the final retreat of the Danes, theſe large figures may repreſent the reconciled monarchs."

"On the edge below the fretwork, are ſome rows of figures joined hand-in-hand, which may alſo im-

* Malcolm II. king of Scotland, who began his reign in 1004, and Canute the Dane, afterwards king of England.

ply

ply the new degree of confidence and security which took place, after the feuds were composed, which are characterized on the front of the pillar. But to whatever particular transaction it may allude, it can hardly be imagined, that in so early an age of the arts in Scotland, as it must have been raised, so elaborate a performance would have been undertaken, but in consequence of an event of the most general importance; it is therefore surprising, that no distincter traditions of it arrived at the æra when letters were known.

" The height of this monument (called king Sueno's stone) above the ground is 23 feet; besides 12 or 15 feet under ground. Its breadth is 3 feet 10 inches, by 1 foot 3 inches in thickness."

About 6 miles north-east from Forres, on the sea side, is the burgh of Murray, a very antient and respectable fortress, at the extremity of a narrow promontory or head-land, projecting into the firth, and appears to have been the usual landing place of the Danes and Norwegians, in their descents on that province.

The extremity of the peninsula was formed with an island, by means of a great ditch cut across. An immense mound of earth and stones surrounds the æra of the fort, and will be a lasting memorial of the labour bestowed on making it impregnable. The triple ditch and rampart, which defended the creek, are yet entire. The top had been defended by logs of oak piled on one another. This place seems to have been fortified about the end of the 10th century.

Three miles below Forres is the port of Findorn, which hath 10 or 12 coasting vessels. On the bay of Findorn, are the ruins of Kinloss's abbey, where some labourers employed lately to clear away the rubbish, discovered several rows of finely fluted pillars, that had supported roofs of great extent, of which no vestiges now remain. Near the abbey is an

 orchard

orchard of apple and pear trees, at leaſt coeval with the laſt monks; numbers lie proſtrate; their venerable branches ſeem to have taken freſh root, and are ſtill loaded with fruit. This abbey was founded by David I. in 1150, and was the burying place of ſome kings.

The views of the lofty coaſt of Sutherland begin to open at this place, as far as the Ord of Caithneſs.

Proceeding eaſtward we come to Elgin, the county town, antiently the ſeat of the biſhops of Murray, at preſent a ſolitary and partly ruinous place, with little trade, but remarkable for its eccleſiaſtical antiquities. Of theſe the magnificent ruins of the cathedral are admired by every traveller. Many parts of the building ſtill remain pretty entire, of which Mr. Cordiner hath given three elegant views. This cathedral, formed by Andrew biſhop of Murray in 1224, was built in the form of a croſs; its length 264 feet; breadth 35; the length of the traverſe 114; it was ornamented with 5 towers, 84 feet in height, excluſive of the ſpires; the great tower in the center 198 feet. Four miles ſouth-weſt of this place, in a ſequeſtered glen, is the abbey of Pluſcarden, a fine edifice in the form of a croſs, pretty entire, with a ſquare tower of aſhler work. Eleven miles from Elgin is the river Spey, the largeſt in the north, and abounding in ſalmon, whoſe progreſs from the ſea is interrupted by cruives placed at the entry, though a few ſtraggling fiſh force their way many miles by their well-known dexterity in leaping. This river iſſues from a little inland lake beyond Fort Auguſtus; and after a courſe of 50 miles, fertilizes the beautiful, extenſive and populous valley called Strathſpey, where it becomes the boundary between Murray and Banffſhire, and falls into the ſea at Caſtle Gordon.

This ſeat is the reſidence of the dukes of Gordon, and hath been lately modernized in a neat ſtyle of architecture, extending near 600 feet in front.

It

It is situated in an extensive park, on the east side of the river, near the sea, and hath a beautiful effect amidst the full-grown trees, with which the park is richly ornamented.

On the opposite side of the Spey, stood the miserable village of Fochabers, which will soon disappear, if not already demolished, the duke having begun a new town at a more convenient distance, upon a regular plan, and gives every encouragement to those who undertake to build substantial, neat dwellings.

From the Spey eastward, the towns are situated close on the shore, and are mostly sea-ports. The first is Cullen, a royal borough, situated in a beautiful, well-improved country, owing to the indefatigable exertions of the late earl of Finlater, one of the first improvers in Britain. The farm-houses, barns and yards are neat, commodious, and well constructed. The hedges strong and well kept; and the roads on all sides broad and well made. No man knew better how to lay out his money than lord Finlater; no man laid it out with more œconomy; but he knew that to starve improvements, was the ready way to make them useless, and hurt himself. His lordship did every thing in the proper season, and never scrupled the necessary expence. His greatest difficulties arose from the obstinacy of his tenants against innovations. At length he got the better of their prejudices, not by arbitrary mandates, through the channel of his stewards, but by going himself from farm to farm, advising rather than directing, how to proceed.

"Be diligent," said he, "your time is your stock; follow rational methods, and you will all get rich; it is what I wish, and will help you to, if you do not prevent me by your obstinacy. I wish not for a rent which a man cannot pay and live; I would have you live well; he that works, has a right to eat." By living well, his lordship meant,

 that

that inſtead of poor ſoup-meagre, ſuch as the generality of the farmers in that kingdom have for dinner, he wiſhed his tenants ſhould eat fleſh-meat every day, hot or cold; and thoſe who did not fare thus ſumptuouſly, he conſidered as indolent drones, and refuſed to renew their leaſes; obſerving, that the rents of his eſtate were calculated to admit meat at every man's table.

In the country round Cullen are numerous cairns or barrows, the places of interment of the ancient Caledonians, and the Danes, the method being common to both nations. At Kil-hillock, or the hill of burial, a very remarkable one was demoliſhed ſome years ago. Its diameter was 60 feet, the height 16, formed intirely of the ſtones brought from the ſhore, as appears by the limpets, muſcles, and other ſhells mixed with them. The whole was covered with a layer of earth 4 feet thick, and that finiſhed with a very nice coat of green ſod, incloſing the whole. It ſeems to have been originally formed by making a deep trench round the ſpot, and flinging the earth inwards: then other materials brought to complete the work, which muſt have been by a whole army. On breaking open this cairn, on the ſummit of the ſtony heap beneath the integument of earth, was found a ſtone coffin, formed of long flags, and in it the complete ſkeleton of a human body, lain at full length, with every bone in its proper place: and with them a deer's horn, the ſymbol of the favourite amuſement of the deceaſed.

In ſeveral other cairns, which have lately been opened, were found urns containing charcoal, aſhes, burnt bones, flint arrows heads with almoſt vitrified ſurfaces, The materials of the urns appear to have been found in the neighbourhood; and conſiſt of a coarſe clay mixed with ſmall ſtones and ſand, and ſeem to have been only dried, and not burnt.

At the diſtance of 6 miles from Cullen, is Portſoy, from whence conſiderable quantities of grain are annually

annually exported, partly in consequence of the before-mentioned improvements by the earl of Finlater, and the example he set to the surrounding districts.

Vessels are also fitted out from this place for the Hebride white fishery, of which some particulars have already been given. A manufacture of stocking thread is likewise carried on to a considerable amount for the London and Nottingham markets. Industry is the characteristic of this extensive line of coast, encouraged liberally by the fostering hands of the nobility and gentry, who seem to be actuated by one general spirit of benevolence.

These remarks are particularly applicable to Banff, the county town, situated about 7 miles from Portsoy, where the inhabitants import annually 3500 matts of Dutch flax, at, upon an average, 3s. 5d. each. The flax is beat in water-mills, and then heckled, which operation employs 60 men; this, when given out to spin, employs 4000 women of all ages, and yields 150,000 spindles of yarn, which circulates about 10,000l. among the spinners. The doubling and twisting the yarn is done at Banff, and employs about 200 women and children, and 40 more at the bleach-field. These threads, when sent to Nottingham or Leicester, for stockings, bring in return cash or goods to the value of 30,000l. Such is the dependance, mutual aids and reciprocal benefits of the industrious towns in both kingdoms, however distant their situation from each other.

This place stands at the mouth of the river Devron, remarkable for its salmon fisheries; but the harbour is small, and the entrance uncertain, owing to the shifting of the sands by the storms, which rage on this bare shore with incredible violence. A circular pier is therefore placed on the outside, leaving only a narrow passage with the harbour, which this precaution does not however wholly screen from the enraged waves.

The views from the riſing grounds around Banff are ſingularly great, and have been lately enriched by a magnificent ſtructure, built by the earl of Fiſe, upon a beautiful plain waſhed by the Devron, whoſe lofty banks, cloathed with wood on the oppoſite ſide, afford a delightful contraſt to the ſoft vale underneath.

The diſtant views on the north and eaſt, are thoſe of the great ocean bounded by the horizon, whoſe waves, with northerly winds, roll majeſtically from the deep, over an extenſive ſandy beach, till they reach the ſhore, when they evaporate in foam and ſmoke.

The weſt view is bounded by the lofty mountains of Roſs-ſhire, Sutherland, and part of Caithneſs, whoſe blue tops are ſcarcely diſtinguiſhable from the clouds. This view, while the ſun is cloſing his diurnal journey, is the moſt magnificent that can be conceived, and ſeldom fails of impreſſing the mind with a deep ſenſe of the great works of God.

On leaving Banff, we croſs the Devron over a handſome new bridge of 7 arches, and enter Aberdeenſhire; though a ſmall ſlip on the coaſt, ſtill forms, with great impropriety, a part of Banffſhire. From Inverneſs to this place the coaſt is remarkably low, inſomuch that the ſea hath overwhelmed ſome thouſand acres, and is ſtill making new depredations.

Immediately after croſſing the Devron, the country riſes to a conſiderable height above the ſea, though not mountainous; the ſhores bold, rocky and precipitous; abounding in caverns and deep receſſes, ſimilar to thoſe of Sutherland and Caithneſs.

This coaſt is lined with ſmall fiſhing towns; the firſt is Down, ſituated at a ſhort diſtance from the Devron, a neat place, the creation of the preſent earl of Fiſe, * who, beſides accommodating the in-

* His lordſhip hath altered the name to that of Macduff, the name of his family, and well known in Britiſh hiſtory.

habitants

habitants with a chapel, hath contributed liberally towards the extenſion of their harbour, the moſt improveable refuge for ſhipping between Kinnaird's head and the firth of Cromarty; and, as ſuch, hath a claim to the attention of government.

An excellent mineral ſpring hath lately been diſcovered near Down, to which many perſons reſort in ſummer, for whoſe accommodation the earl of Fiſe hath built a handſome lodging-houſe.

From this place eaſtward is Gardenſtoun, ſo called from Alexander Garden, eſq. the ground proprietor; Cruvie, Achmedden, Roſehartie, Pitulie, Broadſea and Fraſerſburgh, ſituated immediately under the famous promontory of Kinnaird's head, ſo fatal to the ſhipping of theſe kingdoms, from the want of a light-houſe, and good harbour, as will appear from the following memorial:

Memorial reſpecting the Port of Fraſerſburgh, 1785.

Fraſerſburgh is a ſmall ſea-port town in the county of Aberdeen, containing about 1000 inhabitants, and is ſituated in a cheap and populous country, on the point of land called Kinnaird's head, which is the ſouthern extremity of the Murray firth.

The coaſt on both ſides of that point is generally low and rocky, and ſo dangerous for ſhipping, that ſcarce a winter paſſes without ſeveral wrecks happening on it. The Expedition, of Stockton, of 400 tons burden, was wrecked within three miles of Fraſerſburgh, in December 1784, in the night time.

Kinnaird's head is a high land projecting out to ſea, and from the ſituation of the coaſt, is generally the firſt land made by ſhips coming from the north or eaſt ſea, to the eaſtern coaſt of Scotland. From this

this point the land trends due weſt on the one hand, and greatly to the ſouthward of eaſt on the other.

It has been always thought by mariners, that a light-houſe erected there would tend materially to the preſervation of the ſhipping engaged in commerce upon the coaſt, as a light ſo ſituated, would be ſeen from the weſt, the whole length of the Murray firth; from the north at ſea as far almoſt as the Orkneys, and immediately on doubling the point of land called Buchanneſs, from the eaſt and ſouth. And indeed there is no part of the coaſt where a light could be placed with more propriety and advantage *.

Fraſerſburgh has a ſmall good harbour, made and kept up at a conſiderable expence by the proprietor and the town. According to the tide, there are 11 to 15 feet water within the harbour, and 20 feet immediately without at ſpring-tides: without is a tolerable road for ſhipping, in a bay nearly a league in length, and half a league in depth, with good anchorage in a ſandy bottom. Veſſels of about 200 tons burden enter the harbour at preſent.

Fraſerſburgh is well ſituated for trade with the eaſt coaſt of Europe. The town has lately advanced conſiderably, and requires only encouragement to render it a port of ſome conſequence on the coaſt of Scotland. At preſent it carries on a ſmall trade to the Eaſt ſea, ſeveral manufactories are forming in its neighbourhood, and the port is well adapted for building of ſmall veſſels.

Stations on the coaſt for the veſſels and perſons employed in the cod and herring fiſheries are much wanted, and often talked of being eſtabliſhed.—Fraſerſburgh is well calculated for a ſtation, the fiſhing banks for cod commencing right off Kinnaird's head, about ten leagues out at ſea, and the herring ſhoals paſſing every year cloſe under the

* Seldom a winter paſſes, ſays captain Kyd, without ſhipwrecks; laſt winter, a ſhip from the Baltic to Dublin, was loſt on Ratra Head, near Kinnaird's Head.

coaſt;

coast; the Dutch are in the constant practice of fishing on these banks.

The great deficiency of wind-bound ports on the coast of Scotland, from the firth of Forth to that of Cromarty, is acknowledged. A pier built on the Ellie rock at Frasersburgh, would render it such a port as is desired, and most serviceable to the wind-bound ships going to the Baltic, or north about. That rock lies at a little distance from the present harbour, to which there are two channels of access, the north and the south, and it is proposed to extend the north pier to the end of that rock, and to build an intire new pier on the south, at a greater distance from the other pier than the present, whereby the harbour will be considerably enlarged in size, and an increase of near four feet water will be got in that part of it, and there will then be at the entrance and in the south channel 24 feet water at spring-tides, although on the north channel there will not be more than 16 feet water, which arises from the south channel being of a sandy bottom, and opening out to the bay; but the north is on rock, and runs close by the coast to Kinnaird's head point. The distance from the Ellie rock to the rock called the Inch, on which it is also proposed to build a break to the sea, is a channel of about 20 or 25 yards width, with 19 feet water on it at high streams, and is the entrance by the north channel to the harbour, after the new pier shall be built. For a further explanation, reference is made to a plan herewith produced, by which it appears that there will be in the proposed addition to the harbour, considerably upwards of 20 feet water at spring-tides, and from 15 to 16 at ordinary ebb-tides, the flow of stream-tides being here from 5 to 8 feet. Was the proposed pier on the north, with the break on the Inch only executed, it would be of material service in rendering the harbour secure, and sheltering vessels under it in stormy weather; and indeed the harbour never can be very safe from the roll of the sea with a north-east wind, without

without this pier on the Ellie rock, while with it the roll would be prevented perhaps intirely. The expence of building the pier and breaker, it is supposed, would be near to 3000l. sterling, estimating at 3s. per square yard.

If such piers were built, vessels could at low water run under the Ellie rock and pier, where they would be safe from all winds, and would have about ten feet water. The bay is only exposed to a north-and-by-east wind; but the point of Kinnaird's head, and the Ellie rock and pier on it, would shelter them from these winds if they run under it, and small vessels are at present in use of laying there to enter the harbour with the tide. Against all other winds but the north-and-by-east, the bay is secured. It is necessary to observe, that with a westerly wind, no vessel going west, can, from the situation of the coast, pass Kinnaird's head point, nor proceed further when going south, with a south-east wind, but are often obliged to remain wind-bound for a considerable time; and such vessels as draw too much water to enter the port of Frasersburgh, are obliged to return to other ports at a considerable distance, till the wind becomes favourable for their voyage; but Frasersburgh being in possession of two channels of entrance to the harbour, one or other of which, from their situation, can always be taken, might be made very serviceable to our commercial navigation as a wind-bound port, by carrying the above proposal, of increasing the depth of water, and security of the harbour into execution.

There was in the south channel of the harbour, a rock called the Beacon, covered at high-water, and dangerous for shipping, but within these few years it has been partly cleared away by the town at a considerable expence, and by what is now proposed, all dangers from it will be removed.

It has been long in agitation to build these piers, but the want of money has hitherto prevented it.

The

The expence of building both these piers, as now proposed, is estimated at four thousand pounds sterling, a sum far above the abilities of the town's people; but they would most chearfully contribute such a proportion as they can afford, if they had hopes of obtaining a partial assistance from government.

Such assistance is humbly expected; and if no other fund arises, it is submitted, whether a part of the money which will be paid into the exchequer in Scotland, in consequence of the late act, disannexing the forfeited estates, and which is thereby made subject to the future disposition of parliament, for public purposes in Scotland, may not with propriety, and for the advantage of both kingdoms, be applied to forward the work here mentioned.

The utility of a light-house at Kinnaird's head is further explained in the evidence to the committee upon the fisheries, by Captain Kyd, an experienced naval officer, who hath been stationed many years between the Forth and the Orkneys.

From this place to Inverness, the coast lies due west; the Highland mountains are therefore still observable on the high grounds, like a ridge of blue clouds at the edge of the horizon, nor is it easy sometimes to distinguish *terra firma* from the aerial vapours. The distance between this place and the Ord of Caithness, is 70 miles in a straight line, across the sea, and it is probable that some of the back mountains perceivable here, may lie 30 miles within land, if not more. The Orkney islands, though not so lofty as the Sutherland mountains, are also seen in clear weather; the distance is 90 miles.

Of the East Coast of Scotland, from the Murray Firth to Berwic.

On leaving Kinnaird's head, we bid adieu to the prospects of the North Highlands, which division of of the kingdom immediately disappears. We now enter what is called the east coast, comprehending a line of 120 miles; the seat of great patience, and indefatigable industry. The country is populous, the towns are numerous, some of them large and commercial, trading with Norway, Denmark, Sweden, Russia, Dantzick, Hamburg, the Prussian dominions, Holland, France, Spain, Portugal, and England, to a considerable extent, and which will be greatly increased so soon as a complete system of fishery laws shall be established, the duties on coals and salt abolished, and the navigations opened to the western ocean. The inhabitants of the west are expert in the herring fisheries, but mere dabblers in the white fisheries; here the habits and genius of the people have rendered them expert in the white fisheries, while those of the herrings have been, for a series of years, carried on by open boats, and little understood. But the inhabitants of this coast chiefly excel in manufactures, particularly linen, yarn, thread and stockings, in all their varieties; upon which, however, the working people earn with difficulty a mere subsistence. Many thousands know not the luxury of butchers meat, wheaten bread, or even small beer. The weekly earnings of the men in spinning or knitting, are from 4 to 6s. of the women, 1s. 6d. sometimes 1s. 8d. a few, a very few, have cleared, by uncommon application, 2s.

The first town of any note on this coast is Peterhead, which stands on the most easterly point in Scotland, and from thence, due west, we have the greatest breadth of that kingdom, viz.

	Miles.
From Peterhead to the point of Ardnamurchan, in Argyleshire —	180
But if we include the Hebride isles, the breadth will be —	231

Peterhead is the nearest land to the northern continent of Europe, and lies within 300 miles of the cape called

called the Naze of Norway, at the entrance of the Baltic.

Through this channel the grand body of the herrings pass, in their annual migrations, from Shetland and the north seas to the more southern latitudes, attended with the all-devouring cod and ling, on which account Peterhead, or as it is sometimes called, Buchanness, hath always been the second station of the Dutch busses, after leaving the Shetland islands. Tradition says, that some hundred years ago, the Dutch offered lord Mareschal, then the proprietor of the coast, to cover a small island, called Inch Keith, with silver, for the property of it to carry on their fisheries, which, for obvious reasons, could not be accepted. Be that as it may, the Dutch still frequent the coast, in July and August, and sometimes 100 sail are seen within sight of land, busily employed in the herring and white fisheries. The natives, to whom this treasure properly belongs, have lately made some attempts towards the white fishery, of which they cure and vend, chiefly at the London markets, 4000 barrels of delicate small cod and ling, annually. They also fit out some vessels for the Hebride fishery off Barrahead, for the Barcelona market, and they claim the merit of having taught the islanders how to take and cure the large fish, which abound on their coasts.

Few harbours in Great Britain are of more importance to navigation than this of Peterhead, as in case of violent storms from the easterly points, large vessels embayed betwixt this and the mouth of the Forth, have not a port that they can safely take at every time of the tide, that of Aberdeen excepted. If therefore, they cannot make their way to sea, in the teeth of a strong easterly wind, or double this head-land that they may gain the Murray firth, they must inevitably come on shore. This harbour lies on a spacious bay, where vessels of any burden may ride in all other winds, and is therefore the general

neral rendezvous of the ſhipping which frequent the northern ſeas, where they caſt anchor on clean ground, and ride ſafely till the ſtorms have abated. But though nature hath done ſo much for the benefit of navigation, ſomething is left for the exerciſe of human aid. The harbour can, at preſent, contain in perfect ſafety, 40 or 50 ſail of veſſels drawing 12 feet water, and is capable of being extended, ſo as to admit a greater number of ſhips, drawing 20 feet, by which means, not only caſual merchantmen, but ſmall ſhips of war, with their convoys, would find this a moſt deſirable refuge, when purſued by ſuperior force.

Peterhead is a neat well-built town, celebrated for the ſalubrity of its air *, and the virtues of its mineral waters; on theſe accounts, as well as the ſalt-water bathing, it is the reſort of genteel company during the ſummer months, and hath every appearance of a thriving, plentiful, and happy place.

The coaſt from Peterhead, ſouthward, exhibits al-

* Aberdeenſhire hath the reputation of being remarkably healthy, and the inhabitants are diſtinguiſhed for their longevity. Of this, I had two inſtances in one day, ſome years ago, when travelling in that country; the firſt was a venerable looking man then in his hundredth year, as I found by various particulars, as well as his own declaration. The ſecond inſtance was ſtill more extraordinary. Having been informed that a farmer had reached the age of 130, I paid him a viſit, and received the following particulars from himſelf in anſwer to my queſtions: That he was born in 1648; being too young in Cromwell's time for carrying arms, he was ſent to the woods to cut ſhafts for halberts; at other times, he was ordered to aſſiſt at the blackſmith's forge; that he married his laſt wife at the age of 120, and was able to go about the farm, till within the laſt two years, when his ſight failed him. In this ſituation I found old Peter Garden, who, as I had taken the liberty of aſking ſeveral queſtions, thought he had a right to aſk my name, from whence I came, and where bound, hoping I would not be offended, if an old man beſtowed his bleſſing, which he did with much gravity. His wife confirmed every particular, and ſaid, that ſhe had been his ſervant, and afterwards married him, for a bit of bread. The old man died the enſuing winter. His portrait is in the poſſeſſion of ſome nobleman or gentleman of that country, whoſe name I do not remember.

moſt one continued ſcene of promontories and cliffs, lofty, precipitous, and picturesque, * affording much entertainment to travellers, whoſe curioſity leads them thither in the ſummer months; though in that ſeaſon they only give a ſpecimen of the ſcenery which the winter hurricanes diſplay. It is probable that the ſloping earth amidſt theſe cliffs have been waſhed away by the continued action of the ſea in eaſterly winds. That the waves being checked by the perpendicular rocks, would break in with redoubled rage, upon every opening, thereby forming thoſe diſmal caverns ſo frequent upon the eaſt coaſt, and which have been accurately deſcribed by Mr. Pennant, Dr. Johnſon, Mr. Cordiner, and other gentlemen of literary abilities. Of theſe ſubterraneous openings, that called the bullers of Buchan, is the moſt extraordinary. Its entry is a rude and high arch, under which boats enter in calm weather with ſuch perſons as chooſe to explore this awful region.

" We ſoon turned our eyes, ſays Dr. Johnſon, to the buller, or *bouillior* of Buchan, which no man can ſee with indifference, who has either ſenſe of danger or delight in rarity. It is a rock perpendicu-

* About 50 tons of kelp, ſays Mr. Cordiner, are annually ſent from Peterhead to Newcaſtle. The proceſs of making it is thus: The rocks, which are dry at low water, are the beds of great quantities of ſea-weed; which is cut, carried to the beach, and dried: a hollow is dug in the ground 3 or 4 feet wide; round its margin are laid a row of ſtones, on which the ſea-weed is placed, and ſet on fire within, and quantities of this fuel being continually heaped upon the circle, there is in the center a perpetual flame: from which a liquid, like melted metal, drops into the hollow beneath: when it is full, as it commonly is ere the cloſe of day, all heterogeneous matter being removed, the kelp is wrought with iron rakes, and brought to an uniform conſiſtence, in a ſtate of fuſion. When cool, it conſolidates into a heavy, dark-coloured alkaline ſubſtance, which undergoes, in the glaſs-houſes, a ſecond vitrification, and aſſumes a perfect tranſparency; the progreſs by which, thus, a parcel of ſea-weed, formerly the ſlimy bed of ſeals, or dreary ſhelter of ſhell-fiſh, is converted into a cryſtal luſtre for an aſſembly-room, or a ſet of glaſſes for his majeſty's table, is a metamorphoſes that might be a ſubject for an entertaining tale.

larly tubulated, united on one ſide with a high ſhore, and on the other, a riſing ſteep, to a great height above the main ſea. The top is open, from which may be ſeen a dark gulph of water which flows into the cavity, through a breach made in the lower part of the incloſing rock. It has the appearance of a vaſt well, bordered with a wall. The edge of the buller is not wide, and to thoſe that walk round, appears very narrow. He that ventures to look downward ſees, that if his foot ſhould ſlip, he muſt fall from his dreadful elevation, upon ſtones on one ſide, or into the water on the other. We, however, went round, and were glad when the circuit was completed.

" When we came down to the ſea, we ſaw ſome boats and rowers, and reſolved to explore the buller at the bottom. We entered the arch which the water had made, and found ourſelves in a place, which, though we did not think ourſelves in danger, we could ſcarcely ſurvey without ſome recoil of the mind. The baſon in which we floated was nearly circular, perhaps 30 yards in diameter. We were incloſed by a natural wall, riſing ſteep on every ſide to a height which produced the idea of inſurmountable confinement. The interception of all lateral light cauſed a diſmal gloom. Round us was a perpendicular rock, above us the diſtant ſky, and below an unknown profundity of water. If I had any malice againſt a walking ſpirit, inſtead of laying him in the Red-ſea, I would condemn him to reſide in the buller of Buchan.

" But terror without danger is only one of the ſports of fancy, a voluntary agitation of the mind that is permitted no longer than it pleaſes. We were ſoon at leiſure to examine the place with minute inſpection, and found many cavities which, as the watermen told us, went backward to a depth which they had never explored. Their extent we had not time to try; they are ſaid to ſerve different purpoſes. Ladies come hither ſometimes in the ſummer with collations, ca[illegible]ions, and ſmugglers make them ſtorehouſes for clandeſtine merchandize. It is hardly to be doubted but the pirates of ancient times often uſed them as magazines of arms, or repoſitories of plunder."

On this coaſt is a fiſhery of ſea dogs, which begins the laſt week in July, and ends the firſt in September. The livers are boiled for oil, the bodies ſplit, dried, and ſold to the common people, who come from great diſtances to purchaſe this coarſe fare. Excellent turbot are taken on this ſhore.

The ſalmon fiſheries of Scotland have of late been conſiderably improved by extending them to the open ſea, as well as rivers. A ſucceſsful fiſhery hath been ſet up upon this plan among the ſandy bays below Slains. The proceſs is very ſimple, and only requires a greater extent of netting. It is performed by long nets, carried out to ſea by boats, a great compaſs taken, and then hauled on ſhore. It is remarked, that the ſalmon ſwim againſt the wind, and have a higher flavour than thoſe taken in freſh waters. This may be owing to the richneſs of the fiſh when at ſea, being then in the beſt condition.

At a ſhort diſtance from the bullers is Slains caſtle, the ſeat of the earls of Errol, chief of the Hayes. * A few miles further is Ellon, a thriving populous village, waſhed by the river Ythan, where much ſalmon is taken. In the neighbourhood is Ellon-houſe, a large fine ſeat belonging to the earl of Aberdeen. At the mouth of the river is the village

* The family of Errol trace their deſcent to a memorable victory gained by the bravery of their anceſtor and his two ſons, over the Danes at Loncarty in Perthſhire, in the reign of Kenneth III. about the year 980, for which ſervice the family were promoted to the order of the nobility, in which rank they have remained ever ſince. The king alſo, as a reward for their valour and merit, gave them as much land in the fertile carſe of Gowrie, as a falcon, ſet off a man's hand, ſhould fly over without ſtopping. The falcon flew over 6 miles of ground in length, which was afterwards called Errol, and hath been the poſſeſſion and chief title of the Hayes and their ſucceſſors ever ſince.

of Newburgh, which is accommodated with a harbour and pier, where veſſels of ſmall burden can load and unload. We now arrive at the river Don, over which a fine Gothic arch is flung from one rock to the other. This arch, ſaid to have been built by a biſhop of Aberdeen about the year 1290, is 67 feet wide at the bottom, and 34 feet 6 inches high above the ſurface of the river, which, at ebb tide, is here 19 feet deep. The building is admired for its light appearance. Paſſing this bridge we arrive at Old Aberdeen, a place of little conſequence, though the ſeat of a college, founded by biſhop Elphinſton in 1494. One mile further ſtands New Aberdeen, at the mouth of the Dee, in 57 deg. 12 min. N. lat. 107 miles from Edinburgh, and 485 from London. Aberdeen is a place of great antiquity; if tradition be true, it was a place of note in the reign of Gregory king of Scotland, from whom, about the year 893, it received ſome privileges, but the oldeſt charter now remaining, was granted by Alexander II. in 1217. By this charter the king grants to Aberdeen the ſame privileges he had granted to his town of Perth. In 1004 Malcolm II. founded a biſhoprick at a place called Mortlick in this county, in memory of a ſignal victory which he there gained over the Danes; which biſhoprick was tranſlated to Old Aberdeen by David I. and in 1163, the then biſhop of Aberdeen obtained a new charter from Malcolm IV.

In Scotland there are only 4 cities, viz. Edinburgh, the metropolis; Glaſgow, the firſt place of trade and manufactures; Aberdeen, the ſecond in ditto; and St. Andrews, now in ruins. Aberdeen, including the Old Town, is ſuppoſed to contain 25,000 people; it is a handſome, thriving town, but unleſs the inhabitants increaſe and multiply very faſt, the town of Paiſley, though it hath neither harbour nor ſhipping of any kind, will ſoon eclipſe Aberdeen both in magnitude and the number of the people. New

Aberdeen

Aberdeen is the ſeat of a college founded by George earl mareſchal, in 1593, which, as well as that of Old Aberdeen, hath been the nurſery of ſcience, liberal arts, and eminent men. The remains of antient buildings, ſome of them in good perfection, diſplay the former conſequence of theſe towns, but however we may admire the venerable Gothic pile, the bold arch, or the ingenious carving; the preſent age hath the merit of a work which, if not ſuperior, is at leaſt equal to any erection in that kingdom, whether eccleſiaſtical or civil, and is thus deſcribed by an intelligent native of that place.

" The harbour of Aberdeen, ſays he, was long a great detriment to its trade, and occaſioned the loſs of many lives, and much property. A ſtranger could never depend upon finding it as he left it; while veſſels lay at anchor in the road, till the tide ſhould make, they have been often wrecked by ſtorms that ſuddenly aroſe. It was very narrow at the mouth, having the eaſterly rocky point of the Grampian mountains on the ſouth, and a flat blowing ſand on the north, extending along the coaſt for many miles. By the eaſterly and north-eaſt ſtorms, the ſand was driven, in a long ridge, acroſs the harbour's mouth, and formed, what was called the Bar. Upon this bar, the depth of water, at low tide, was ſometimes not above 3 feet. Clearing away the ſand, though but a partial and temporary remedy, was a matter of great expence to the community. If it was cleared one week, ſo as to have 5 or 6 feet of water at ebb, a freſh ſtorm the next week undid all that had been done.

" The town, at laſt, came to the ſpirited reſolution of erecting a ſtone pier on the north ſide of the harbour, ſo ſtrong, that, in all human probability, it ſhould be found effectual to prevent future damage. This pier is 1200 feet in length, and gradually increaſes in thickneſs and height as it approaches to the ſea. Where it begins, it is 20 feet broad at the

 baſe,

baſe, 12 feet broad at the top, and 16 feet high, beſides the parapet wall on the north, which is here 4 feet 6 inches thick, and 4 feet high. The pier continues to increaſe in thickneſs, till it comes to where the rounding of the head begins to be formed, where it is 36 feet broad at the bottom, and 24 feet broad at the top, including the parapet, which is here 8 feet high, and 10 feet broad.

" The head, or rounding of the pier, at the eaſt extremity, is 60 feet diameter at the baſe, and the height to the platform is 30 feet, to which add the height of the parapet, and the perpendicular of the head facing the ſea is 38 feet. As the pier thickens, from the inſide of the parapet wall, ſprings, firſt one, then a ſecond, and at laſt a third footway, broad enough for a ſingle perſon to walk upon, each raiſed about 2 feet above the one below. From one of theſe walks, you can, at any place, overlook the wall. The whole is built of granite * ; many of the outſide ſtones are above 3 tons weight, with hewn beds, and are laid lengthways into the work, ſo that their ends only are outward, no ſtone in it is leſs than 4 feet in length.

" The expence of this great work, amounting to 17,000l. or upwards, is defrayed by doubling the harbour dues, which are chiefly paid by the inhabitants of Aberdeen. A little to the ſouth of the bar they have now a depth of 17 fathoms at low water; and at the harbour mouth, from 8 to 9 fathoms, where they had formerly but a few feet."

After deſcribing this pier, undertaken and completed at the expence of the town, † it is unneceſſary to add any further remarks relative to the ſpirit, magnanimity and good ſenſe of the citizens; whoſe

* Eſteemed the moſt durable ſtone known in Europe, being proof againſt time and elements, and is therefore the moſt proper for bridges, piers and embanking.

† It was built under the direction of Mr. Smeaton, whoſe works, when left to his own judgment, and liberally ſupplied in the means, are always ſolid, maſterly, and great.

example, it is to be hoped, will be followed by the numerous ports of that kingdom at present choaked up, and ruinous.

It is however remarkable, that there is not a single decked vessel fitted out from Aberdeen for the herring, or the white fisheries: here is an excellent harbour, an active people conversant in trade, and possessed of capital; seated within 6 hours sailing of the Long Fortys, and 2 days sailing of the Shetland isles, whose sole fishery is confined to a few open boats; the captures are insufficient for the supply of the inhabitants *.

This inattention to the fisheries is the more extraordinary, as the exports of Aberdeen, though very considerable in salmon, stockings and thread, do not balance the imports, in value. The herring and white fisheries therefore, if prosecuted with vigour, cured and dried with judgment, would not only extend the scale of exports, but also furnish the outward bound vessels with freights, and better assortments for the foreign markets.

The removal of certain obstructions to the fisheries, now under consideration, and the further aids proposed to the attention of the legislature, will if granted, leave these eastern shores without any excuse, should they still neglect these branches, for which their situation, capital, and general traffic gives them such superior advantages. The salmon of

* Great quantities of fish are therefore brought to town from villages to the south and north, even as far as Newburgh, 15 English miles distant, upon womens backs, in baskets, with a breast-rope fixed to them. These poor drudges will thus travel 15 miles before breakfast, with a heavy load upon their backs; and such is the force of habit, that they would think it a punishment, to be obliged to return home with an empty basket. If therefore, they have neither goods nor provisions to carry home, they generally take in ballast of stones, equal in weight to a third of their outward bound cargo, and thus they trudge homeward with four shillings in their pockets, the produce of the fish; which, if purchased from fishermen, produces a clear profit of one shilling.

the Dee * and Don, are taken in great abundance, cured in the higheſt perfection, and greatly valued at the European markets. If the merchants, in addition to theſe, ſhould alſo export the cargoes of 50 or 60 veſſels conſtantly employed in the herring and white fiſheries, the port of Aberdeen would, in a few years, become the moſt celebrated mart of fiſh now exiſting.

Three miles ſouth from Aberdeen we croſs the Dee, over a fine bridge of 7 arches, built by the famous Gavin Dunbar, biſhop of that city.

In paſſing this bridge we leave Aberdeenſhire, the moſt extenſive and populous county in the Lowlands, next to Perthſhire; waſhed on the eaſt and north by the ocean, abounding in ſea-ports, from whence there is a ſafe and ready paſſage to the Orkneys, and Shetland iſles; the Greenland fiſheries, Norway, and the regions around the Baltic; the German coaſt, Holland, Flanders, France, England and Edinburgh: watered alſo by numerous ſtreams, all of them the reſort of ſalmon, and whoſe banks diſplay the moſt extenſive plantations, as well as natural woods, † in theſe kingdoms; whoſe proprietors, or

* The Dee produces the greateſt quantity, and employs from 40 to 50 boats. The fiſh of the Don are taken in cruives above the bridge; a practice contrary to the antient laws of the kingdom, unleſs where the nature of the water rendered the net fiſhery impracticable. In the *Regiam Majeſtatum*, the oldeſt body of Scottiſh laws now extant, ſaid to be compoſed in the reign of Malcolm II. the ſubjects were obliged to leave a free paſſage for the fiſh from Saturday evening till Monday morning, and this was called the *Saterdayes ſloppe*. Alexander I. enacted, "That the ſtreame of the water ſal be in all parts ſwa free, that ane ſwine of the age of 3 zeares, well fed, may turne himſelf within the ſtreame round about, ſwa that his ſnowt nor tail ſal not touch the bank of the water." The laws of Robert I. ſpeaking of fiſh of different ſizes, and the dimenſions of the rivers, that the fiſh may paſs up the river: "Cruives, &c. ſhall have their hecke 2 inches wide, that the fry may paſs." The laws of Robert III. and James IV. ſay, "That ſlayers of reide fiſh or ſmoltes of ſalmond, the third time, are puniſhed with death. And ſic like he quha commands the ſamine to be done."

† Theſe are finely deſcribed by Mr. Pennant, and Mr. Cordiner.

the

the greatest part of them, have the good sense to stay at home, where they are respected and honoured, instead of impoverishing themselves and their families, amidst the promiscuous crowd of an overgrown capital.

The county of Mearns, into which we now enter, is of small dimensions, and being the eastern extremity of the Grampian mountains, it is chiefly composed of hill and heath. That part however, called the *Hollow of the Mearns*, and which lies near the coast, is both fertile and pleasant, highly cultivated, full of seats, and finely ornamented.

At the distance of 15 miles from Aberdeen we come to Stonehaven, or as it is usually termed, Stonhive, situated on the south side of Cowie bay, a small harbour, into which vessels of 100 tons burden may enter at high water. Sail-cloth, and knitted stockings are the manufactures of the place, but no fishery.

About a mile from this place is the seat of Robert Barclay, Esq; of Urie, great grandson of the famous Barclay, the apologist for the quakers, whose writings, particularly his dedication to Charles II. will ever endear his memory to all good men. The descendant of that great philosopher is no less eminent for the pattern he hath set his countrymen in temporal improvements. "This gentleman, says Mr. Pennant, by the example he sets his neighbours, in the fine management of his land, is a most useful and worthy character in his country. He has been long a peripatetic observer of the different modes of agriculture in all parts of Great Britain; his journies being on foot, followed by a servant with his baggage on horseback. He has more than once walked to London, and by way of experiment has gone 80 * miles in a day. He has reduced his remarks to

* This I conceive to be an error of the press. Forty miles a day is great walking, and he who accomplishes 60 miles must be a prodigy.

practice,

practice, much to his honour and emolument. The barren heaths that once furrounded him, are now converted into rich fields of wheat, beans or oats; and his clover was at this time, Sept. 2d, under a fecond harveft.

" He is likewife a great planter; he fills all his dingles with trees, but avoids planting the eminencies, for he fays they will not thrive on this eaftern coaft, except in fheltered bottoms. The few plantings on the upper grounds are ftunted, cankered and mofs-grown.

" Mr. Barclay firft fet about his improvements in 1768; fince which he has reclaimed about 400 acres, continues to finifh about 100 annually, by draining, levelling, clearing away the ftones, and trimming. Thefe, with the plowing, feed, &c. amount to the expence of 10l. an acre. The firft crop is commonly oats, and brings in 6l. an acre; the fecond, white peas, worth fometimes as much, but generally only 4l. turnips are the third crop, and ufually worth 6l. the fourth is barley, of the fame value; clover fucceeds, worth about 4l. and laftly wheat, which brings in about 7l. 10s. an acre, but oftener more.

" As foon as the land is once thoroughly improved, it is thrown into this courfe: turnips, barley, clover, and wheat; fometimes turnips, barley, clover, and rye-grafs. He fometimes breaks up the laft for white peas, and afterwards for wheat, and fometimes fallows from the grafs, and manures it for wheat, by folding his fheep.

" The land thus improved, was originally heath, and that which was arable, produced moft miferable crops of a poor degenerate oat, and was upon the whole not worth 2 fhillings an acre; but in its prefent improved ftate is worth 20, and the tenants would live twice as well as before the improvement.

" Some of the fields have been fallowed from heath, and fown with wheat, and produced large crops. One

One field of 34 acres, which had been mostly heath, was the first year fallowed, drained, cleared of the stones, limed, &c. and sown with wheat, which produced in the London market 270l. clear of all expences. Mr. Barclay has lately erected a mill for fine flour, the only one in the county, which fully answers, and has served to encourage many of his neighbours to sow wheat where it was never known to be raised before. At present near 800 bolls are annually produced within 10 miles of the place.

" The first turnips for feeding of cattle were raised by this gentleman; and the markets are now plentifully supplied with fresh beef. For that of Aberdeen, there are frequently 50 fat beeves slaughtered in one day, from Christmas to the first of July, generally weighing 40 stones Scots a-piece. Before that period fresh meat was hardly known in these parts, during the winter and spring months. Every person killed his cattle for winter provision at Michaelmas; and this was called *laying-in, in time.**"

Such are the beneficial effects of judicious management in the various branches of husbandry; in which however the east-side of the kingdom hath a manifest advantage over the west, being less subject to those heavy rains which are an insuperable obstruction to successful agriculture.

At a short distance from this place are the ruins of Dunnoter, the antient seat of the earls mareschal. The annotator of Cambden speaks of the stately rooms in the new buildings and the library; at present nothing remains but naked walls, with some carved works, cornices, and coats of arms scattered among the ruins. Nothing seen but rocks on one side, and the ocean on the other; nothing heard but

* The usual practice at present of such of the farmers as can afford to eat butchers meat 6 months in the year, and who compose about a twentieth part of that class of men throughout the kingdom.

winds,

winds, waves, and fea-fowl. Places which gave birth to heroes famed over all Europe for martial atchievements in defence of their country and liberties, are now the folitary habitations of the feathered creation. A coat of arms, a date, timberlefs walls, and the ruinous arch, afford an affecting monument of human viciffitudes. The family of Keith was among the moft antient in Europe. In 1010 the Scots gained a complete victory over the Danes at Camus-town, in Angus; king Malcolm II. as a reward for the fignal bravery of a certain young nobleman who purfued and killed Camus the Danifh general, beftowed on him feveral lands, particularly the barony of Keith in Eaft Lothian, from which his pofterity affumed their firname. The king alfo appointed him hereditary great marefchal of Scotland, which high office continued in his family till the year 1715, when the laft earl engaged in the rebellion and forfeited his eftate and honours; and thus ended the family of marefchal, after ferving their country, in a diftinguifhed capacity, above 700 years*.

The

* The late earl marefchal, when laft in Scotland, fent his fecretary to examine the ftate of Inverugie caftle, but would not go himfelf, probably becaufe it muft have been diftreffing to behold his once fplendid place of refidence, now in ruins, defolated and forlorn. The earl, during his exile, took up his refidence in Pruffia, where being greatly efteemed by the king, he was appointed to the government of Neufchatel, and it was owing to the preffing folicitations of the Pruffian monarch, that he recovered his eftate in Scotland, to which he made a fhort vifit; during this period he received the following curious letter from his kind friend and benefactor.

" I cannot allow the Scots the happinefs of poffeffing you altogether. Had I a fleet, I would make a defcent on their coaft, and carry you off. The banks of the Elbe do not admit of thefe equipments; I muft therefore have recourfe to your friendfhip, to bring you to him who efteems and loves you. I loved your brother with my heart and foul: I was indebted to him for great obligations: this is my right to you, this my title. I fpend my time as formerly; only at night I read Virgil's Georgics, and go to my garden

The annotator of Cambden speaks of a church at Dunaster, the burial place of St. Palladius, who in 431 was sent by pope Celestine, to preach the gospel amongst the Scots. Here also, was preserved the regalia of Scotland, during Cromwell's usurpation, of which some particulars have already been given.

The rocks on which this castle stands, form the eastern extremity of the Grampian mountains; from whence they extend, in a south-west direction, as far as Loch Lomond in Dunbartonshire, composing a ridge of more than 100 miles in length. A low, and, in general, a fertile tract of ground, stretches in front of these mountains, from the one extreme to the other, distinguished by differen tnames, as the hollow of the Mearns—Strathmore—Stormont—Strathcrne—and the banks of the Forth, above Stirling. This extensive tract composed the main strength of the antient Caledonia beyond the Forth; and is at present still more famous for the manufacturing spirit of the inhabitants, from Perth eastward, in yarn, thread, linen, osnaburghs, and sail-cloth.

Among the list of improvers in this tract, the late earl of Strathmore, lord Kaimes, lord Gardenstone, and Messrs. Scott, merit particular notice.

den in the morning, to make my gardener reduce them to practice; he laughs both at Virgil and me, and thinks us both fools.

"Come to ease, to friendship, and philosophy; these are what, after the bustle of life, we must all have recourse to." The earl obeyed the friendly summons, and died soon after.——*These are what, after the bustle of life, we must all come to*, says his majesty. That is, after our ambition and thirst of dominion have destroyed thousands of people, desolated provinces, ruined cities, churches, palaces; and, in short, done mankind every mischief which cannon, bombs, and 2 or 300,000 armed slaves could perform, with us at their head, we betake ourselves at the close of life, to ease, to friendship, and philosophy. Germany seems fertile in this sort of philosophers; no sooner hath one hero performed his part in the bustle of life, than another appears with a new scroll of claims upon some devoted province or circle, and thus one of the finest countries in Europe, seldom enjoys the blessings of peace for any considerable length of time.

Nine miles from Stonehaven ſtands Bervy, or Inverbervy, the county town, and a ſmall ſea-port; but manufactures have yet made little progreſs.

A mile ſouth of Inverbervy is the village of Gourdan, which hath a harbour and pier, where ſmall veſſels may load and unload. A few miles further is John's-haven, a conſiderable fiſhing village; and at the mouth of the river South Eſk, 13 miles from Inverbervy, is the elegant, populous, and thriving town of Montroſe, a royal borough of great antiquity, as appears from a charter granted by David I. who began his reign in 1124. Montroſe lies in the county of Angus, and is the ſecond town in manufactures, ſhipping, and general commerce. Its fiſheries were formerly very conſiderable, and gave employ to above 500 boats and decked veſſels, who were alternately engaged in the herring, cod, and ling fiſheries, which they cured and exported to the Baltic, Hamburgh, Holland, France, and England, under the general name of Habberdyn (Aberdeen) fiſh.

Beyond the Long Fortys, which ſtretch in a parallel line with the whole eaſtern coaſt, lies a conſiderable bank with 6 pits in it of uncommon depth, being from 40 to 100 fathoms, and ſwarming with cod, ling, turbot, &c. but, ſtrange as it may ſeem, the inhabitants of Montroſe have abandoned the fiſhing buſineſs, which is thereby transferred to the Dutch and Hamburghers.

The two rivers, South Eſk and North Eſk, furniſh the town with ſalmon, which they export to London and foreign parts, to the value of 6 or 7000l. annually. A ſmall village called Uſan, ſupplies them amply with lobſters, of which, from 50,000 to 100,000, are ſent annually to London. Very beautiful agates are gathered beneath the cliffs, and ſent to the lapidaries in London.

Montroſe lies in the neighbourhood of a fertile, well-improved country, and exports, in good ſeaſons grain,

grain, flour, oatmeal, and malt, to a great amount. Such are the advantages which this happy place derives from nature; to which, if we add the produce of industry, as white and coloured thread, linen, lawns, cambricks, diapers, osnaburghs, and sail-cloth, the general exports must be very considerable. After crossing the entrance of the harbour, we arrive upon one of the best improved districts in that kingdom, chiefly the work of two brothers, of the name of Scott, who, about 50 years ago, began the experiment of improving upon an estate of 8 or 900l. a-year value, which is now rented low at 3000l.

First improvers have, in all countries, many difficulties to struggle with; the large sums expended, the slow returns, the obstinacy and ignorance of servants, the woeful chapter of accidents, the envy and malevolence of narrow, illiberal minds: messrs. Scott, animated by public virtue, and a love of their country, were proof against all these discouraging circumstances, and the whole county have followed, and are following the example, in proportion to the abilities of the respective proprietors. They were the first who introduced lime as a manure, of which they had abundance on their own lands, but they severely felt that they were two or three miles on the wrong side of the Red-head, where all coals passing beyond that cape northward are subject to a duty of 5s. 4d per chaldron, to the infinite prejudice and discouragement of agriculture, arts, and manufactures, particularly where nature, as at this place, hath denied them peat and wood. Those, therefore, who use lime, are obliged to bring it by water carriage from the earl of Elgin's lime-works upon the river Forth, at the extravagant expence of 17 pence per boll, upon the shore; from whence it is carried by horses or little carts, sometimes to the distance of 20 or 30 miles, thereby engrossing the time of the farmers, their servants, and cattle, which, were it not

for

for the heavy, though unproductive duty on coals, might be faved. Of the many evils under the fun, this is not the leaft, in a country where the farmer who dies worth above 100l. is faid to die amazingly rich.

The coaft from Montrofe fouthward is high, bold, and rocky, and hath many curious openings, and fubterraneous caves, worthy the attention of travellers; fome are open to the fea, with a narrow entrance, and inftantly rife within into lofty and fpacious vaults, and fo extenfively meandering, that no one hath had the courage thoroughly to explore them. Others fhew a magnificent entrance, divided in the middle by a vaft column, forming two arches, of a height and grandeur that fhame the works of art, in the moft ftupendous of the Gothic cathedrals. The cavern called the Geylit-pot aftonifhes every ftranger; where he embarks in a fubterraneous voyage, finds himfelf amidft the moft folemn fcenery imaginable, proceeds on till he comes in fight of the clouds, fun and fky, and lands amidft corn fields, at a confiderable diftance from the fea, where he embarked. Many of the ftupendous peninfulated rocks of the coaft are joined to the land by narrow defiles, where only two or three perfons can pafs a-breaft, and whofe tops were, in barbarous times, formed into rude fortifications, of which fome veftiges ftill remain. On the promontory of Red-head are the ruins of an antient caftle, once a refidence of William the Lion, who began his reign in 1165. It ftands on the fouth fide of Lunan bay; a fine femicircular bafon, open to eafterly winds, but where many diftreffed veffels are glad to take fhelter.

Fourteen miles from Montrofe, ftands the antient royal borough of Arbroath, or Aberbrothic, in a fine bottom, at the mouth of the fmall river Brothic. It is a fmall manufacturing town, particularly in ofnaburghs, white and coloured thread; which, with barley and wheat, compofe its principal exports. A

natural

natural harbour, a tolerable artificial one hath been formed of piers, where, at neap-tides, veſſels of 80 tons may enter, and 200 tons at ſpring-tides.

But the glory of this place was its antient abbey, whoſe poor remains ſtill exhibit ſome traces of its former magnificence. It was founded by William the Lion, in 1178, and dedicated to the famous Thomas a Becket. The king was buried here, but no remains of his tomb are now perceiveable. The ordinance for the yearly proviſion of the houſe, will convey ſome idea of the great charity and hoſpitality of the place, and alſo of its fiſheries, now diſuſed.

In the regiſter for the year 1530, there was an order for buying,

800 weathers,	82 chalders of malt,
180 oxen,	30 ——— of wheat,
11 barrels of ſalmon	40 ——— of meal.
1200 dried cod-fiſh.	

Beſides the produce of the abbey-lands, or what their tenants brought in. This profuſion of ſtores may ſeem very extraordinary, on being informed that the number of monks did not exceed 25; but the wonder will ceaſe when it is conſidered that thoſe houſes were open to all, the poor as well as the rich, and that charity and hoſpitality were the diſtinguiſhed characteriſtics of eccleſiaſtical communities.

Leaving theſe venerable remains, we proceed through a pleaſant, well-improved country to Dundee, ſituated moſt beautifully on the north banks of the Tay, from whence the country gradually riſes to a conſiderable height, affording extenſive views of the ocean, the river, and the oppoſite coaſt of Fifeſhire.

The mouth of the Tay is much encumbered with ſands, and the entry is difficult. From thence to Dundee the width is 2 miles, and the depth ſufficient for ſhips of the largeſt burden. Above Dundee it widens conſiderably, and hath the appearance of a capacious inland lake, 10 miles in length by 4 in width, environed by picturesque landſcapes, and fertile ſhores, particularly the Carſe of Gowrie, the granary of Scotland, and not inferior to any part of England. This river is celebrated for its ſalmon and pearl fiſheries, both of which have, however, fallen off within theſe few years paſt, but wherever there are ſands, or a gravelly bottom, the ſalmon will reſort, though there may be an occaſional ſcarcity of that fiſh from cauſes which human ſagacity cannot unfold.

The ſituation of Dundee, amidſt the riches of land and water, implies a conſiderable export trade in grain, oatmeal and flour, to which we may add potatoes, which are ſhipped in conſiderable quantities for Norway and Sweden. Of manufactures, the inhabitants export white and coloured thread, to a great amount, particularly to London; alſo to the ſame mart, an incredible quantity of oſnaburghs, partly for home ſale and partly for cloathing the negroes in the Weſt Indies. Soap, ſhoes, leather and ſaddlery goods, contribute likewiſe to the aſſortment of exports from this ſeat of induſtry: but reſpecting the herring and white fiſheries, we have not a word to ſay, though of old theſe compoſed the principal riches of the whole eaſtern coaſt.

The antient records of this place having been deſtroyed by Cromwell's army, the only exiſting veſtiges of its high antiquity are the remains of its Gothic church, which was founded by David earl of Huntingdon, brother to William king of Scotland, on his return from his third cruſade, in which, with above 500 Scotſmen, he accompanied Richard I. of England in the year 1189. This prince after ſuffering various calamities incident to ſuch diſtant expeditions, was in great danger of being ſhipwrecked on his return, near the mouth of the Tay, which he with difficulty entered, and in memory of his deliverance, began the pious work of founding one of the moſt extenſive churches in Chriſtendom, as appears by the wide ſpaces between the parts which yet remain.

Having

Having been a warm champion of the Christian faith, he readily obtained a mandate from the pope, still to be seen in the Vatican, recommending a general collection throughout Europe towards forwarding the building. Of this church only the choir, called the Old Kirk, now remains; to which is joined another building divided into 2 churches, and seemingly of a later date. But the most striking object is the venerable tower, of 186 feet in height, and a proportionable width, which, from its construction, seems to bid defiance to time. Though during the enthusiastic phrenzy which destroyed these beautiful and costly edifices, the people of Dundee were the most violent, yet their posterity were glad to seek protection within the apartments of this tower, when the town was besieged in 1651, by Cromwell's army, and plundered to an incredible amount, besides the capture of 60 vessels in the road and harbours. The present generation, however, seem to atone for the impiety and madness of their ancestors, in the neat and commodious churches which now adorn that place. The same attention, elegance, and solidity, is perceived in all their public erections, particularly their harbour, which was formed at a considerable expence, sufficient to admit 200 sail at a time. The depth at spring-tides 14 feet. Vessels of larger burden lye in the road at a short distance, or unload part of their cargo, before they take the harbour.

Leaving this agreeable place, we immediately embark for the opposite shore in Fifeshire, from whence there is a pleasant ride to St. Andrews, formerly a considerable city, populous and rich, abounding in merchandize and shipping; the resort of strangers from various nations of Europe, to traffic for fish, grain, skins and other produce of the kingdom; at present a heap of ruins, without trade, shipping, or even a key. So late as the reign of Charles I. this place had 30 or 40 trading vessels, and carried on a considerable herring and white

 fishery,

fishery by means of busses, in deep water; which fisheries had for ages been the grand source of their commerce, wealth and splendour.

After the death of the king, this whole coast, and St. Andrews in particular, became a scene of murder, plunder and rapine: every town suffered in proportion to its magnitude and opulence; nor were these hypocritical ruffians satisfied with the shipping, merchandize, plate, cattle, and whatever came within their sight; they also laid the whole coast under contribution; St. Andrews was required to pay 1000l. but the inhabitants not being able to raise that sum after being thus plundered, the general compounded for 500l. which was raised by a loan at interest, and hath remained a burden upon the corporation I believe ever since.

The gulph or bay of St. Andrews, is of great extent, being, from the point of Fifeness on the south, to Red head on the north, 24 miles over; and when ships have the misfortune to be forced into it by stress of weather, with the wind at east or north-east, it is difficult, and sometimes impossible for them to escape: they dare not attempt the river Tay, on account of the shallow water and the sand-banks, which often shift in tempestuous weather; besides the great seas which continually happen at the mouth of that river, when those winds blow. From thence to Aberdeen, lying almost a degree north, there is not a harbour which can be attempted with safety by ships of burden. On the south side of the bay lies the great river Forth, where all the ships of Europe could find ample sea-room; but vessels embayed off St. Andrews, might as well attempt to sail across the Grampian mountains, as to double the cape of Fifeness, with strong easterly winds. Ships thus circumstanced, are often stranded or lost; some of them in day-light, and within 100 yards of this ruinous harbour, in the view of the citizens, who can afford

no

no relief to the unhappy persons on board, whose cries are distinctly heard from the town.

In the opening of this harbour there is deep water, and in the entry of it, there is from 11 to 13 feet at neap-tides, and from 19 to 22 at spring-tides. The bason, throughout the whole, hath above 12 feet at neap, and 21 at spring-tides. Some time before the year 1728, the magistrates of St. Andrews consulted certain architects and masons respecting the expence of rebuilding the harbour as far out as the furthest point of the rocks at low-water mark, and thereby rendering it a safe retreat, of easy access to all vessels forced into this bay by stress of weather, when the report, delivered upon oath by the architects, stated the expence at 8734l.

This port, says Mr. Douglass, in his publication of 1728, is equally distant from the rivers Forth and Tay; and the great bay in which it is situated, abounds not only in cod and other white fish, but in herrings also, in their season. It is observed of late, the white fish lie further out at sea than formerly, which is the reason the fishers of this town, who ply in open boats only, have so very bad success; they dare not venture out to sea, in blowing weather, which they might easily do *in busses or covered vessels*. So these poor people, though willing to work, are half starved for want of business; and were the inhabitants able to fit out busses for that purpose, they could not any where be better served with good hands, and more reasonable wages. Fifty-seven years have elapsed since the publication of those judicious observations, but St. Andrews, its harbour and fisheries, remain in *statu quo*.

On leaving St. Andrews, the coast edges in a south-east direction, till we come to Fifeness, the north entrance of the Forth, one of the largest rivers in Great Britain, unincumbered with shoals, shallows, or hidden rocks, and in general affording good

 anchorage

anchorage and deep water for ſhips of the line*. The north entrance of this noble river is diſtinguiſhed by the iſle of May, a large rock, 3 miles in circumference, which affords ſafe riding for ſhips in weſterly ſtorms, and hath a light-houſe. Immediately oppoſite the iſle of May on the ſouth ſide is the Baſs Iſland, a tremendous rock, which alſo affords ſhelter for ſhipping, and good anchorage.

The Forth is at this place 9 miles wide, opens within land to 18 miles; contracts at Edinburgh to 5 miles; and, at the Queen's-ferry, above Edinburgh, to leſs than 2 miles; widens again to near 4 miles; is navigable for merchantmen as high as Alloa, 50 miles from the ſea; and for coaſters as far as Stirling, 24 miles further by water, though only 4 by land, in a direct line.

The river ſtill exhibits a ſeries of ſerpentine meanders for ſeveral miles above Stirling, but the tide flows only a full mile higher, to a place called Craigforth, where the proprietor intercepts the paſſage of the ſalmon by a cruive or weir, very injurious to the large tract of country, which ſtretches as far as Ben-Lomond weſtward. The river, from Stirling to the bridge of Aberfoil, at the entrance into the Weſt Highlands, is only paſſable for man or horſe at few places, and theſe in dry ſeaſons. It glides gently through a dead flat, from Gartmore eaſtward, and on theſe accounts it might be made navigable for barges, at a trifling expence to the proprietors of the lands, an improvement much wanted in a rich, extenſive and populous valley, without market towns, coal and lime.

Suppoſing this work to be executed, of which there is ſome probability, the whole extent of navigation on the Forth, will, including all its windings,

* In 1781, admiral Parker's fleet lay ſome days oppoſite to Edinburgh, accompanied by 500 ſail of merchantmen, the whole in full view of the city and caſtle.

exceed

exceed 200 miles, through a coast of nearly 100 miles; fertile, populous, industrious, and from Stirling eastward, almost lined with towns, antiently the seats of commerce and navigation, till they were ruined by the English depredations, in which miserable state some of them still remain, while others begin to resume the appearance of business. The principal object of these towns was the fisheries, which they prosecuted with great vigour as far as Iceland, till the time of the union, from which period the eastern fisheries gradually dwindled away; and the poor fishermen, unable to subsist themselves upon air and water, took up the trade of smuggling; but so soon as the fishery laws shall be amended, the salt duties abolished, and an adequate bounty extended to boats, as well as busses, these people will readily fall into the track of their ancestors, live by honest industry, and add new vigour to our naval strength.

Many of the ports are nearly choaked up, others want repairs, which neither the individuals, nor the corporations of these decayed places, can accomplish.

Though the harbours on the Forth are in general small, the depth of water might be made sufficient for vessels of 200 tons burden, which fully answers the purposes of their coasting and Baltic trade; but to obtain this, or even a less depth of water, an aid of 50,000l. would be requisite.

Leaving this great river, and its much-neglected harbours, the first town from the south entrance is Dunbar, an antient royal borough in East Lothian, famous antiently for its fisheries, and particularly its red herrings, this place being the Yarmouth of Scotland, in that branch. Dunbar shared, however, in the same fate with the eastern ports already mentioned; its boat-fishery decayed; and its herring-houses were locked up, or appropriated to other uses. The herrings having returned to that coast, hath

 given

given new ſpirits to the inhabitants, who have reſumed their former buſineſs of pickling and drying.

Though the town be ſmall, the efforts of the people are great. They are concerned in the Shetland white fiſheries, and others on the eaſt coaſt, from the Tay to Berwick. They have alſo red herring-houſes at Staxigo, in Caithneſs, much to the benefit of the poor natives; and, of late, they have made a ſpirited attempt at the Greenland whale fiſhery.

They ſtruggled hard to participate in the weſtern commerce, by means of a deep-water canal between the Forth and the Clyde, but all their efforts were fruſtrated, through influence and narrow views. Their harbour is ſmall, and its entrance remarkably narrow. It would be endleſs to enumerate the ſhipwrecks which happen on this eaſtern coaſt, from the want of good harbours, to which veſſels might fly when embayed. In December 1784, the whole eaſtern coaſt, from Yarmouth to the Forth, was covered with wrecks. Some ſhips were thrown upon the ſands, others broke upon the rocks, and many foundered.

At this time an Engliſh ſhip appeared off Dunbar, in great diſtreſs, ſtruggling ſeemingly to make a harbour, which could not receive her. She was now embayed, and at the mercy of the waves; the inhabitants beheld the melancholy event of her being wrecked, without ability to afford relief, in a ſea which run mountains high. Probably one half of the property thus loſt, would have rendered Dunbar harbour a ſafe retreat. At neap-tides it admits, veſſels drawing 10 feet; and 14 at ſpring-tides. Three feet more could be gained at the expence of 2000l.

From Dunbar we come to St. Abb's head, on the ſouth ſide of which is the ſmall port of Eymouth, in the Merſe, where conſiderable quantities of herrings have lately been taken by boats belonging to the Engliſh, as well as the Scottiſh coaſt.

On the melancholy occaſion above-mentioned, one of the Leith traders, on her return from London,

don, made for this little harbour at the height of the tide, and thus saved a valuable cargo of merchandise, worth, possibly, 15 or 20,000l. besides the vessel. Had she attempted the harbour an hour earlier or later, she must have been broke to-pieces; and this affords another strong instance of the absolute necessity of rendering these harbours more commodious for navigation in general, by extending the piers, where practicable, by which several feet of water will be gained, and ships of burden find a safe entrance at different periods of the tide.*

A few miles further, stands Berwic, formerly the capital of Berwickshire, now the Merse, and is the last port on the Scottish side of the Tweed. Its harbour is good and secure, but its entrance is so greatly encumbered with sands, that no vessel of burden dare approach it. The exports of Berwic are chiefly grain, salmon, eggs, and wool. Of eggs they export to the amount of 10,000l. annually. They are collected from the southern parts of Scotland, as far west as the head of the Solway firth, packed up in boxes, with the thick end downwards, and sent to London, for the use of the sugar refiners.

Abridgment of Answers from most of the Collectors of Customs in Scotland, to Mr. Commissioner Buchannan's Queries, respecting the State of the Fisheries at their several Ports.

Cromarty. In the Murray firth, and along the east side of Ross and Sutherland shires, to the northernmost point at the head of Pentland firth, there are from 2 to 300 boats employed in fishing, with 7 or 8 hands to each: these boats do not go to any great distance; and as the coast is very populous upon a considerable part of this tract, few of the fish are sent to any distant or foreign market.

Aberdeen. The fishing near the shore at this port is not considerable; but if proper vessels were employed, that could go from 10 to 30 leagues from the

the coaſt, there is not a doubt but their ſucceſs would be very great, as there is vaſt abundance of cod and ling on that coaſt; and as large ſhoals of herrings come from the northward, in the months of July and Auguſt, a moſt beneficial fiſhery might be expected from them: alſo ſmall bounties for a few years, to encourage the inhabitants to make trials, is ſtrongly recommended. The ſalmon fiſhing on this coaſt is greatly on the decline for ſome years paſt.

Montroſe. There are about 40 ſmall boats employed in fiſhing upon this coaſt, and from 6 to 8 men in each boat. Their fiſh is all conſumed by the country in the neighbourhood. The account of the fiſhery here is pretty much the ſame as at Aberdeen.

Dundee. There are only 3 ſmall fiſhing boats at this place, and what they take is inſufficient for the towns on the coaſt, and they uſe no lines for great cod and ling. About Mar's bank, and the cape, they ſay there are great plenty of theſe fiſh; but they would require decked ſloops to do things to purpoſe there.

Dunbar. Formerly there was a very conſiderable cod and ling fiſhery carried on from this place, as far ſouth along the coaſt, as Holy Iſland in Northumberland. The fiſh were plenty, and the profits very large: the ſtages and houſes are ſtill kept in repair. It is reckoned, the uncertainty of the herring, on which they feed, coming on the coaſt, is a great reaſon why the cod and ling do not come in ſuch numbers. There is this year a better appearance of cod and herrings, than has been on the coaſt for a long time. A bounty is ſtrongly recommended to be given to veſſels fiſhing for herrings in the Dutch way, which is hauling their nets at ſea into the veſſels, and prohibiting the uſe of boats altogether *.

* The writer probably means only the ſhip's boats, as the Dutch uſe none in their herring fiſheries. To prohibit a boat fiſhery unconnected with buſſes, would be cruel and unjuſt.

Of the Interior Country which joins the two Kingdoms, usually called the Borders, extending from Berwic to the Solway Firth.

On leaving Berwic we bid adieu to the eastern shores, and cross the neck of land which unites the two British kingdoms, comprehending an extent of more than 70 miles in a straight line, to the Solway firth, which falls into the western ocean. It is a country famed in British history for the bravery of the inhabitants, who, inured to military exercises, by the frequent wars between these kingdoms, as well as the freebooting inroads of individuals, composed the flower of the Scottish armies, and generally led the van, under the banners of chieftains, whose deeds in war were beheld with admiration by all the states of Europe. These were the Douglasses, Scotts, Kerrs, Johnstones, Humes, Maxwells: names formidable even to royalty itself, and who sometimes shook the throne, particularly in the reign of James II. when the earl of Douglass marched against his sovereign at the head of 40, some say 60,000 men.

The two kingdoms, though not separated by water, are nearly divided by a natural rampart called the Cheviot hills, which stretches in a south-west direction from near Berwic to the Solway firth. The above-mentioned inhabitants on the Scottish side, were therefore called the Cheviots on the border, and celebrated above all others for archery*. But martial atchievements were not the only character-

* Of whom an old song says:

> "The Cheviots——all the border
> Were bow-men in good order,
> Told enemies, if further,
> They mov'd, they'd ne'er return."

Another song begins with

> "Ye stout men of Tiviot dale,
> Close by the river Tweed,"

istic

iſtic of theſe borderers. Love and muſic ſoftened the noiſy ſound of the trumpet, and to thoſe heroes we owe the gentle tales of love, ſo highly painted in Tweed-ſide, and other paſtoral airs, which take their names from the rivers and hills of this country.

The moſt conſiderable of theſe rivers is the Tweed, which riſes at no great diſtance from Edinburgh, and receives all the waters on that ſide of the kingdom, as the Tiviot, the Leeder, the Galla, and the Yarrow.

The Tweed ſeparates the two kingdoms from Berwic to Coldſtream, the diſtance 14 miles. Here, as at Berwic, one end of the bridge ſtands in England, and the other in Scotland. The adjoining village on the Engliſh ſide is called Cornhill, and that on the Scottiſh ſide, Coldſtream.

Thoſe who travel on the ſouth ſide of the river, now quit Northumberland, and enter the ſhire of Roxborough, a large, and in general a fruitful, level county, ſheltered on the ſouth by the Cheviot hills, and watered by many conſiderable rivulets, which fall into the Tiviot. The men of the preſent age are generally robuſt, and fond of reciting the gallant fates of their anceſtors. The black cattle are nearly equal in ſize to thoſe of Northumberland, but the county is open, the farm-houſes are mean, and the country in general hath made little progreſs towards repairing the ravages of the Engliſh armies, though (excepting Cromwell's exploits) two centuries have elapſed, ſince queen Elizabeth put an end to theſe deſolating expeditions.

The north ſide of the Tweed, from Berwic to Kelſo, hath the marks of recent improvements, and excellent cultivation.

The natural appearance of the country, riſing gradually from the river, to the diſtance of 8 or 10 miles northwards, ſets off theſe improvements, to great advantage, and here nature and art exhibit, upon the whole, a proſpect little inferior to the beſt

parts

pass of England. This agreeable tract extends as far as Kelso, 24 miles west from Berwic, and 10 from Coldstream. At this place the traveller, after emerging from the mountains of Northumberland, by the Wooler road, perceives one of the softest landscapes in nature, the Tiviot meandering through a rich, level district on the south, and the Tweed flowing gently from the west, unite at the bridge of Kelso, where the Tiviot loses its name, and both roll in one stream to Berwic, meeting the tide about 8 miles above that port.

Kelso is a neat, but inconsiderable market-town, the granary of this fertile district, from whence much grain is sent to Berwic for exportation. The want of inland navigation is a considerable misfortune to this fine country, and to the extensive districts westward. Here is no coal, and little turf or lime. These, and various necessaries of life, must be conveyed from Berwic, Northumberland, or the neighbourhood of Edinburgh, to which places, the natural produce of the country must be sent, by the same tedious and expensive mode of conveyance. It is therefore worthy of inquiry, whether the Tweed could not, consistent with the preservation of the salmon fishery, be rendered navigable for flats or barges, to Kelso.

Property being now secured to the inhabitants, the country populous and fertile, the rivers swarming with salmon, the hills producing the finest wool in the kingdom, afford ample scope for speculation, were the navigation thus opened.

In former times this country was more populous than at present, and here stood the large, antient town of Roxborough, and its potent castle, of which scarcely a vestige now remains. They were destroyed in the reign of James III. king of Scotland, to prevent their falling into the hands of the English, who had often wrested them from the former, in their hostile attempts to subdue that kingdom. This country

abounds,

abounds, alſo, in Roman remains, as encampments and highways, deſcribed by Gordon, and other antiquaries. Its eccleſiaſtical ruins are numerous and elegant, particularly the abbey of Melroſs, founded in the year 1136, by David I. and minutely deſcribed by Mr. Pennant.

On leaving Kelſo,* we croſs an elegant new bridge, and enter Roxboroughſhire, where we are accompanied by the Tiviot to Jedburgh, which, though the county-town, and ſituated in a fertile country, is half in ruins, depending, it is ſaid, upon the precarious reſort of travellers to and from England, where a new road is now forming from Boroughbridge in Yorkſhire, to Edinburgh; which, when completed, will open the fourth communication between the two kingdoms.

The road I am now deſcribing, is called the croſs-road, from its direction eaſt and weſt between the two ſeas, and thereby croſſing the kingdom, and conſequently the main roads from London to Edinburgh.

The firſt ſtage after leaving Jedburgh, is Hárvic, lying on the line of the famous Roman highway called Watling-ſtreet, which extended from Dover to Scotland, and may be diſtinctly traced in many parts.

At this place we leave the plains, and find ourſelves in a paſtoral country, amidſt pictureſque vallies, hanging woods, and moſt beautiful mountains, riſing frequently in a conical form, ſo regular in their direction, and uniform in their appearance, as to reſemble the works of art.

At Harvic, we are in the centre between the two ſeas, the diſtance by the road, on each ſide, being about 40 miles. On the weſt ſide there are only two

* The duke of Roxborough hath a ſeat at this place. Alſo Sir John Douglas.

ſtages,

ſtages, viz. Moſſpaul and Langholm; from thence we arrive at the loweſt bridge upon the river Eſk, which divides the two kingdoms, and from whence the river, now called the Solway firth, gradually widens, till it is loſt in the Iriſh channel.

The tract through which we have paſſed, feeds incredible flocks of ſheep, whoſe wool is the ſtaple of the country, and which, with the ſheep and lambs, afford the inhabitants of theſe beautiful vallies, a ſcanty ſubſiſtence. The ſouth of Scotland produces the beſt wool in that kingdom, but it falls off in quality towards the weſt, owing, it is alledged, to the rains and moiſture which prevail on that ſide, though Ireland, which lies more upon the Atlantic, produces wool, from which ſuperfine cloth is fabricated at Dublin, to an extent far exceeding the general belief of mankind. We alſo find wool of a ſecondary quality, in ſome of the Hebride iſlands, which are ſituated on the line of Ireland, but the quantity is inconſiderable.

Of the towns and manufactures between Berwic and this place, little can be ſaid. We are now 80 miles diſtant, by the road, from Berwic on the eaſt, and 76 from Dalkeith near Edinburgh, on the north, in which ſpace lie the ſhires of the Merſe, Roxborough, Peebles, Selkirk, and part of Dumfries; yet there is not, in this great diſtrict, a town equal in ſize to thoſe of the fifth claſs in England.

The places called towns, are in general a ſet of poor, thinly inhabited, inſignificant villages, though ſome of them, as Lauder, Selkirk, Peebles, and Jedburgh, have the title of royal boroughs. The petty traffic carried on, is chiefly in grain, wool, ſheep and black cattle; the two laſt are ſent moſtly to England. Some feeble attempts have lately been made towards the manufacture of their wool, which in ſeveral parts is thus conducted; they ſend the wool to Yorkſhire

to

to be combed, it is then returned to be ſpun into yarn of different griſls; this done, it is ſent to the manufacturing towns of England to be woven and dreſſed, from whence a great part of it, thus manufactured, is again ſent into Scotland for ſale.

Of the Coaſt upon the Solway Firth, comprehending the Counties of Dumfries, Kirkudbright, and Wigtown.

But however deplorable the counties we have been deſcribing, may appear, in regard to manufactures; we are on the verge of a region to which, comparatively, the eaſtern diſtrict is a Yorkſhire, in manufactures and induſtry.

We are now upon Engliſh ground at Longtown, ſituated immediately at the ſouth end of the bridge. The appearance of this village, laid out in regular ſtreets, the houſes uniform, and white-waſhed, the people eaſy and comfortable, afford a ſtriking contraſt to the villages we have left, and thoſe through which we are immediately to paſs. This place owes its elegance and conveniencies to the late Mr. Graham of Netherby in Cumberland, whoſe munificence extended alſo to every farm-houſe, yard, and incloſure, on both ſides of the river, over a tract of ſome thouſand acres; inſomuch, that the property of this family appears like enchanted ground, amidſt dreary ſolitude, wretched ſmoaky hovels, naked fields, ſtarved cattle, and a dejected people, who lament their ſituation on the north ſide of the river*.

This

* Upon my expreſſing ſome ſurprize at the contraſt between the appearance of Mr. Graham's farms, and thoſe of the neighbourhood on the Scottiſh ſide, a countryman archly obſerved, "Gude troth, Sir, we are on the wrang ſide of the water; gin ye be an Engliſh man we wad be very glad to niffer lairds wee you, gif it could be done. Your lairds do meeckle gude both to themſelves and the tenants; but our lairds do naething for us, and are ne'er

 ſatisfied

This contrast will appear the more extraordinary to those who attend to the soil on the Scottish side, and the excellent crops produced on those spots when cultivated by persons of property. From Longtown bridge to Dumfries, and even to Drumlanrick on the west, a tract of near 50 miles in a straight line, and from the Solway firth, to a great distance northward, the country consists, in some parts, of a dead flat, in others, of gentle risings, but the whole is destitute of trees and hedges, excepting the districts around Dumfries, which, in crops, verdure, planting, and hedges, rivals England; a proof that the naked appearance of this extensive tract of low country is owing to the frequent irruptions of the English armies in former times, and the neglect in the proprietors to repair those misfortunes.

The first village on the road, next to Longtown, is the famous Gretna Green, where the rite is dispensed by a blacksmith, joiner, or fisherman, which is to give the decisive turn or cast to future happiness or misery. When the young couple arrive, they fly up stairs, on the wings of love, and should they be overtaken by the incensed pursuers, before the ceremony hath been performed, they are advised to slip into bed, and in this manner shew themselves to the pursuers, who supposing that all is over, make up matters, or depart in rage, imploring all the evils of Egypt to fall upon the ungrateful daughter, and the object of her choice. The price demanded by the priest upon these occasions, is from a glass of whisky to two or three guineas. When gentlefolks arrive in a carriage, and seemingly in a great hurry he leaves the price to their honours, of whose rank he hath generally a hint from the postillion from Car-

satisfied till they have turned us out of doors without a bawbee in our pouches. Yet they are ay poor and ay seeking mair siller for their lands. Gif they wad stay at hame, instead of dangling about the toon of London, where they are nae meikle thought on, we wad fare the better, and they ne'er a bit the worse."

liſle; who, ſhould the prieſt be from home, will undertake the friendly office, purely from the ardour of his regard to quality ſo generous and good.

After travelling a few miles on a level good road, we arrive at Annan *, a ſmall royal borough, pleaſantly ſituated on a river of the ſame name, abounding in ſalmon, and navigable, within half a mile of the town, for veſſels of 250 tons burden. It was formerly a place of trade, but lying contiguous to the Engliſh border, and in the track of their weſtern incurſions, it was often pillaged, deſtroyed, or burned; the laſt of theſe deſtructive inroads was in the reign of Edward VI. when lord Wharton, preſident of the marches, burned the town and demoliſhed the church.

The export trade of Annan at preſent, conſiſts of grain only, and that in no great quantity. The Solway firth is, at this place, above 2 miles in width; the incloſures, planting, and verdure on the Engliſh ſide afford a delightful proſpect, and a moſt ſtriking contraſt to the naked fields on this ſide. Appearances begin however to mend, as we approach Dumfries. On the left is Comlongam, the birth-place of lord Mansfield; the antient part of the building, though the walls are above 12 feet in thickneſs, hath yielded to time, and is moſtly in ruins.

At a ſhort diſtance we arrive at Lockermoſs, a flat of 10 miles in length, and 3 in width; which, from the proſtrate large trees and other appearances, ſeems to have been an extenſive foreſt, overwhelmed by the ſea; but we have no light from hiſtory or tradition, at what time this great inundation happened. Some canoes, hollowed with fire, having been found in the moſs, ſeem to carry that event to a very remote period.

* On a line with Newcaſtle, and nearly a degree to the ſouthward of Berwic.

The

The inhabitants of Dumfries have lately divided the town's share of this morass, and the individual property being thus ascertained, some successful attempts have been made in raising grain, hay, willows, and other vegetable productions suited to mossy soils.

On the left, near the Solway firth, is the antient castle of Caerlaveroc, which, though frequently besieged by the English, from the year 1300, when it was taken by Edward I. is still in better condition than most of the old fortresses of that kingdom. It was the property of the antient and warlike family of Nithsdale, who, from the number of beds, amounting to 80, found in the castle by Cromwell's troops, seem to have lived in great state. The great hall is 91 feet by 26. On the walls are various carvings, as coats of arms, legendary tales, and Ovid's fables, all neatly executed.

The castle stands on the edge of the Solway firth, which now widens to 9 miles, and receives the river Nith, a copious stream, furnished, 6 miles below Dumfries, with a harbour sufficient to admit vessels of 250 tons burden; small craft go with the tide as high as the town. The banks of the Nith on both sides, between Dumfries and its port, are beautifully ornamented with villas, groves, natural woods and well-enclosed fields; the whole forming a rich landscape, and a most delightful outlet to the inhabitants of Dumfries, a small, but elegant town, capital of the county, and of the south of Scotland between the two seas. It was antiently a place of considerable commerce, though often ruined by the English, who made Dumfries their head quarters, from whence they extended their ravages to the western extremity of Airshire, where the firth of Clyde bounded these excursions.

The inhabitants of the last age attempted the Virginia trade, which they were obliged to resign to Glasgow, Whitehaven and Liverpool, since which period

period they have lived by one another, without commerce, ſhipping, or manufactures worthy of being mentioned. Many of the inhabitants are, however, in eaſy circumſtances, and few places in Great Britain are better calculated for being the reſidence of thoſe who prefer a tranquil, to a buſy life. The town is neat and clean; the country and river are delightful; butchers meat, poultry, ſalmon and other fiſh, are good and cheap; and the place, though not a ſeat of trade, is enlivened by the reſort of travellers to and from Ireland, Airſhire and Glaſgow.

On leaving this agreeable town, by the Port Patric road *, we croſs the Nith over a bridge of 9 arches, and enter the ſhire of Kirkudbright, which, with that of Wigtown, compoſed the antient province of Galloway, a name ſtill retained by the natives and their neighbours. It gave its name to a numerous breed of ſmall ſtout horſes raiſed in this country, though now applied indiſcriminately to all horſes of that ſize.

The aſcent of the road, after croſſing the bridge, affords a rich proſpect of the windings of the Nith, through an extenſive well-improved country, bounded on the north by mountains, but open on the eaſt, as far as the eye can reach, the neareſt mountains on that ſide being the weſt end of the Cheviots. Having reached the ſummit, we enter upon an open mooriſh country, and have a diſtant view of England as far as St. Bee's Head, near Whitehaven, the moſt weſterly land in that diviſion of the kingdom.

* The earl of Hillſborough preferring the paſſage by Port Patric, was the chief promoter of this road, for which the whole country is under the greateſt obligations to his lordſhip. Previous to this improvement, Galloway was little known; the old deſcriptions given by Buchannan, Boethius, and other writers, are extremely defective; no traveller hath attempted a modern account, and of the coaſt, after leaving the main road to Port Patric we are almoſt entirely in the dark. I was therefore deſirous to viſit theſe unknown ſhores, and to follow the directions of the capes and bays, however inconvenient, either on horſeback or on foot.

At

A the diſtance of 15 miles from Dumfries we arrive at Carlingwork, a ſmall village, ſituated between the river Orr, on the eaſt, and the Dee, on the weſt. Theſe rivers approach within 8 miles of each other, and both of them being navigable for craft, it is propoſed to join them by a ſmall canal, which is already begun at the expence of the proprietors of the lands, and when completed, will realize many acres of very improveable ground.

At this place I left the main road, and took a ſouthern courſe for Kirkudbright, the ſhire town, and formerly a conſiderable trading port, at preſent the ſeat of poverty and indigence. It ſtands on the eaſt ſide of the Dee, where ſhips of conſiderable burden may lie in perfect ſecurity from all winds. The bay that forms the entrance of this river gave ſhelter to king William's armament during the Iriſh wars, and is honoured with the reſidence of the earl of Selkirk, whoſe ſeat and gardens it environs at high tides. From this place the country is various, to Gatehouſe, a ſmall village on the river Fleet, which falls into a bay of the ſame name, but without trade of any kind. This place is accommodated with an inn, not only commodious, but elegant; and here it may be proper to remark, that the whole croſs country from Berwic to Gatehouſe, is furniſhed with inns and ſtabling equal to thoſe of England in their appearance, and greatly ſuperior in the quality of their wines and liquors.

From Gatehouſe to Creetown, the beſt and moſt agreeable road lies cloſe upon the ſhore. It is a fine level coaſt, lined with gentlemens ſeats on one ſide, and enriched with ſea views on the other. But the ſhorteſt way is through the moors, where a military road hath lately been formed, with little judgment, over hills and mountains by which the cattle are fatigued, the paſſengers diſguſted, and the journey unneceſſarily protracted.

Creetown is a ſmall village on the eaſt ſide of

 Wigtown

Wigtown bay, near the mouth of the river Cree, which is navigable ſome miles higher, to Carty port, near Newtonſtewart, a conſiderable village, pleaſantly ſituated in a fertile country, abounding with all the real neceſſaries of life, particularly extenſive woods of full-grown trees, which overhang the banks of the Cree, and the waters which fall into it from the north.

We are now in Wigtownſhire, which is ſeparated from Kirkudbright by the Cree; it is the moſt ſoutherly county in Scotland, almoſt ſurrounded by water, and hath 3 capacious bays, viz. thoſe of Wigtown, Glenluce, and Stranrawer, uſually called Loch Ryan. The poſt road leads directly through the centre of the county to Port Patric, but my intention being coaſt-ways, I kept along the weſt ſide of Wigtown bay to the ſhire town of that name, an inconſiderable place, beautifully ſituated at the mouth of the river Bladenoch, and ſurrounded with extenſive fields, producing large crops of wheat, oats, and barley.

Little can be ſaid in favour of the port of this place, but after a ſhort ſtage through a rich country due ſouth, we come to Garlieſton, a village ſituated on the edge of a ſmall bay, where veſſels of conſiderable burden may ride in perfect ſecurity, on good anchoring ground. This place is the property of the earl of Galloway, whoſe family reſidence lies at a ſhort diſtance. The gardens and pleaſure grounds, extend to the edge of the bay; and command extenſive views of land and water.

The ſame appearances of fertility continue to Whitehorn, an inland royal borough, antiently the epiſcopal ſee of Galloway, founded, according to Bede, by St. Ninian, and famous for its noble priory and other eccleſiaſtical buildings. Of theſe edifices ſcarcely a veſtige remains by which we can trace their magnitude and ſituation. The town alſo, exhibits a melancholy picture of decay, and ſeems to have ſuffered

fered greatly in the general wreck of the kingdom. The houses have the marks of venerable age; some in ruins, others open at the roofs, and the streets partly overgrown with grass. As this place lies at a considerable distance from the main road, and there being no allurements for English riders, I was not much offended at the curiosity of the inhabitants, who were eager to know the motives of a stranger's appearance at the royal borough of Whitehorn.

Three miles south-east is the small isle of Whitehorn, separated from the continent by a narrow channel, and here vessels of burden may find safe ancharage. This district, from Wigtown southward, is properly a peninsula, formed by Wigtown bay on the east and Glenluce bay on the west, and is upon the whole a rich corn country; ornamented with gentlemens seats, planting, and well-enclosed parks. The extremity of the peninsula is called Burrowhead, and lies in a line with the mull of Galloway, which forms the west entrance of the bay of Glenluce.

Having got to the *ne plus ultra* of the kingdom, I proposed to return northward along the west coast of the peninsula, washed by the bay of Glenluce, abounding in small creeks and ports, particularly Port William, a handsome village, rising into consequence through the liberal assistance of Sir William Maxwell, the proprietor of that district.

From Port William we still keep along the coast to Kilfillan bay, the port to Glenluce, an antient and seemingly decayed town at the bottom of the bay, and here we again fall in with the road to Port Patric, which contributes to enliven this otherwise solitary place. The town lies on the east side of the river Luce, which having crossed, we travel through an almost continued avenue, and a well-improved country, to Stranrawer, at the distance of 10 miles.

The proprietors who have thus distinguished themselves for the benefit of their families and country, are Sir Thomas Hay, whose grounds we enter

 upon

upon croſſing the river Luce; Meſſrs. Adair, Roſs, Cathcart, Dalrymple, and the earl of Stair, reckoned among the firſt improvers in the kingdom, whoſe reſidence is at Culhorn, on the ſouth ſide of the road; but the antient family ſeat was at Caſtle Kennedy on the north ſide, one of the moſt entire caſtles now exiſting in Scotland, ſurrounded almoſt with water and pleaſure grounds, kept in excellent order, and affording an agreeable view to every traveller.

This road croſſes the country to Stranrawer, and from thence to Port Patric, but the coaſt road lies upon the weſt ſide of Glenluce bay, where veſſels ride ſecure in all winds, the eaſtern points excepted. This direction leads to the mull of Galloway, a promontory well known to mariners who navigate the Iriſh channel; and here we are again in the latitude of Burrowhead, which now appears at the diſtance of 10 miles eaſtward.

Theſe two capes are ſituated in north lat. 54-44, nearly on a line with Belfaſt, Whitehaven and Durham.

North from	Dublin	96 geographical miles.
————	Amſterdam	164
————	London	226
————	Paris	413
South from	Copenhagen	68
————	Edinburgh	84
————	Stockholm	336
————	Peterſburg	371
————	Bergen	383

Being upon a medium, half way between the capital of France and thoſe of the northern ſtates of Europe.

Such a ſituation implies an extenſive commerce, and flouriſhing manufactures; and ſtill more ſo, when natural advantages, ariſing from a coaſt of 82 miles in length, without including the curves occaſioned by headlands; which coaſt is furniſhed with above 50 ports or creeks, ſome adapted for veſſels of burden, as thoſe of Annan, Dumfries, Kirkudbright, Garlieſtown, the iſle of Whitehorn; others, ſufficient, or which at a ſmall expence might be made ſufficient, for the admiſſion of fiſhing buſſes, or ſmall decked veſſels. On the land-ſide we perceive a ſhore fertile in grain, of which many cargoes are annually exported to Greenock, the Highlands, Dublin and Liverpool *.

The back country is leſs fertile, being compoſed chiefly of rock, thinly covered with earth, producing only heath and ſhort graſs, on which, however, an incredible number of ſmall ſheep, black cattle and horſes, are annually raiſed, both for the home and Engliſh market.

The marine productions are ſalmon, eels, white fiſh, and generally herrings, in greater or leſſer quantities.

Here, therefore, is a ſufficiency by ſea and land, for the ſupport of the people, and a ſurplus for the relief of others; with every natural conveniency of ports and harbours for facilitating fiſheries and commercial intercourſe.

We are next to conſider the relative ſituation of this coaſt with other countries, and the advantages of its local ſituation for trade and fiſheries. It lies in the centre of the three Britiſh kingdoms, nearly at an equal diſtance from Land's End on the ſouth, and the Pentland firth on the north; alſo, between the Britiſh ſea on the eaſt, and Ireland on the weſt. It is (taking the centre of the coaſt as the medium diſtance) within half a day's ſailing of Whitehaven, Workington, Maryport, and other trading towns in

* In the memorable year 1782, this country ſent ſeveral cargoes of grain and meal to Greenock and Port Glaſgow, which contributed to keep the people from ſtarving; they alſo ſent conſiderable quantities of barley to Liverpool and Dublin, at great prices. Their crops happened to be good, and their harveſt was early, while other parts of theſe kingdoms experienced the reverſe.

Cumberland—the counties of Down and Antrim, the ſeats of manufactures, bleacheries, fiſheries and navigation in Ireland—the iſle of Man, remarkable for its great herring fiſheries—within two days ſailing of Glaſgow, Liverpool, Dublin and the Iriſh fiſheries—and within three days ſailing, with a fair wind, of the Hebride fiſheries. We may alſo notice its very favourable ſituation for the American and Weſt-India trade, opening immediately to the Atlantic, and enjoying all the advantages of the Clyde, and the coaſts on the Iriſh channel.

Having thus enumerated the bountiful diſpenſations of the Author of Nature, to this coaſt, we ſhall now ſtate the improvements of ſuch gifts, by the inhabitants.

Of ſhipping, and foreign trade, they have none, the exports of grain and meal, by barks and ſloops excepted.

Of buſſes, for the Iriſh and Hebride fiſheries, they have not a ſingle veſſel.

Of manufactures in ſilk, cotton *, wool, linen, thread, iron, copper, lead, ſteel, ſalt, leather, ſoap, &c. they have not the ſmalleſt appearance.

Hearing theſe circumſtances repeated, without variation, at every village, town, or royal borough, I loſt all patience: "Unhappy beings! how in the name of wonder, do you get a ſubſiſtence?" "We do a little," anſwered they, "in the ſpirit way; we ſmuggle a little:" A proof, among many others, that of all trades, that of ſmuggling, however flattering to ſpeculation, is the moſt fallacious in the experiment.

Previous to the union, this coaſt, as before obſerved, had ſome traffic and ſhipping. Some of the ports were reſpectable, when Greenock, Rothſay, and Campbeltown, were compoſed of a few thatched cottages, and when Port Glaſgow had no exiſtence. The high duties to which Scotland ſub-

* I have juſt been informed that cotton mills are now building at Annan, and Newtonſtewart.

jected

jected itself at the union, held out allurements too flattering for human avarice, and many persons who had procured a livelihood by trade and fisheries, betook themselves to illicit practices, of which we see the fatal consequences wherever that custom prevails, but more particularly on this coast, from one end to the other. This will be further illustrated in the comparison between the present state of these ports, and the four places above-mentioned.

The former took to smuggling; they are beggared, and many of their towns are in ruins. The latter applied to trade, manufactures and fisheries—they are comparatively opulent—elegant buildings; and regular streets occupy the place of straggling thatched huts—their bays are now accommodated with excellent keys, wharfs and storehouses, and a foundation is laid for extensive commerce with Europe and America.

Similar causes will produce similar effects on the Solway firth, as soon as the inhabitants shall apply to ship-building, the making of sails, nets, ropes, salt, casks, and whatever is necessary for the complete equipment of fishing and coasting vessels, in which they have the example of their neighbourhood, in Cumberland, Ireland, the isle of Man, Campbeltown, and Rothsay.

In 1772, the small town of Campbeltown fitted out, and entered for the herring fishery 95 decked vessels, which employed 1235 seamen, and gave employment to persons of all ages belonging to the town and its neighbourhood, from 6 to 80 years or upwards. Now, supposing that the inhabitants of at least 150 miles of coast, including the curves, upon the Solway firth, shall begin to build and equip the same number of vessels, (which, I believe, will be nearly 2 vessels upon an average, for each port or creek) the good effects of this first attempt, would be quickly felt amongst a people who have been long devoted to sloth and indigence, while the returns on the sale of herrings, would incite new enterprizes.

4 Persons

Perſons of both ſexes, and of all ages, would be fully employed and well paid; the whole coaſt would aſſume a new appearance, and joy would gladden every face, inſtead of that dejected gloom which is the preſent characteriſtic of the people of Galloway.

Such would be the conſequences of exchanging the idle habits of ſmuggling for the more certain profits which the ſea affords; and while the inhabitants of the ſhores were thus engaged in the various branches depending on the fiſheries, which may be called the maritime ſtaple of Scotland; ſome attempts might be made towards introducing induſtry through the inland parts of this diſtrict, where the trade of grazing gives employment to a few hands only, while the main body of the people drag out a life in idleneſs and penury. The great national ſtaple of Scotland is the linen manufacture, linen-yarn, and thread; for which there is an unbounded demand in both kingdoms; but ſuch is the inattention of theſe ſouthern inhabitants to induſtry, that while, in 1783,

	Yards.	Value.
The linen ſtamped for ſale in the whole kingdom was	15,348,744	775,100
In the county of Angus alone	6,742,387	177,105
In the counties of Dumfries, Kirkudbright and Wigtown, to which the habitable part of Angus is as 1 to 8, only	47,519	2,167

If the neglect of the fiſheries by theſe people, while all their neighbours are riſing into conſequence by means of that branch, afford matter of ſurprize; the neglect of the linen manufacture muſt appear equally unaccountable in a province furniſhed with ſome hundred ſtreams, many of them conſiderable, and all of them proper for bleaching.

This

This coaſt alſo lies within ſight of that part of Ireland, where the greateſt manufacture of linen in the known world is carried on, by the deſcendants of Scotſmen, chiefly from theſe ſouthern coaſts. The weſtern extremity of Galloway approaches ſo near the counties of Down and Antrim, that the bleachers of the latter may be diſtinctly ſeen with the naked eye. To thoſe bleacheries the farmers of Galloway and Cantire ſend their webs to be whitened, for the uſe of their families, ſaddled with the expence of carriage by land and water.

Upon the whole, theſe countries ſeem to be little removed from a ſtate of nature; it would therefore be meritorious in the board of truſtees at Edinburgh, to encourage certain experienced perſons to inſtruct the people in ſpinning, weaving, bleaching; alſo, in manufacturing materials for the fiſheries.

The coaſt, or the greateſt part of it, labours under ſome natural impediments to infant manufactures, which may in part be removed, with little or no expence to the public. It hath neither coal, lime, turf, nor freeſtone. The coal is therefore brought from Whitehaven, burdened with a high duty, beſides freight and port dues, in loading and unloading. The lime is ſubject to the ſame expenditures, the duty excepted. When theſe articles arrive at the ports, another expence attends the carriage to the inland parts, which is performed by little carts, each drawn by a ſmall horſe, * ſometimes two.

* "The carriages in common uſe," ſays Dr. Johnſon, in his Tour through Scotland, "are ſmall carts drawn by one little horſe; and a man ſeems to derive ſome degree of dignity and importance from the reputation of poſſeſſing a two-horſe-cart."

Theſe carts are, however, ſubject to the ſame duty as carts in England, which contain four times the quantity. The ſame obſervation is applicable to the duty on horſes. In Scotland the horſes in general uſe amongſt the farmers, are not, upon an average, worth above 7l. each, being generally ſmall and lean, from hard labour, upon a ſcanty ſubſiſtence; in England the farm horſes are large, well-fed, and able to draw againſt 2 or 3 of the former, on which accounts theſe duties ſeem unequally levied.

On

On theſe carts, which, when drawn by a ſingle horſe, carry a quantity equal to the load of two London wheel-barrows, a duty was laid in 1783, of 2s. each; and in 1784, it was enacted, that the half-ſtarved farmers who ride theſe half-ſtarved horſes, ſhall pay a duty of 10s. for each horſe ſo rode upon; which duties on horſes and carts, in a country thus miſerably circumſtanced, have occaſioned univerſal diſcontents and murmurings, while the revenue derived therefrom, after deducting the expence of collecting, &c. is ſcarcely worth bringing to account.

The people of theſe parts alſo behold, with much concern, the unequal prices, between that coaſt and Ireland, of candles, ſoap, ſalt, leather, iron and other neceſſaries, for manufactures, fiſheries and common uſe, owing to the high duties to which the Scottiſh nation are ſubject.

Abridgment of Anſwers, &c.

Dumfries. The cod fiſhery in the Solway firth is very inconſiderable, owing to the rapidity of the tides, and the bottom being all looſe and ſandy. Upon the Engliſh ſide it is better, the bottom being harder and firmer, and of courſe more food for the fiſh. The ſalmon fiſhery is the moſt conſiderable on this coaſt. They have alſo a little herring fiſhery, moſtly towards the iſle of Man, but of no great conſequence.

Kirkudbright. The cod fiſhing on this part of the coaſt, is alſo very poor, and the herring fiſhing trifling. The beſt are the ſalmon fiſheries, one of which alone is let for 384l. and is moſtly carried to the Liverpool and Whitehaven markets, and a few to the Weſt Indies.

Wigtown. The cod fiſhing near this, is better than in the two former ports, but not very conſiderable. The herring fiſhery very indifferent, and the

the ſalmon fiſhery good. It appears plain to me, that the ſmallneſs of the fiſhing on the coaſt of theſe parts, is more owing to ſmuggling, than want of fiſh, and that if proper veſſels were ſent farther out to deep water, they would find no ſcarcity of fiſh.

Of the Firth of Clyde, from the Mull of Galloway to Greenock, including the Coaſt of Airſhire, Renfrewſhire, and Part of Wigtownſhire.

Soon after leaving the mull of Galloway, we enter the eaſtern coaſt of the firth of Clyde,* which ſtretches 90 miles in a ſtraight line northward to Greenock, the principal port on that river, and of the whole kingdom, near which place it ceaſes to be navigable for ſhipping.

This coaſt lies in the form of a creſcent, part of Wigtownſhire compoſing the headland on the ſouth; Renfrewſhire on the north; and Airſhire in the centre.

The proſpects from the hills around the mull of Galloway, are magnificently grand. We have here extenſive views of the Atlantic, the firth of Clyde, and the Iriſh channel. On the north appears the craig of Ailſa, riſing from the firth of Clyde in a conical form, to a great height; weſtward is the far-projecting peninſula of Cantire, which ſtretches within 13 miles of the county of Antrim; beyond, on the north-weſt are ſeen Ilay, and the paps of Jura; due weſt the county of Antrim; on the ſouth, is the county of Down, the coaſt of Cumberland, and the iſle of Man. Some writers affirm that this coaſt may be ſeen from Snowdon in Carnarvonſhire, with the naked eye; but, as the diſtance between that lofty mountain and Galloway, is 115 miles, it is probable that the land ſeen from Snowdon, is the mountains of Mourne, in the county of Down, which may, at ſuch a diſtance, be very eaſily miſtaken for the Scot-

* This extenſive coaſt is alſo undeſcribed by travellers.

tiſh

tiſh coaſt. No part of Wales is diſcernible from the latter.

The weſt coaſt of Galloway, facing the Atlantic, abounds in ſmall bays, but being expoſed to the violence of the north-weſterly winds, theſe openings are little frequented, excepting Port-Patric, a ſmall harbour oppoſite Donnaghadee in Ireland, from which it is diſtant ſcarcely 20 miles, and is thereſore the ſtation of the packets to and from that kingdom. Perſons of diſtinction, to avoid a ſea voyage of 60 miles between Holyhead and Dublin, frequently go round by Port-Patric, where they are waſted over in 3 or 4 hours. This place is 90 miles from Glaſgow; 132 from Edinburgh; 136 from Dublin; and 419 from London, by the Carliſle road.

We now turn the Fairland point, which forms the ſouth entrance of Loch Ryan, one of the moſt commodious bays in theſe kingdoms; very acceſſible; well ſheltered from all winds, excepting the north-weſt; with good anchoring ground, of ſufficient depth, in ſome parts for men of war, and in general for merchantmen. It is near 8 miles in length, and 1½ at its entrance, from whence it widens to 2½ miles. At the head of the bay lies Stranrawer, a royal borough, admirably ſituated for trade and fiſheries, eſpecially in ſeaſons when the herrings viſit the bay; of which they availed themſelves, as appears from their exports in 1758, amounting to 13,121 barrels; they alſo attempted the Hebride fiſheries by decked veſſels, but that trade is at preſent nearly extinguiſhed, though the inhabitants are ſtrongly diſpoſed, and well qualified for a maritime life.

The road for Airſhire continues about 8 miles on the north edge of the bay, and hath a commanding view of the oppoſite coaſt, which, owing to the good taſte of certain perſons of diſtinction, is finely laid out and well incloſed with thriving hedges. The coaſt at the north entrance of the bay being loſty, and almoſt perpendicular rocks, waſhed by the ocean, does

does not admit of a road for travellers; the gentlemen of this county, and Airſhire, have therefore formed a good road through Glen-Nap, a moſt ſequeſtered valley, ſeveral miles in length, watered as uſual by a meandering river, which, after collecting the tributary rills of the mountains on each ſide, loſes itſelf in Loch Ryan.

Upon emerging from this glen, the coaſt of Ireland, Cantire, Ailſa, Arran, and other objects, riſe gradually to view. We are now in Airſhire, which conſiſts of three great diviſions, viz. Carric, on the ſouth; Kyle, in the centre; and Cunningham, on the north; the whole compoſing one of the largeſt counties in the ſouth of Scotland; for the moſt part fertile, highly cultivated, incloſed with hedge-rows, ornamented with numerous ſeats, parks and pleaſure grounds of nobility and gentry; abounding in grain, large well-fed cattle and ſheep, coal, limeſtone, and timber.

Its rivers are numerous, ſome of them conſiderable, and generally ſtocked with ſalmon. Its extenſive coaſt, of 60 miles in a line, is ſometimes viſited by the ſhoals of herrings, frequently by fiſh of the leſſer whale kind, and is at all times the repoſitory of white fiſh. Nature having done ſo much by ſea and land, we ſhall next ſtate the *per contra*, on the part of the inhabitants.

After a ſhort ride upon the high lands above Glen-Nap, we deſcend to the coaſt, where the river Stincher falls into the firth of Clyde, forming a harbour for ſmall veſſels, but in a ſtate of nature.

A poor little village, without any appearances of trade or manufactures, called Balintrae, enjoys, or rather abuſes, this fine ſtation for fiſheries of various denominations. Now and then an old man brings in 10 or 12 dozen white fiſh upon ſpeculation, and if per chance, 2 or 3 travellers ſhould dine or ſleep in the village, his fortune is made for that day, and the next. Sometimes theſe indigent perſons will ſell

 haddocs

haddocs, whitings, and small cod, to the amount of 2 shillings.

From this place to Girvan, at the distance of 15 miles, the road is cut along the edges of verdant mountains rising slantingly from the sea, to a great height, and affording excellent pasture for sheep, whose appearance relieves the timorous mind, for wherever sheep can feed, no danger is to be apprehended in travelling; besides, the edge of the road is fenced with a low wall. In some parts the road rises, seemingly, to the height of 300 feet from the sea; while above, there appears to be more than double that height. Every object, whether above, below, or at a distance, is enchanting to the sight, and the whole composes, in clear weather, one of the finest prospects in these kingdoms. Cumberland and the isle of Man, now disappear; Ireland is faintly seen at a great distance due west; but Ailsa, Cantire, Arran, and the Highland mountains, are in full view. The shipping passing to and fro, contribute to enrich the prospect.

Girvan, a large and populous village, is situated at the mouth of the river Girvan, which also forms a natural harbour where fishing vessels might find sufficient water. From this coast the craig of Ailsa lies 9 miles west, and 19 miles from the opposite coast of Cantire. This rock is 2 miles in circumference at the base, is accessible only at one place, and rises to a great height in a pyramidical form. A few goats and rabbits pick up a subsistence among the short grass and furze; but the importance of the rock consists in the great variety and boundless numbers of birds, by which it is frequented, particularly the gannets or solan-geese, whose young are used at the best tables, and bring a good price. Other birds are caught, for their feathers. The rock is rented from the earl of Cassils at 33l. per annum. The depth of water around the base is from 7 to 48 fathoms. It is surrounded with excellent banks, well stocked with cod and other white fish; but such is the infatuation of the people on the coast of Airshire, that these banks are little frequented. There are two roads from Girvan to Air; one by the shore, which, in some parts, leads over the sands, and is only passable at certain times of the tide; it is properly a horse-road, and that only for persons acquainted with the coast. The best, and most frequented, though not the shortest road, is by Maybole, distant 15 miles.

On leaving Girvan we lose sight of the firth of Clyde, and its distant prospects; the road is entirely inland, through an extensive, beautiful, and populous valley, watered by the river Girvan, affording an agreeable variety, after the hair-breadth escapes, and distant views in the former stage. Of the seats in this valley and neighbourhood, that of Sir Adam Fergusson exceeds all others in situation, elegance and taste. The grounds are beautiful, the planting is considerable, judiciously ranged, and in excellent condition. Other particulars could be mentioned, which give still a higher degree of pleasure, but as these speak for themselves, every where around, we shall not attempt further explanation.

Towards Maybole, the low country opens to a great extent, on the north and east, in which direction the eye scarcely perceives a boundary. Maybole is a small but antient town, with little trade, at the distance of 5 miles from the coast, and 9 from Air. Towards this last place we cross the river Don, over a bridge of one arch, said to be wider than that of the Rialto at Venice. A little further, is the large river Air, on which stands the capital of this extensive county, formerly a place of good trade, and seat of fisheries; all of which have vanished, and the people live by one another. Air appears, from history and other documents, to have been a considerable place at the time of the Norman conquest; the vouchers of its antiquity are corroborated by an elegant building, called the Cross, which hath escaped the destructive rage of the laſt and preceding century. The date on this fragment of antiquity is 1055, conſequently it hath ſtood in its place above 730 years, and it is to be wiſhed that the majority of the inhabitants will unite in preſerving it from being deſtroyed by perſons who have expreſſed a ſtrong deſire to that purpoſe. In 1557, the tax levied upon Air was 236 pounds Scots; upon Glaſgow only 202. In 1771, Air was aſſeſſed at 15s. ſterl. and Glaſgow at 18l. 10s. In 1751, the pickled herrings exported from Air, were 6624 barrels; ſince the year 1777, none. Theſe revolutions appear the more extraordinary, when we conſider the very advantageous ſituation of Air, both by land and water; the fertility of the country; the riches of the ſea; its contiguity to the weſtern fiſheries, on one ſide, and to Glaſgow, on the other; the large returns for cattle, grain, and coal; the ample revenues of the town; and particularly the conveniency of its harbour for fiſhing veſſels of every conſtruction. It may however, be preſumed, that a ſober, intelligent people, ſtrongly diſpoſed to induſtry, will avail themſelves of the propoſed regulations to unfetter the fiſheries, annihilate cuſtom-houſe impoſitions, and facilitate the home markets. Completing the great canal, will alſo facilitate the revival of a commercial ſpirit on this coaſt; while on the weſt, a ſhort and ſafe paſſage to the Hebrides will not only open new enterpriſes in the herring and white fiſheries, but alſo enable the inhabitants of Airſhire to ſupply the poor Highlanders with grain, meal, and coal, of which the former have a redundancy, thereby opening new ſources of traffic, to the mutual benefit of the rich as well as the poor country.

Twelve miles due north lies Irvine, a neat ſmall port, which formerly had ſeveral buſſes in the herring fiſhery. At preſent that branch is given up, but the inhabitants ſtill employ a number of brigs in the coal trade to Ireland. Some years ago, it was reſolved to pull down the old church of this pariſh, and erect another on its ſite, when the workmen diſcovered a cemetery con-

taining

taining a number of ſtones, whereon were cut the effigies of armed knights, as large as life, in excellent workmanſhip, with inſcriptions in the Saxon character, ſuppoſed to import the name, quality, and other particulars of the warriors, whoſe remains had been there interred; but ſuch was the ignorance of the inhabitants, that the effigies and writings were effaced, to prepare the ſtones for the new building.

Six miles further, is Saltcoats, whoſe fiſheries have dwindled from 12 to 5 buſſes; but the inhabitants have not loſt their ſpirit; they employ ſeveral veſſels in the coal trade to Ireland; and have eſtabliſhed ſome ſalt-works, a rope-work, and the trade of ſhip-building.

Saltcoats is the laſt and moſt northern town in Airſhire, from whence decked veſſels are fitted out. It is alſo the only port along the extenſive and very dangerous coaſt between Loch Ryan and Greenock, that admits of improvement, for the protection or ſhelter of veſſels, in all kinds of weather, and in every time of the tide. To the want of a ſafe aſylum on this bare coaſt, none of the harbours having more than 13 feet water at ſpring tides, hath been owing the loſs of many ſhips and valuable cargoes, among which were the Ann, the Jeany, and Murdoch, of Glaſgow, and the Thomas of Hull, within theſe few years. Had a fourth part of the value thus loſt, been applied to the enlargement and deepening of this harbour, theſe accidents would have been prevented.

Nature hath almoſt completed the work, by running out two low rocks in the form of a horſe-ſhoe, to the depth of 16 to 18 feet water, on which piers might be built at no great expence to the public, though far beyond the abilities of a ſmall town without revenues, and whoſe main ſtaple, the fiſheries, is almoſt extinguiſhed. The expence of extending the piers, and deepening the harbour will not exceed 8000l.

From this place to Greenoch, diſtant 28 miles, the

the coast becomes lofty, affording no protection in strong westerly winds, for vessels of any size, a small channel, called the Fairly road, excepted. Neither is there any place, that can with propriety be called a town, upon that shore, or within 20 miles of it *.

Between the main land of Airshire and the coast of Cantire, is the isle of Arran, 14 miles in length, and 9 in its greatest breadth, where are the remains of salt-works, coal-works, and other appearances of trade; but at present the whole island exhibits one continued scene of poverty and dejection, bordering on despair. This island is surrounded with fisheries of various denominations; and here are the bays of Lamlash, Brodie, and Ranza, where ships of any burden may safely ride in all weather. At the bottom of the bay, was a fine circular pier, now in ruins. In 1558, the earl of Sussex carried his fleet into this bay, where he landed, burned, and destroyed the whole country around; having performed this service, he proceeded to the small island of Cumbray, which he served in the same manner.

I shall close this survey of the western coast, with the following remarks:

* So late as the year 1263, the Norwegians made a fresh invasion on the west of Scotland, with a fleet of 160 sail, and an army of 20,000 men, commanded by Haquin king of Norway, whose ravages on the coast of Air, Bute, and Arran, reaching the Scottish court, an army was immediately assembled by Alexander III. and a bloody engagement ensued at the village of Largs facing the island of Bute, when 16,000 of the invaders were slain in the battle and flight, with 5000 Scots. Haquin escaped to the Orkneys, where he soon after died of grief. The entrenchments of the Norwegian camp may still be traced along the shore of this place. The Scottish commanders who fell in battle were buried in a rising field, near the village; 3 or 4 persons were interred in one grave, on each side of which was a large stone, a third was placed across the grave, supported at the extremities by the side stones, and in this rude manner the warriors lay entombed. Some years ago the proprietor of the field demolished these repositories of the dead, leaving only one, (a special favour!) which serves to give an idea of the whole.

	Miles.
That between Berwic and the head of the Solway firth, a tract of more than,	70
The head of that firth and the mull of Galloway, a coast of - -	82
The mull of Galloway and Greenock, ditto	90
Also the isle of Arran, whose circumference may be estimated at - -	40
The whole containing, in a straight line,	282

On which tract, and shores, there are no manufactures, trade, fisheries, or shipping, (a few brigs in the coal trade excepted) worthy of notice. Nor is there, on the whole coast, a three-masted ship, or a town whose inhabitants amount to 7000; if therefore, we make allowances for the difference in soil and climate, the situation of the inhabitants in general, is not much preferable to that of the Highlanders; and this, as well as the preceding survey of the Scottish shores, confirms the former observation, that the traffic and business of the kingdom, doth not at present extend beyond the limits of the three navigable rivers, and a portion of the east coast; but even the shipping of these ports is comparatively trifling to that of the neighbouring states of Holland, Hamburgh, and the Baltic.

Ships of 500 tons burden are unknown in Scotland, excepting for the purpose of transporting emigrants to America, and these are purchased from England, Hamburgh, or Russia; consequently, ship-building hath not yet been carried to that extent which it would be the interest of government to raise it, and which the combined maritime strength of France, Spain, Holland, and other states, with whom we may be at war, seems to require.—"It was recollected, says an intelligent writer, that the fitting of our fleets had been retarded, by the combination of carpenters, at the commencement of the late war; that both public and private bodies had been obstructed by similar agreements among the coopers;

at a time too when the journeymen coopers on the Thames, were receiving for their labour 15s. a day, without having raiment for themselves or shelter for their wives. When a body of troops were sent from the Clyde, in 1776, Scotland could not furnish coopers enough to answer the speedy demand for packages, though staves abounded; and the intelligent and active men, who were entrusted with the victualling of that body of troops, collected coopers from the most distant parts of England. An armament then may be delayed or even defeated, amid the pressures of war, by the paucity, or the combination of coopers, which may be procured equally by the incitement of our factions, or by the money of our foes. But, combinations can only be prevented by augmenting the numbers of the defective classes. The augmentation of numbers can alone be gained by additional employments; and thus combinations among tradesmen may be prevented, or beat down, by raising up many competitors among the extravagant workmen, whose services are wanted the most, both in peace and war. It is surely wiser to guard by foresight against public disappointment, than to solace our misfortunes by the downfall of a minister, who may have been merely unable, from the scarcity, or combination of coopers, carpenters, and sailors, to execute a measure without the reach of possibility." The same author, speaking of the great encouragement given by this country to ship-building in America, says,—" Of the 679 vessels, which were required to transport the great West India cargo of 1772 to Britain, much more than two thirds had been built in our colonies; to so great an extent had we resigned the most useful of all our manufactures to our colonies, contrary to the remonstrances of the wisest men of their time. We have been sufficiently solicitous about the manufactures of wool, of hats, and of iron in the colonies; but we have cared little, during the last century, for the more important pertant manufacture of ships. This had been a melancholy remark, were it not that we may derive consolation from reflecting, how much the public wisdom may convert misfortunes into benefits. We may now regain the business of ship-building to no small extent, which our imprudent kindness had given away: our safety requires, that we ought to retain every advantage, which a signal revolution has happily thrown in our way." *

The late war almost annihilated the Scottish shipping, particularly those belonging to Glasgow, Greenock, and other ports on the Clyde, of which,

* It may be agreeable to men of business, as well as to men of speculation, to be informed of the present rates of ship-building, in the southern harbours of England and Wales; as they were communicated by an intelligent person, who made a tour with a view to discover the ship-yard, the cheapest and best.

In the Thames and British Channel.

	per ton.		
At Gravesend, Broad Stairs, Dover and Folkstone,	£. 8	0	0
At Hurstake, Cowes, Southampton, Weymouth, Tingmouth, Bridport, Topsham, Shoreham, Dartmouth and Cawsand, 7l. to - -	7	10	0
In the Bristol Channel, on the English side.			
At Biddeford and Barnstable - -	6	10	0
In the Bristol Channel, on the Welch side.			
At Newenham, Gatecomb, Chepstow, Newport, Hythe and Swansey, 6l. 10s. to -	7	10	0

For those prices the workmen engage to compleat the hull and joiners work, carved work, and the work of painters, glaziers, &c. without any extra charge. At those ship-yards, and indeed all the ship-yards of the kingdom, have been full employment, since the peace. It is this fulness which creates many other ship-yards; and it is the establishment of new ones, which, by means of competition, reduces the price of manufacture to the lowest possible point. We are told that the ship-builders of New England will contract to build ships at 3l. sterling per ton, including the joiners work. If an American-built ship will last 7 years, and a British-built ship 21, surely the latter will prove the cheapest. On such topics it is not worth while to argue about farthings. Even after the American-built ships had arrived in the Thames, they used to require expensive additional joiners work, &c, on the hull.

The above paragraph was inserted by mistake in another place.

it

its asserted, 313 vessels of various sizes, were captured; while other circumstances, as the loss of the exclusive trade to America; the non-payment of the American debts; the superior advantages of Ireland for the supply of that country, and the West Indies; with the decay of the fisheries, all happening at the same period of time, have been heavily felt by the merchants and traders of that coast; every individual suffered in a greater or lesser degree, and hundreds were utterly ruined by that war and the subsequent revolution.

Notwithstanding these adverse circumstances, the commercial spirit of Glasgow and Greenock seem not in the least abated; ship-building, as merchantmen, brigs and sloops, is carried on with the utmost alacrity; numbers of young men, who, from the want of employment at the plow, must have embarked for America, are at present fully engaged in the dock-yards; of whom the proportion to experienced carpenters is as three to one. Every lad thus employed may be considered as adding something to the British navy; and should the business of ship building become general and permanent in that kingdom, as well as in England, navies might be raised almost instantaneously, to the astonishment of mankind, and the terror of united enemies. The obstructions to the success of our naval operations, from the scarcity of seamen, carpenters, coopers and transports, will be more or less removed in proportion to the encouragement given to fisheries, and ship-building in that kingdom. Since the reign of James IV. all the exertions in the latter branch have been made by the people only, unassisted by government in any respect whatever; while in England, Ireland, and the maritime nations of Europe, the public money hath been judiciously and liberally applied to this great object.

There is not in the whole kingdom of Scotland a dock for building or repairing ships of the line. An effort was made some years ago, at Leith, whereby the

the navy was re-inforced with a frigate, the only instance of ministerial favour to that or any other port in Scotland, since the union of the two kingdoms in 1706. The launching of this vessel, a sight so new and extraordinary, drew to Leith, the whole inhabitants of Edinburgh, with the adjacent country; and when we consider the long period of time between the reign of James IV. and his present majesty, it is not to be wondered, if, at the launching a ship of war some untoward events should happen. The wedges were removed, but the frigate, instead of flying into Neptune's arms, with the velocity of an eagle, disappointed the gazing multitude, as if to upbraid their country for its supineness and disrespect to the navy.

Having in this manner attempted to describe the present state of the maritime parts of Scotland, with a view to the extension of fisheries, navigation and ship-building, the following sketches of the interior country properly follows, and from these accounts some idea may be formed of the natural and commercial situation of that antient and very improveable kingdom.

REMARKS

REMARKS

ON THE

SHORT TOUR OF SCOTLAND,

COMPREHENDING THE

SOUTHERN DIVISION OF THAT KINGDOM,

AND A CONSIDERABLE PORTION OF THE HIGHLANDS.

AMONG the benefits arising from turnpike roads, is that of travelling for health or pleasure over this extensive and beautiful island. It is an amusement by which an overgrown, luxurious capital, distributes a portion of its superfluous riches through eighty-five counties, and an incredible number of villages, some of whom consider the money thus acquired, as their staple or main support.

On the other hand, the traveller finds his curiosity gratified, his knowledge extended, or his health restored; while the scenes of penury and distress which often present themselves to view, especially in the countries which we have been describing, will, in the comparison, impress his heart with gratitude towards the Deity, and teach him a lesson of contentment, which, till then, he possibly never had the pleasure of enjoying so completely.

Thus travelling diffuses reciprocal benefits, from the centre, to the most remote corners of Britain; and partly with a view to this important end, as well as to lay open the internal state of the kingdom, I have

have drawn up the following remarks upon that part of the road which is least known, though not the least conducive to health, as all those who have made the experiment, readily acknowledge.

Travelling through the interior parts of Scotland, is no longer attended with the dangers and insurmountable difficulties; the want of necessaries, and other in conveniencies, which deterred our ancestors from visiting these mountainous regions. The people are studious to oblige. Provisions, especially fish, tame and wild fowl; small, but delicate beef, mutton and lamb, are plenty, to those who can afford to pay for them; wines, and spirituous liquors, are yet unadulterated in that country; bed, and table linen, far exceed the expectations of every stranger; but these observations are only applicable to the main roads, which are now generally accommodated with carriages.

The best season for an excursion into Scotland, is, from the middle of May, till the first of August. The weather is then generally dry and clear, a circumstance of the first importance to those who travel either for health or pleasure. The glory of Scotland is its picturesque views, and romantic scenery; which, to explore with satisfaction, requires both a clear sky, and ample time: whoever hurries along in a close carriage, arriving late, and setting out early, must return with a very superficial knowledge of the country, and the manners of the people.

There are 4 roads which lead from London to Edinburgh; viz.

By Berwic, on the east, distance	388
— Wooler, in the centre	378
— Jedburgh ditto, not yet completed, and	
— Carlisle, on the west	396

The difference between all these is trifling; whoever therefore leaves London merely from motives of curiosity, health or information, may set out by the east road, and return by the west. The English counties

counties and principal towns through which he passes on the east road are;

Middlesex.
Hartfordshire.
Bedfordshire.
Huntingdonshire.
A small part of Northamptonshire.
Ditto of Rutlandshire.
Lincolnshire,—Stamford,—Grantham.
Nottinghamshire,—Newark.
Yorkshire,—Doncaster,—YORK.
Bishopric of Durham,—Darlington,—DURHAM.
Northumberland,—NEWCASTLE,—Morpeth.

The county of MIDDLESEX, which extends to Potter's Bar, a little way beyond Barnet, consists of small verdant fields, and the noted Finchley common, where travellers in the night time, are frequently eased of their gold, watches, and other superfluities which gentleman of the road stand in need of.

Hartfordshire, is a beautiful and highly-improved corn county, though destitute of coal, lime, and stone; on which account, living is high, and the villages are mean, being chiefly composed of timber, or timber and clay; yet there is a neatness within, which we look for in vain, either in Scotland, Ireland, or any where on the continent, except Holland.

The same appearances extend as far as Stamford in Lincolnshire, where we first meet with houses built of stone. The country, which, from Hartfordshire to this place, appears low and swampy, is now more agreeably diversified with hills, prospects, and considerable towns.

Passing Grantham, and Newark on the Trent, we arrive at Bawtree in Yorkshire, distant 154 miles from London. Hitherto the inns have every convenience for travellers of all denominations, but their wines are adulterated, and their charges are high. In Yorkshire, and

and from thence northward, the articles are better, the charges are lower, the people more obliging.

Yorkshire exceeds in dimensions any two counties of the kingdom; it is also blessed with a fruitful soil, and an intelligent people, through whose indefatigable industry, the various branches of agriculture, manufactures, and commerce, continue to flourish, though under the heavy pressures which the exigencies of the state, have from time to time, laid upon them. Equally happy is this county in the number of its navigable rivers, which with the aid of artificial navigations, convey the produce of the most remote parts, to the Humber, from whence they are shipped at Hull, to London and the various markets of Europe and America.

The rivers over which the traveller passes in his northern tour, are

The Idle, at Bawtree.
—— Dun, at Doncaster.
—— Alder and Aire, united at Ferrybridge.
—— Wharf, at Wetherby.
—— Nyd, near Welsford.
—— Ure, at Boroughbridge.
—— Swale, at Topclif; and the Tees, which divides Yorkshire from the bishopric of Durham.

On the right of the great road to Edinburgh, is the ancient city of York, the capital of the north, which, though lying a few miles off the great road, every traveller of taste or curiosity, should visit, to behold that stupendous pile, called the Minster, which in magnitude and sculpture hath no equal in these kingdoms, nor is it exceeded by any Gothic edifice amongst the nations of Europe.

York is situated at the distance of 198 miles from London, and in the centre between that city and Edinburgh. The district from York to Durham is one continued tract of rich inclosures, luxuriant in grain and pasture, inhabited by an opulent tenantry, accommodated with elegant lodgings, rich orchards, well

well-furnifhed tables, and handfome geldings to ride upon to church or market, worth from 20 to 50 guineas each.

Durham, capital of that bifhopric, hath alfo an antient edifice, built partly by the munificence of David king of Scotland; and here, at the Red Lion, the traveller firft perceives the rural beauties of the northern rivers, rolling over beds of maffy ftones, between precipitous, craggy banks, ornamented with trees, fhrubberies and viftas, enlivened with the chorufes of the feathered creation, proclaiming their gratitude to the Author of thefe fylvan habitations.

From this reprefentation of the northern rivers, it may be fuppofed that the defcent on one fide, and the afcent on the other, are fomewhat diftreffing and inconvenient, efpecially to thofe who travel in carriages, and who cannot, or will not, walk a little way, either for their own fafety, or the eafe of the horfes.

The ftage from Durham to Newcaftle being upon high ground, commands the richeft, and moft extenfive profpects on the road from London to this highly-cultivated country. The Tyne, a copious ftream flowing from the weft, clofes thefe enchanting views. On croffing this river we enter the county of Northumberland, which extends 64 miles due north to Berwic, where it borders with Scotland.

Newcaftle is a county of itfelf, large, populous, commercial, and flourifhing. It is properly the firft mart of the north, in exports, imports, and fhipping, befides its coal-trade, which is immenfe. Its principal manufactures are thofe of glafs, bottles, hardware, fhip-building, and falt-works. Ships load and unload as high as the bridge, between which and Shields, 7 miles below, the river forms one continued harbour, furrounded with an extenfive country, rich in grain and pafturage. Provifions are plentiful, good and cheap. But the glory of Newcaftle is its charitable foundations, though thefe being

ing ſo very general over the whole kingdom; in every town and village proportioned to the abilities of the inhabitants, renders minute deſcription unneceſſary.

The country from Newcaſtle northward, ſeems to excel, were it poſſible, thoſe we have paſſed, in beauty, fertility, and huſbandry.

Morpeth, a large handſome market-town, ſtands on the river Wanſbeck, from whence its exports in grain are very conſiderable.

Some years ago, a road was formed from this place to Edinburgh, by private ſubſcription, through Wooler and Kelſo; which, though it ſaves 10 miles, and affords the traveller a view of the Cheviot hills, Kelſo, the Tweed, and the Tiviot, muſt yield to the Berwic road, both in goodneſs and the variety of pleaſing objects.

Therefore, leaving the Wooler road on the left, we advance to Alnwic, a neat market-town on the river Alne, the reſidence of the antient, the heroic, the opulent and magnanimous family of the Piercies, earls of Northumberland, who, with the Douglaſſes, were long the admiration of Europe; and often the dread of their reſpective ſovereigns. The family ſeat at this place is built in the Gothic ſtyle, moſt ſumptuouſly furniſhed and ornamented; and is open to every ſtranger or traveller who chooſes to walk in. Here the duke lives in ſtate, entertains all ranks of people liberally, from the jolly votary of Bacchus, to the decayed labourer. Nor is the munificence of this family confined to mere acts of charity; the town of Alnwic, and the whole country, have been greatly improved by the preſent owner.

The lands are finely incloſed, planting is riſing on every ſide; the farm-houſes have been moſtly rebuilt in a handſome ſtyle, the roads are kept in good repair, and every circumſtance for the conveniency of the tenants, or the embelliſhment of the eſtate, hath its due ſhare of attention. This great

N n expence

expence neceſſarily requires an increaſe of rent, which, however, does not exceed the bounds of reaſon, humanity, and moral juſtice. Though the rent-roll hath increaſed from 25 to near 60,000l. per annum, this extraordinary ſum is punctually paid, and all parties are ſatisfied. It is not paid in kind, as formerly, but in caſh or bank notes, at the family ſeat, every 6 months, when the tenants in their Sunday's clothes, have an audience of the ſtewards, who give receipts, and take memorandums of repairs and other works to be done. On theſe occaſions, a kind of jubilee is held for 12 or 14 days. The ſpits and the kettles are kept in full employ; the great tables groan under the weight of the mighty ſirloin, the capacious plumb-pudding, and a hundred articles beſides, in butcher's meat, fiſh, paſtry, &c. which are waſhed down in copious potions of wine, punch, or home-brewed ale, ſo old and ſo powerful, as to conquer every man, however ſtout, who gives it a fair trial. In theſe particulars we perceive that the antient hoſpitality and manners, have not intirely fled old England.

The riſing ground on the north ſide of the river, gives a full view of this princely ſeat and its pleaſure-grounds. Weſtward, the mountains ſeem to draw towards the ſea, of which we have a full view; affording an agreeable variety to the generality of travellers, and a new ſight to many.

The laſt ſtage is Belford, a modern village, where the houſes are regularly built, and numbered on the doors, as in London. To Berwic there is nothing remarkable, excepting Holy Iſland, a ſmall ſpot, ſeparated by a narrow channel from the main land, whereon ſtands the antient caſtle of Bamborough. "The iſland was purchaſed from the Foſters, by lord Carew, biſhop of Durham, and with other conſiderable eſtates, left veſted in truſtees, to be applied to unconfined charitable uſes. Three of theſe truſtees are a majority: one of them makes this

2 place

place his residence, and blesses the coast by his judicious and humane application of the prelate's generous bequest. He has repaired and rendered habitable the great square tower: the part reserved for himself and family, is a large hall, and a few smaller apartments; but the rest of the spacious edifice is allotted for purposes which make the heart to glow with joy when thought of. The upper part is an ample granary; from whence corn is dispersed to the poor without distinction, even in the dearest time, at the rate of 4 shillings a bushel; and the distressed, for many miles round, often experience the conveniency of this benefaction.

"Other apartments are fitted up for the reception of shipwrecked sailors; and bedding is provided for 30, should such a number happen to be cast on shore at the same time. A constant patrole is kept every stormy night along this tempestuous coast, for above 8 miles, the length of the manor, by which means numbers of lives have been preserved. Many poor wretches are often found on the shore in a state of insensibility; but by timely relief, are soon brought to themselves.

"It often happens, that ships strike in such a manner on the rocks, as to be capable of relief, in case numbers of people could be suddenly assembled: for that purpose a cannon is fixed on the top of the tower, which is fired once, if the accident happens in such a quarter; twice, if in another; and thrice, if in such a place. By these signals the country people are directed to the spot they are to fly to; and by this means, frequently preserve not only the crew, but even the vessel; for machines of different kinds are always in readiness to heave ships out of their perilous situation."

I have given the history of this charity on a double account; first, that it may stimulate others to follow the example in hazardous situations for shipping; and secondly, as a rebuke to such of the Scottish

 travellers

travellers as enter England with narrow-minded religious prejudices againſt the eſtabliſhment of that country, and particularly that learned and reſpectable body, the biſhops, who, in the opinion of enthuſiaſts, will be denied the felicity of a future ſtate. Let all ſuch perſons hide their faces, and tremble for their unchriſtian diſpoſition towards their fellow-creatures, and the miſchievous conſequences to ſociety, wherever ſuch preſumption gains the aſcendant.

A few miles further, opens a view of the ſweet winding Tweed; little indebted, however, at this place, to human induſtry, in the planting of trees and other decorations. Berwic now appears riſing from the north ſide of the river, over which there is a handſome bridge of 16 arches. Berwic is ſituated 335 miles from London, and 53 from Edinburgh.

It was antiently a place of great ſtrength, ,and of more conſiderable dimenſions than at preſent; often taken by the Engliſh, and as often retaken; at length it was finally wreſted from the Scots in 1482, and is now a county of itſelf, governed by the Engliſh laws, though ſituated in Scotland. Its harbour, ſalmon-fiſheries, and exports, have formerly been mentioned. On leaving this place, we have to aſcend a hill, which riſes, as uſual, to a great height from the river, and affords a variety of proſpects; on the eaſt is the main ſea, on the ſouth is Berwic, the Tweed, and the coaſt of Northumberland; and on the ſouth-weſt are the Cheviot hills.

We are now in the ſhire of Merſe, formerly Berwicſhire: it conſiſts of two diviſions, the lower and the upper; the lower diviſion ſtretches along the north ſide of the Tweed near 30 miles in length, and is in general a pleaſant well-improved country; the upper part is that through which we paſs to Edinburgh, and being moſtly high lands, the air is ſharp, and the ſoil indifferent.

A few

A few miles from Berwic, we arrive at Eyton, on the river Eye, where a gentleman of the name of Fordyce hath begun the laudable work of hedge inclosures, which in a few years, will have a pleasing effect; but of trees there is a scarcity, excepting dull clumps of firs, a mode of planting very common in that kingdom, though scarcely deserving the name of ornamental planting. Dr. Johnson, who expressed his sentiments freely on this subject, hath thereby given great offence, though he only spoke what all Englishmen think, when they first perceive the naked state of that country. The old custom of inclosing with stone dikes, begins, however, to be exploded by gentlemen who have any regard for the ornament of their country, the warmth of their grounds, and the protection of the cattle, from the piercing winds of winter, and the flies in summer.

Experience hath convinced them that hedge rows, interspersed at proper distances with spiral trees, are incomparably preferable, in respect of beauty, utility, and duration. This hath long been the practice in most parts of England, where all the branches of husbandry are carried to the highest perfection. Here every field affords shade and shelter; the crops are great, and the pasture is rich. The thorns are planted in double or treble rows, properly fenced from the cattle; the soil is occasionally turned up; and the weeds are carefully taken out. A strong, impenetrable hedge soon repays the first cost, in the warmth of the grounds and the condition of the cattle, and no expence is required in repairs, to which stone dikes are ever subject. The planting of hedges and trees was considered of such consequence in antient times, that the states of Scotland enforced it by laws and penalties*.

From

* "The lords thinkis speedefull, that the king charge all his free-halders, baith spirituall and temporall, that in the making of thei

From Eyton we arrive at Coldingham-moor, the eastern extremity of a ridge of hills, which, under various

their Whitsundayis set, they statute and ordaine, that all their tennentes plant woodes and trees, and make hedges, and saw broome, after the faculties of their maillinges, in place convenient therefore, vunder sik paine as law and vnlaw of the barronne or lord sall modifie. James II. anno 1457."

"It is statute and ordaned, anent policie to be halden in the cuntrie, that everilk lorde and laird, make them to haue parkes with deare, stankes, cunningares, dowcattes, orchardes, hedges, and plant, at the least, ane aicker of woodde, quhair there is nae greater woddes nor forrestes." James IV. anno 1503.

There is not a word in these laws respecting stone dikes. We may therefore suppose Scotland to have been a well-inclosed country, till the death of James V. in 1542, when Henry VIII. and the subsequent regency, not finding their proposals of a marriage relished by the Scots, between Edward VI. and the young queen Mary, laid the country waste from sea to sea. In a report made to Henry VIII. by the English wardens of the marches, containing the particulars of their destructive incursions between the 2d of July and the 17th of November, 1544, is the following account:

Towns, towers, stedes, barnekyns, parish-churches, bastel-houses, cast down or burnt — —	192
Scots slain — — — —	403
Prisoners taken — — — —	816
Nolt, or horned cattle taken — — —	10,386
Sheep — — — —	12,492
Nags and geldings — — —	1,296
Goats — — — —	200
Bolls of corn — — —	850
Insight geare without measure.	

In another inroad by the earl of Hereford, between the 8th and 23d of September, 1545, that nobleman rased and destroyed in the counties of Berwic and Roxburgh only

Monasteries and friar-houses — — —	7
Castles, towers, and piles — — —	16
Market towns — — — —	5
Villages — — — —	243
Milns — — — —	13
Hospitals — — — —	3

But these were only petty exploits compared to the rough courtship during the subsequent regency, after Henry's death.

The attention of the people being engrossed with ecclesiastical affairs during the succeeding reigns, no care was taken to repair these misfortunes; objects of national utility and ornament were neglected;

various names, extends from Coldingham to the firth of Clyde on the west, thereby crossing the kingdom from sea to sea, and dividing the south of Scotland into two parts. No traveller can therefore reach Edinburgh or Glasgow, without passing these hills; but the trouble of ascending them is amply repaid by the grandeur of the prospects which they command, in the descent northwards.

In this moor the traveller is happy to find a decent inn and good accommodations, called Press-inn, 12 miles from Berwic. The ascent still continues through a bleak tract of 3 miles, when the road takes a slanting north-west direction, on the declivity of the hills, and gradually opens a most extensive view of the north-coast, as far as the promontory of Red-head, in the shire of Angus, distant above 50 miles, due north. That coast is, however, soon intercepted, by the coast of Fife, which stretches along the north side of the Forth, from Fifeness, the eastern point, as far westward as the eye can perceive. The entrance of the Forth is distinguished on the

neglected: the country being laid waste, remained in that state till the beginning of the present century, when the religious ferment subsided, and peace and security being established, the gentlemen of the Lothians, began to direct their attention to inclosures, and other rural improvements, but without any regard to the laws of their country: instead of hedges, they put themselves to considerable expence in building dikes of stone and lime; which served to confine the cattle from wandering, but not to give them shelter or protection; the consequence is, that in hot weather they run from one side of the field to the other, during the greatest part of the day, and thus waste themselves; to this, therefore, as well as the scarcity of grass and sustenance, is owing the general leanness of the cattle in that country. Neither are these fields so well supplied with water as in England. This example of the Lothians, soon became general in the kingdom, where pitiful dikes of loose pebbles, collected from the corn-fields, were called fences, and the grounds inclosed therewith, honoured with the name of parks. At length the Glasgow merchants seeing the inefficacy of those miserable expedients, and ashamed of the appearance of their country, struck into the wise plan of hedging and planting, recommended in ages which we call barbarous.

north ſide, by the iſle of May, and on the ſouth by the Baſs iſland, a rock of 300 feet in height, covered with an incredible number of ſolan-geeſe, and was antiently a ſtate priſon. The Baſs, from whatever direction ſeen, is one of the principal objects in the magnificent views which theſe hills afford, whether by the Berwic or the Kelſo road; it is alſo ſeen diſtinctly from Stirling-caſtle, 50 miles weſt. This rock is only acceſſible at one place, and that with difficulty, and in moderate weather, yet old people remember an orchard on the ſummit.

A fertile country, and decent farm-houſes, with well-filled yards, now begin to appear on every ſide*. The farms let from 2 to 500l. per annum.

Had this country, which for ſeveral miles lies in a ſloping direction to the edge of the ſea, been incloſed and ornamented after the Engliſh manner, the road to Edinburgh having ſuch commanding views of planting, water, and ſhipping, would have drawn the admiration of every traveller.

The deſcent from Coldingham-moor terminates with a glen called the Peaſe, formerly the terror of female travellers, but now rendered perfectly ſafe by means of a bridge juſt completed, which extends from one ſide of the frightful chaſm to the other, and is of itſelf a curioſity.

It conſiſts of 4 arches, and 3 piers, 2 of which are built on rock; the height of the arches, including the battlements, is 137 feet; and the length of the bridge 325. The expence of the whole, which hath been generouſly raiſed by the gentlemen of the adjacent country, amounts to 1500l. The glen above and below is filled with well-grown trees.

We are now within 36 miles of Edinburgh; the

* Happening to paſs through this country in November laſt, I took particular notice of the farm-yards, all of which were well filled with large handſome ſtacks, placed in rows with mathematical exactneſs, and amounting in number, from 30 to 36.

road

road is good and the country level; bounded on the south, by a lofty chain of hills; on the north by the Forth; having the opposite coast of Fifeshire always in view.

Dunbar, 27 miles from Edinburgh, is a handsome royal borough, antiently the residence of the potent earls of Hume, of whose castle, which gave shelter to Edward II. in his flight from Bannocburn, scarcely a vestige remains. At this place are preserved some of the Scottish pikes, 6 ells in length, the unwieldy implements of attack and defence in former ages. "As easily," says an English writer who was at the battle of Pinkey, "shall a bare finger pierce through the skin of an angry hedge-hog, as any encounter the front of their pikes."

From this place the road is perfectly level to Haddington, the capital of the county of East Lothian, formerly a place of trade and consequence, at present a poor royal borough.

A few miles further, we pass the field of Preston Pans, where the brave colonel Gardener lost his life near his own garden walls, when 3000 half-armed Highlanders, defeated, and almost cut to-pieces, the royal army, commanded by general Cope. At a short distance stands the large village of Musselburgh, at the mouth of the river Esk. The Forth at this place, hath the appearance of an inland sea, widening from 9 miles at its entrance, to 18 miles between Musselburgh and Largo Bay, in Fifeshire. Though now within 6 miles of Edinburgh, the traveller perceives no part of that city till he hath arrived at the base of Arthur's seat, where he finds himself at once amidst smoke and business.

This metropolis is situated in 55 degrees, 57 minutes north latitude, and 3 degrees, 14 minutes, longitude from London.

Distant from that city, by Carlisle, 396 miles; } 388
——by Wooler and Kelso, 378; by Berwic }

Distant

Diſtant from Glaſgow, by Calder, 44; by Falkirk —— ——	48
——Dungſbay-Head, in Caithneſs ——	273
——Port-Patric, in Galloway ——	132
——Dublin, by ditto —— ——	268

It ſtands in the centre of that fine tract of land which ſtretches 50 miles along the ſide of the Forth, called the Three Lothians, and within 2 miles of the ſpacious Forth, having thereby the benefit of ſea-breezes, which, in winter, blow pretty freſh on a city of ſuch elevation.

The country around being alſo finely variegated with hill and dale, contributes to the health of the citizens. Here agues, and ſome other diſorders common in England, are little known.

The ſite of the old town is extremely ſingular; a ridge or hill, riſes from the weſt ſide of Arthur's ſeat, by a gradual aſcent, and in a weſterly direction, to the height of 180 feet. It ſtretches above a mile in length, and terminates in a perpendicular rock of 300 feet from the baſe. This rock being inacceſſible on all ſides, except the eaſt, naturally ſuggeſted the expediency of a fortreſs on the ſummit, conſiſting of an area of 6 Engliſh acres; in what age, or by what people it was made a place of ſtrength, hiſtory is ſilent. From this origin we may, however, trace the progreſs of the city; firſt, in houſes built contiguous to the fortreſs or caſtle, by which they might be protected, and there increaſing, from age to age, extended at length to the oppoſite or lower termination of the ridge, near the bottom of Arthur's ſeat. The old city therefore conſiſts chiefly of one ſtreet, built on the ſummit of this ſloping ridge, and extending from one hill to the other. It is ſtraight, well-built, and conſidered by the inhabitants as magnificent. The houſes are generally 5 or 6 ſtories high in front, and from 6 to 10 ſtories backwards, owing to the narrowneſs of the ridge, and its rapid declivity on each side*. The whole, at a distance, having the appearance of vast buildings, crowding for security under the wings of the castle.

The views from Edinburgh are its glory; as its incommodious buildings; its narrow dirty lanes, there called wynds and closses, are its disgrace. An open space between the main street and the gates of the castle, called the Castle-hill, affords the citizens an airing before breakfast, dinner, or in the evening, with an extensive view of the new town, the Forth, the shipping, and the adjacent countries. From the castle itself, the views are still more magnificent; but these must yield to a circular walk on the summit of the Calton hill, which affords prospects of town and country in every direction, so variegated and enchanting, as even to surpass the extravagant descriptions in romance; yet these views, however improbable it may seem to persons who have not been at Edinburgh, are lost in the comparison with what Arthur's seat commands.

This hill, as before observed, forms the eastern boundary of the town, from whence it rises to the height of 700 feet, being more than double the height of the cross on the top of St. Paul's, London, which is 340 feet. It terminates in a point, where the traveller may sit down, and survey at his ease, the centre of the kingdom; besides a compleat view of Edinburgh, and its castle, on which he looks down, as if seated among the clouds. These near views have been greatly heightened by the buildings lately erected, and will receive additional splendour from those now in contemplation.

The city being chiefly raised upon a narrow ridge, with one main street extending along the summit, a number of narrow lanes, upon the declivity on each

* The front of the exchange is 60 feet; the back-wall 100; but there are back walls that seem much higher than the exchange, where I have reckoned 11 or 12 stories.

side,

fide, where neither carriages nor horfes could pafs without danger, thereby loft, in a great meafure, the advantages arifing from the refort of perfons of rank or fortune, many of whom took up their winter refidence elfewhere, and thus the balance procured by the induftrious manufacturers with foreign nations, was regularly drained away by the opulent and idle, to the feats of diffipation, in diftant climates. At length, feveral public-fpirited gentlemen and citizens, beholding with concern, the miferable condition of their metropolis, and perceiving the advantages which nature offered for its improvement and extenfion, publifhed a plan of a new city, in a more eligible fituation, for the refidence of the higher ranks in life, and totally unconnected with the old town.

The defcent on the north fide of this ftrange mafs of buildings, terminates in a narrow valley called the North Loch, from its having been formerly covered with water. This valley extends the whole length of the town, from eaft to weft, and is bounded on the north by a rifing ground, which ftretches in a parallel direction with the old city, three quarters of a mile in length, the breadth fufficient for three ftreets to run in the fame direction; the fummit is flat, the foil is gravel, and the air is pure, of which Boreas frequently fends copious drafts from the north-eaft and fouth-weft. This fine fpot is bounded weftward by a romantic fteep glen, fhaded with trees, under which the water of Leith flows towards the town of that name, and forms its harbour. Thus bounded on the fouth by the North Loch, on the weft by the water of Leith, on the north by the fame river at a fhort diftance, nature could not have formed a place more fuitable for enlarging an over-crowded capital; and, confequently the magiftrates, in 1767, obtained an act for extending the royalty over the faid grounds; marked the outlines of a new town, upon a regular plan

plan of architecture; a view of the ſame was publiſhed on copper-plate; and lots of ground were immediately taken by the nobility, gentry, and principal inhabitants, upon building leaſes, ſubject to quit rents payable in perpetuity to the corporation. The houſes were to be of ſtone and ſlate; commodious, elegant, uniform, and the height limited to three ſtories. The ſtreets were to be from ninety to one hundred and twenty feet wide, perfectly ſtraight, and to croſs each other at right angles. Each end of the town was to terminate with a ſquare; churches and public buildings, were to be erected in the moſt conſpicuous places, for ornament as well as conveniency. The North Loch, at preſent an unwholeſome quagmire, was to be formed into a canal, bordered by terrace walks, and the aſcent to the new town covered with ſhrubberies, &c.

Thus far the deſign of this intended ſeat of elegance was laid out, and conducted with taſte and judgment. "But when gentlemen had begun to build elegant houſes on the faith of the new plan, they were ſurpriſed to find the ſpot appointed for terraces and a canal, beginning to be covered with mean irregular buildings, and workhouſes for tradeſmen." Thus the magiſtrates, not ſatisfied with an increaſe of revenue, both ſudden and unexpected, had nearly fruſtrated the noble work, by deviating from the magnificent plan which had been publiſhed by their authority. The conſequence, was a ſuit before the houſe of peers, in which the magiſtrates were caſt, with loſs and diſgrace; beſides the mortification of having the management of this buſineſs transferred to the hands of the lord preſident of the court of ſeſſion, and the lord chief baron of the exchequer.

By this equitable and patriotic deciſion of the houſe of peers, in thus wreſting the capital from the hands of Vandals, gentlemen were encouraged to proceed in a plan, which, though ſome deformities have eluded their obſervation, owing to the ſtrange infatuation

tuation of the magiſtrates, ſurpaſſes any pile of buildings in theſe kingdoms, of the ſame extent.

One half of the ground is already covered; and, in a few years, the whole will be engaged. The original plan, which was drawn by an ingenious architect, is ſo judicious in all its parts, as to preclude the poſſibility of improvement thereon, one inſtance excepted; viz. to ſhelter the two outſide ſtreets (each of which conſiſting only of one row of houſes) from the cutting winds of the winter, by planting the deſcents on the oppoſite ſides with quick-growing trees, of the moſt ornamental ſpecies, as beeches, larches, aſpine, Cheſhire thorn, and particularly Lombardy poplars, which for their great beauty are now become univerſal around London. Theſe, in a few years, will riſe above the level of the ſtreets, and gradually ſcreen the firſt ſtories; while the ſummits may be planted with double rows of trees, ſo as to protect the upper ſtories, and afford an agreeable ſhade, in ſummer. Trees thus diſpoſed, will alſo correct the air, embelliſh the town, and form a convenient, healthful walk to the inhabitants, eſpecially thoſe whoſe age or infirmities confine them to the vicinity of their habitations. All ſchemes of covering the open ſide of theſe ſtreets with houſes or ſhops, to the height of one ſtory, as propoſed by an anonymous writer, ought to be conſidered as the deluſive projects of intereſted perſons, more attentive to private views, than the ornament and benefit of their country. The manifold advantages ariſing from theſe improvements to individuals, the corporation, and the kingdom at large, are now generally acknowledged; and ſuch hath been the ſpirit and activity of James Hunter Blair, Eſq. that during the few months of his mayoralty, he hath drawn up a moſt judicious plan of improvements on the ſouth ſide of the town, combated the prejudices and the ſelfiſh motives of oppoſition; and procured an act of parliament empowering the magiſtrates,

gistrates,

giſtrates, and certain truſtees, to carry on the important works ſpecified in the ſaid ſtatute.

It hath already been obſerved, that the old town is built on a narrow ridge or hill, lying almoſt due eaſt and weſt; that a valley or glen runs parallel with this ridge on the north, called the North Loch; and another on the ſouth, called the Cowgate, whoſe banks, though equally ſteep as the former, are crowded with buildings.

The reader may thereſore conceive three towns, ſeparated by nature ſrom each other: The north, or new town; the middle or old town; and a confuſed medley of antient and modern buildings, on the ſouth.

To connect theſe detached parts, and to open ſaſe and ſhort communications ſrom one to the other, became a matter of poſitive neceſſity, however expenſive to a city deeply involved in debts. In 1763, George Drummond Eſq. then Lord Provoſt of Edinburgh, and an ornament of human nature, laid the foundation ſtone of a bridge, to be built acroſs the North Loch, thereby to join the old and the new town. The length of this bridge is 1125 ſeet; the height of the three principal arches ſrom the baſe to the top of the parapet, is 68 ſeet; the breadth 40 ſeet. The whole expence of this great work did not exceed 20,000l. being nearly double the ſum ſor which the architect imprudently engaged to complete it.

The utility of the bridge was immediately perceived; the ſame means became neceſſary to join the old town with the buildings on the ſouth ſide of the Cowgate, and a clauſe is inſerted ſor this purpoſe in the bill lately enacted; by virtue of which, the Lord Provoſt laid the ſoundation ſtone of the *ſouth bridge*, on the firſt of Auguſt 1785; which bridge is to be built in a ſtraight line ſrom the *north bridge*, acroſs the Cowgate; and ſrom thence ſouthward,

ward, a handſome opening is to be made leading to the country.

The univerſity, an irregular motley building, ſcarcely deſerving the name of architecture, is the object of another clauſe in the ſtatute; but the erecting of theſe and other works mentioned in the bill, however laudable and neceſſary, ſeem far beyond the abilities of a corporation ſo involved in debts, and a univerſity having no accumulating revenues. Though ſome millions have been expended, and with great propriety, by government, on the capital of England *, ſince the union of the two crowns; and though

* It would be impoſſible, at this time, to aſcertain preciſely, the public expenditure on works of utility and ornament in this great capital, excluſive of the city expenditures; ſome idea may, however, be formed from a ſtatement of the following parliamentary grants within theſe laſt thirty years.

Building Weſtminſter bridge —— ——	389,000
Repairing London bridge —— ——	100,000
Horſe Guards, probably —— ——	100,000
Somerſet Houſe, if carried on as it ought to be, upon the moſt extenſive plan, will coſt ——	400,000

The expenditures by the Iriſh parliament, on the capital of a dependant province, with little trade and few manufactures, ſeem to exceed credibility; but the gentlemen and citizens of that kingdom have great public ſpirit; they love magnificence, and are fond of embelliſhing their capital upon the models of Greece and Rome. They are equally attentive to the improvement of their harbour; about thirty years ago, or upwards, they began to build a wall equal in breadth to a moderate ſtreet, which, when completed from Ring's End to the Light-houſe in the bay of Dublin, will extend three miles. This great work was undertaken with a view to protect ſhipping in their paſſage to and from Dublin, through an open, and often a fatal bay, as well as to deepen the channel, which at high water hath only eighteen feet. The work is not yet completed, though 2 or 300,000l. hath been expended; probably the whole, when finiſhed, will coſt half a million; and it is propoſed to carry a ſimilar wall upon the north ſide of the channel; if this ſhall be carried into execution, the ſum total will be 1,000,000l. The canal from Dublin to the Shannon, hath coſt upwards of 300,000l. agreeable to the declaration of Sir Lucius O'Brien; though little more than thirty miles are yet completed, being ſcarcely one third of the intended

though more than a million hath been expended by the Irish parliament on the metropolis of that country, its

ended line of navigation. The whole when finished, may cost 800,000l. at the lowest calculation. Another little bit of a job, the custom-house, is now carrying on at an expence of 400,000l. and if parliament throws in another 50,000l. it will be a good guard against conflagration. The building is composed of highly finished Portland stone; and when completed, will display one of the most extensive and magnificent structures in Europe. On the grand front facing the Liffey, are the gods of the twelve rivers in Ireland, having long beards and large piercing eyes, beholding with satisfaction cargoes of Irish produce and manufacture departing from Dublin to feed and cloath the world. A bridge is to be built directly from the custom-house to the south side of the river, from whence a spacious street, possibly a mile in length, is to be carried to the verge of the town, and there terminated by an extensive square, circus or crescent. A trifle of 500,000l will do this business completely.

Dame-street, which leads from the castle to the parliament-house, being too narrow for a general thoroughfare, it was resolved to remedy the inconvenience, not by pulling down a few corner houses, but by erasing the whole south side of the street, about a quarter of a mile in length, and erecting a uniform row of houses, with large elegant shops, suitable to the magnificence of the city. A few hundred thousand pounds will purchase the property and complete the new buildings.

To enumerate bridges, prisons, barracks for 4 or 5000 soldiers, circular roads, hospitals and other works from 5 to 20,000l. each, would encroach upon the reader's time, and life is short. I shall therefore only add some of the parliamentary grants during the sessions of 1785.

To Mr. Cunningham on account of fisheries, store-houses, &c. ——— ———	£. 20,000
To encourage the growth of hemp and flax, —	2,000
For bounties upon home-made manufactures made above ten miles from Dublin ———	20,000
For providing wheels, reels, looms, and other machinery for such manufacturers of Dublin as would remove to the country ——— ———	5,000
For apprenticing out children from charter schools	4,000
Annual funds of the protestant schools to be extended to	10,000
Ditto ——— the foundling hospital ———	14,000
Ditto ——— the house of industry ———	10,000
Ditto ——— the marine school ———	1,000
Ditto ——— the Hibernian school ———	1,000
Ditto ——— the first fruits ———	3,000
Building record offices, and 4 courts ———	3,000
Dublin society ——— ———	5,000
Inland navigations over and above other supplies ———	7,000

harbour, bay and canal; we do not find that the British parliament have ever voted the ſmalleſt moiety towards the relief, the ornament, or the conveniency of the hitherto decayed metropolis of Scotland; nor is there reaſon to hope, that any aſſiſtance whatever will be granted, beyond the trifle allowed from the forfeited eſtates, for completing the regiſter office. The inhabitants of Edinburgh, to the high taxes already impoſed by government and the corporation, muſt take upon themſelves, the expence of theſe improvements alſo; and that not with a ſparing hand, but to the utmoſt of their abilities. Enlightened and animated by two patriotic magiſtrates of taſte and judgment, they are to conſider themſelves as the founders of a great and ſplendid city, which, from the advantages of nature, and a due regard to the embelliſhments of art, may eclipſe in beauty, any city in Europe, thoſe of Italy excepted. Inveſted with almoſt unlimited powers by government, it is now optional in themſelves whether to raiſe a maſs of deformity, or draw thither a reſort of ſtrangers and an influx of money by the elegance and ſymmetry of the private buildings; the magnificence of the public ſtructures; the openneſs and regularity of the ſtreets, and other objects which will occaſionally preſent themſelves.

A third improvement of very eſſential conſequence to this city, ſeems to have eſcaped the notice of the inhabitants. It hath been already obſerved, that the rock on which the caſtle is built, bounds the city on the weſt. The new town, when completed to Leith water, will extend ſome hundred feet beyond the caſtle. A road hath lately been opened in a line from this point of the new town, on the north, to the new buildings on the ſouth.. The intermediate ground between this road and the caſtle, conſiſts of ſloping fields, which extend directly to the baſe of the rock. The fields thus ſituated in the centre between both

town, and on that side of the castle which affords the most magnificent prospect of the rock; lying also on the side of the town, which is least annoyed by smoke, (being, in the sea term, on the windward side, during two thirds of the year) seem intended by nature, as an agreeable outlet to the inhabitants, for health, exercise, society, and amusement.

With a view to these essential purposes, as well as the ornament of the town, and the accommodation of strangers in genteel life, the whole might be laid out in pleasure grounds, with terraces, shrubberies, &c. in the manner of Vauxhall, and inclosed with a dwarf wall, and elegant rails of cast iron.

Though the fields lie at present on the verge of the town, there is reason to suppose, that in less than half a century, they will be nearly in the centre of an extensive, elegant capital, which affords a strong argument in favour of an open area at this place *. Edinburgh begins to surmount its nume-

* Bartholomew Mosse, of Dublin, surgeon and licentiate in midwifery, being moved by the sufferings of the poor women in that city at the time of their lying-in, took a large house in George's-lane, which he furnished with beds and other necessaries, and opened the same in 1745, for their reception, supporting it at his own expence, until its apparent utility, induced several well-disposed persons to encourage the undertaking, by benefactions and yearly subscriptions.

In the year 1750, Doctor Mosse finding the house in George's-lane, too small for the reception of the great number of women applying for admittance, took a lease of a piece of ground in Great-Britain-street, whereon to build a large hospital; and to secure a probability of maintaining it, he first, at the risk of his whole fortune, laid out and finished the present gardens, as a public place of amusement, which is justly admired for its many beauties. In 1751, the foundation stone of the hospital was laid by the lord mayor of the city of Dublin; the doctor carried on the building, and raised money for that purpose by lottery schemes, and on his own credit, until he had expended above 8000l. In the years 1755 and 6, the Irish parliament perceiving his difficulties, voted 12000l. towards the work, and 2000l. for the doctor's own use, as a reward for his services.

In 1756, he obtained a charter from his late majesty, incorpor-
ating

rous misfortunes; manufactures and commerce, the true sources of wealth, are in some degree resumed, by which property will be more generally diffused amongst the inhabitants, which will ultimately centre in ground rents and buildings. But the growth of Edinburgh doth not rest upon the revival of a trading spirit amongst the inhabitants. This city is considered as the modern Athens, in politeness, science and literature. The writings of its professors, divines, and lawyers, are every where read and admired. In the healing art it hath been long and justly celebrated. A seminary thus qualified, will consequently draw thither many students from various parts of Europe

ating a number of noblemen and gentlemen, as guardians, and appointing himself master of the hospital during life. In 1757, it was opened by the duke of Bedford, then lord lieutenant of Ireland, and 52 women, who then attended for admittance, were received. From thenceforward this hospital hath been ranked amongst the the first charitable institutions in that city.

The hospital, chapel, steeple, and rotunda, are much admired by the best judges in architecture. Through the rotunda is a passage to the garden, wherein is a fine bowling green, with beautiful walks and shrubberies. The rotunda and gardens are open three evenings in the week, when there is an excellent concert of vocal and instrumental music; at such times and on Sunday evenings, when there is no concert, there is generally a numerous and brilliant assembly of the first people in the city.

The expences of the hospital are defrayed principally by the receipts of the rotunda, which after deducting the expences, generally amount to 400l. annually; by collections in the chapel, 200l. by balls in the rotunda in winter, and private benefactions; the whole in 1779, amounted to 1159, in which year 1064 women were admitted into the hospital. From this it appears, that the expence of each woman and her child, is about 1l. 1s. 5d. including salaries, repairs, &c.

This was the first hospital of the kind attempted in any part of his majesty's dominions, and the great advantage of it being soon observed, application was made to doctor Moss in 1747, by several persons in London, particularly doctor Layard, for his plan, scheme, and regulations, which he transmitted to him; and the year following an hospital was established in London on the same plan. It is submitted to the magistrates and citizens of Edinburgh, whether a similar plan, on the above mentioned ground, would not be expedient in a capital and neighbourhood containing 100,000 inhabitants.

and America: the present number amounts to 1000, of whom 400 or upwards are in the medical line.

Next in importance is the high school, an antient establishment in this city, consisting at present of a rector and four masters, who teach the Latin tongue with great success, to generally about 400 boys.

Here is also an academy for drawing; for the deaf and dumb; and a riding school.

A society for propagating Christian knowledge; a royal society comprehending various branches of science and literature; an antiquarian society; a medical ditto; a speculative ditto; a botanic garden of five English acres, under the direction of professor Hope, in which is an area, called the school of botany, where several thousand plants are systematically arranged, besides a great number of curious exotics; and in a small inclosure, the professor hath a plantation of the true rhuburb, consisting of 3000 plants, most of them twelve or thirteen years old. An observatory is partly completed on the Calton hill, commanding most extensive views, furnished with the large telescope and all the optical instruments and apparatus which belonged to the celebrated Mr. James Short, F. R. S.

The advocates library contains a valuable collection of books, manuscripts, charters, and other records; elegant prints; 3 or 4000 coins and medals; and among other curiosities, an intire mummy, preserved in its original chest, purchased by the late earl of Morton, for 300l. and by him presented to the faculty of advocates.

Edinburgh is also furnished with a play-house, and several assembly-rooms; one of which is singularly elegant, and nearly 100 feet in length, by 60 or upwards, in breadth. Also a concert-hall, built by Mr. Robert Mylne, architect of Blackfriars-bridge, after the model of the great opera theatre at Parma, but on a small scale. This building is

 greatly

greatly admired, both for the elegance of the architecture and its admirable fitness for music. The expence of the hall was raised by a musical society, who meet weekly.

A new society hath lately been established for the improvement of that warlike music, the bagpipe; the candidates from various parts of the Highlands, ornamented in the proper ensigns of the order, exhibit annually at Edinburgh, before a numerous audience.

There are annual races on the sands of Leith, every July, for a purse of 100 guineas, given by his majesty; a plate of 50 guineas value, by the city of Edinburgh; the noblemen and gentlemen's purse of 100 guineas; the ladies subscription-purse; and other prizes. The races last a week, and are much frequented from both kingdoms.

About 300 nobility and gentry compose the royal company of archers, many of whom meet weekly during the summer, to train themselves in that antient exercise, wherein both English and Scots excelled, and for which they were famed over Europe. They have an annual trial of skill in public, on which occasion they are dressed in tartan, lined with white, trimmed with green and white ribbons; a white sash, with green tassels; and a blue bonnet, with a St. Andrew's cross. They have also 2 standards, whereon are displayed, Mars and Cupid; the motto, "*In Peace* and War." A yew tree, with 2 men dressed and equipped as archers—the motto, "*Dat gloria vires.*" The Scottish arms—the motto, "*Nemo me impune lacesset.*" St. Andrew on the cross—the motto, "*Dulce pro patria periculum.*"

The sight of the archers thus equipped, shooting for the prize, is truly noble.

The company of hunters, called *the Caledonian Hunt*, is also composed of nobility and gentry, who appear in uniform at their meetings; they give an annual

annual ball at the palace of Holyrood-house, where, among other regulations, *no gaming is allowed.*

We shall conclude this list with the company of bowlers—and the company of golfers, each of them being governed by certain regulations.

The hotels in Edinburgh have every claim to recommendation, in respect to the elegance of the buildings and furniture, the variety of dishes, and the quality of the wines most generally used. These houses are built in the new town, and mostly kept by Englishmen. They are also furnished with coffee-rooms, the London and Edinburgh newspapers, with other publications.

Such are the allurements of this rising city—salubrious air, variegated and extensive prospects of land and water; provisions and vegetables cheap and plentiful; spirits and wines unadulterated; coals at 8s. or under, per ton; excellent water; machines for salt-water bathing; respectable schools for both sexes; a celebrated university, in which arts, science, philosophy, and all the branches of literature, are taught on easy terms; academies; literary societies; a flourishing botanic garden; an observatory; public libraries, and all the fashionable amusements. To these, and other circumstances, is owing the constant influx of new inhabitants, and the rapid increase of buildings within these few years past.

People of landed estates, who used to board their children for the benefit of the schools and university, now purchase or hire small commodious houses for a temporary residence, while the numerous amusements of the town, and the pleasure of polite society, engage others to become citizens for life.

When shady walks and pleasure-grounds shall be formed, for which Princes-street, Queen's-street, and the fields already described, are well adapted; and when a penny post-office shall be established (which would also increase the town-revenue) the conveniencies and allurements of this city will be irresistible.

Of the harbour of Leith, though lying upon the capacious river Forth, little can be said in its favour. In appearance and dimensions, it resembles the tower-ditch at London, and hath only 9 feet water at neap-tides, and 16 in high-spring tides.

Were the funds of the city adequate to the expence, several feet water might be gained at the bar, and the harbour made capable of containing 100 sail of ships, and of keeping all vessels not exceeding 12 feet water, constantly afloat. The shipping of the port of Edinburgh, is calculated at 10,000 tons; that of London, 200,000. The largest and finest ships belonging to Leith, are the London traders, who make 7 trips every 2 years at a medium.

It is supposed that the balance in favour of London, and other parts of England, with the Forth, since the increase of buildings, and population in Edinburgh, amounts to half a million annually.

The distance from Edinburgh to Perth is 40 miles, almost due north. The first object that presents itself is the river Forth, which may be crossed at Leith, where it is near 6 miles over, or at the Queen's-ferry, 9 miles above, where the passage is less than two miles. Both of these roads unite at Kinross, a pleasant town on the banks of Loch Leven, a lake of twelve miles in circumference, ornamented with woody islands, on one of which, the unfortunate Mary queen of Scots was imprisoned by her subjects. Thus far the country is very fine, and well improved; consisting of gentle risings, and rich crops of grain, but without those hedge-rows, interlined with trees, which ornament the plains of the south.

From Kinross, the country assumes a mountainous appearance, very proper for sheep, but injudiciously cut up, in many parts, for the raising of slender

crops

crops of grain, a custom too prevalent throughout the whole kingdom of Scotland.

The descent from these hills opens a view of Stratherne, a rich valley, 30 miles in length; bounded on both sides by verdant sheep-walks; interspersed with the seats of nobility and gentry; and beautified by the numerous windings of the river Erne. Cross the bridge, and ascend the base of Moncrief hill, commanding an extensive prospect of Perth, the Tay, and the Grampian mountains.

This is the shortest, and most usual road to Perth; but travellers, who wish to see the remains of a city, celebrated formerly for science and commerce, must, after their passage from Leith, keep along the east-coast of Fifeshire, till they arrive at St. Andrews, whose ruins, at a short distance, exhibit a picture of Gothic magnificence, and Christian barbarity.

The town consisted of 4 streets of considerable length, and proportionable breadth, running parallel to each other, in straight lines. Three of the streets still remain; of the fourth, hardly a vestige is to be seen. Further particulars, respecting this fallen city, would be painful in the recital.

After passing through an open country of 9 miles, the traveller arrives at the banks of the Tay, where that river is 2 miles in breadth; it widens above, to 4 miles; and is navigable for coasting vessels as high as Perth, from whence much salmon is exported to London. The ferry can only be crossed after half-flood, when stout boats are continually plying for passengers to Dundee, a handsome town, finely situated for trade, and long celebrated for the commercial spirit of its inhabitants, who are equally distinguished for their taste, in whatever relates to ornament, or utility.

The distance from Dundee to Perth is 21 miles, through the Carse of Gowrie, esteemed the garden of Scotland, but which, its envious neighbours say, is is denied fire in winter, water in ſummer, and the grace of God all the year. There are 2 roads through this delightful ſpot; the lower and the upper. The lower road is upon the edge of the Tay, and hath a near view of the oppoſite coaſt of Fife, which riſes in a gentle aſcent from the water, and in beauty and fertility is little inferior to the northern ſhore. The upper road commands one of the richeſt views in Great Britain, and is conſequently preferred by all thoſe who travel for health or amuſement. It is carried along the margin of the Gowrie hills, whoſe ſloping ſides are every where covered with rich fields of wheat, clover, or thriving plantations.

Within a few miles of Perth, theſe hills begin to cloſe upon the river; the terrified ſtranger finds himſelf environed by lofty impending precipices, cloathed however to a conſiderable height, with natural woods; a ſpecimen of the rude magnificence ſo frequent in the Highlands, which are now at no great diſtance.

Perth ſtands upon the weſt ſide of the Tay; it conſiſts chiefly of two handſome ſtreets; is, upon the whole, an elegant town, and admits of great improvement. Its ſhady walks on the banks of the Tay, the oppoſite hills covered with riſing plantations, the handſome bridge, from whence there is a view of an extenſive plain bounded by diſtant mountains, compoſe a juſtly admired landſcape.

But no traveller, who is not in a deep decline, ſhould leave this place, until he hath aſcended the hill of Moncrief; where, having gained the ſummit, his labour will be amply repaid. Vain would be the attempt of the moſt fertile imagination, to diſplay, by deſcription, the ſcenery which that hill commands. The ſoft, and the rude touches of nature, are ſo finely blended, that the eye alone can delineate them.

On

On leaving Perth, the Grampian mountains appear in full view, ſtretching in a north-eaſt direction, from Loch Lomond to Aberdeen; having in front, the valley or plain of Strathmore, of conſiderable extent and fertility; the great theatre of Scottiſh valour, in defence of their country and liberties; and is therefore ſtyled, by way of pre-eminence, *claſſic ground.* The Caledonians had long beheld, with deep concern, the encroaching ſpirit of the Romans, in Britain; their vigilance, perſeverance, and progreſſive conqueſts, from the Thames northward, till they arrived at the baſe of theſe mountains. Here the Caledonians, ſeeing themſelves inveſted by ſea and land, with a view to the complete conqueſt of the iſland, made vigorous preparations, to check the further progreſs of thoſe hoſtile intruders. Having collected the force of the nation, and lodged their wives and children in places of ſecurity, they marched forward in good order, and with a bold countenance, till they came within ſight of the Roman legions, whom they no longer conſidered as invincible. While Agricola was animating his veteran ſoldiers, exhorting them to put an end to a ſtruggle of 50 years with one great and important day, the royal Caledonian pathetically addreſſed his countrymen, in a ſpeech of conſiderable length, of which the following abſtract from Tacitus, is here inſerted as a ſpecimen:

" Againſt their pride and ambition," ſaid he, " you will in vain ſeek a remedy or refuge from any obſequiouſneſs or humble behaviour. Theſe plunderers of the earth, theſe ravagers of the univerſe, finding countries to fail them, endeavour to rifle the wide ſeas and the ocean. If the enemy be wealthy, he inflames their avarice; if poor, their ambition. Neither the eaſtern world, nor the weſtern, vaſt as they are, can ſatiate theſe general robbers. Of all men, they alone thirſt after acquiſitions, both poor and

and rich, with equal avidity and paſſion. Devaſtations, murders, and univerſal deſtruction, they by a lying name ſtyle *empire* and government; and when they have ſpread a general devaſtation, they call it peace. Deareſt to every man, by the ties of nature, are his children and kindred. Theſe are ſnatched from us to ſupply their armies, and doomed to bondage in other parts of the earth. Our wives, daughters, and ſiſters, however they eſcape violence from them as from open enemies, are debauched under the appearance of friendſhip. Our goods are their tribute, our corn their proviſion, our bodies and limbs their tools for the drudgery of making cuts through woods, and drains in bogs, under continual blows and outrages.

" The Brigantes*, even under the conduct of a woman, burnt their colony, ſtormed their entrenchments, and, had not ſuch auſpicious beginnings degenerated into ſloth, might have with eaſe caſt off the yoke and recovered their former liberty. Let us, who are yet unſubdued, who ſtill preſerve our forces intire, and want not to acquire, but only to ſecure liberty, ſhew at once, in the very firſt encounter, what kind of men Caledonia has reſerved for her own vindication and defence. Here you ſee a general, here an army; their tributes and mines, with a long train of calamities and curſes, ever attending a ſtate of ſlavery. Whether all theſe are to be for ever impoſed and borne, or we forthwith avenge ourſelves for the attempt, this very day muſt determine. As therefore you advance to battle, look back upon your anceſtors, who lived in the happy ſtate of liberty; look forward to your poſterity, who, unleſs you exert

* The Brigantes inhabited Yorkſhire, Lancaſhire, Durham, Weſtmoreland, and Cumberland. They made a brave defence, under queen Boadicia, and were the laſt of the South Britons who ſubmitted to the Romans.

your valour in this very field, muſt live for ever in a miſerable ſtate of ſervitude."

Many battles were fought in this ſtruggle between the thirſt of empire and the love of freedom. The Roman legions, more through their military knowledge than ſuperior bravery, generally prevailed; but the Caledonians, aided by their mountains and moraſſes, though often defeated, were never completely ſubdued. What the Romans could not, therefore, acquire by the ſword, they endeavoured to accompliſh by policy. Having ſtationed themſelves in the centre of the kingdom, as appears by the camps ſtill viſible in the front of the mountains, they created a diſtinction between the Caledonians of the eaſt, and thoſe of the weſt ſide of the country. To the former they gave the name of *Picti*; to the latter, that of *Scoti*. In order more effectually to divide the nation againſt itſelf, they prevented all ſocial intercourſe, fomented jealouſies, and encouraged feuds, themſelves acting as auxiliaries, as occaſions required, and prudence dictated.

When the Romans were called home, in the fifth century, to defend the centre of their tottering empire, againſt the unceaſing attacks of Goths, Vandals, and other barbarians; the two nations of Scots and Picts, who had long been the tools of Roman policy, became, in their turn, zealous, not for freedom, but for conqueſt. Thoſe plains remained the theatres of fierce conflicts, till the middle of the ninth century, when the Scots finally prevailed, and the whole country, now re-united under one monarch, took the name of Scotland. The ſeat of government was transferred from Rothſay, Dunſtaffinage, Inverlochy*, and other caſtles of the antient Scottiſh princes, to

* There ſtill remains a fragment of the caſtle of Rothſay, and a conſiderable part of Dunſtaffinage. They are conjectured by antiquaries to be nearly coeval with the Romans in this iſland. The caſtle of Iverlochy ſeems, by its architecture, to be of later conſtruction.

Scone,

Scone, and its neighbourhood, as being more inviting, and also more centrical and commodious, for repelling the ravages of the Danes, a people who had carried terror and desolation throughout the whole kingdom, but more particularly the eastern coast facing the Baltic. Those districts were, therefore, still devoted to the rage of war, which was rendered more destructive, from the aversion of the Danes to Christianity. The Scots proved generally victorious; and, at length, the invaders, tired out with fruitless enterprises, abandoned their precarious conquests, about the middle of the eleventh century, during the reign of the famous Macbeth. No place therefore, in Britain, affords so great a variety of antient remains; such delicious morsels, whereon the antiquary may gratify his curiosity, and the critic display his learning *

Twelve

* They consist chiefly of *Roman Encampments*, at Strageth, Ardoch, Comerie, and Delvin. *Roman Highways* are also visible in many parts, connecting the different encampments and the lesser stations.

Caledonian Fortresses. These were generally placed on, or near the summits of the Grampian hills, and commanding extensive views of the vallies underneath. They were surrounded with ramparts formed of loose stones, having entrenchments or ditches on the outside. Here the Caledonians lodged their women and children in times of danger, while the young and the brave gave battle to the Romans. The most conspicuous of these posts are at Blairgown, the two hills of Catter-thun, and Denoon castle.

Historical Pillars or Obelisks. These are both instructive and curious. They were erected in commemoration of signal victories gained by the Scots over the Danes, and are generally ornamented with a rude sculpture, or bas-relief of men on horseback, and other emblematical figures and hieroglyphics, which have been accurately described by the antiquaries of the last and present century. These obelisks derive a particular consequence from their being found upon this north-east side of Great-Britain, and no where else. Some of these stones are erected at Aberlemni near Brechin. Other pillars of curious workmanship, representing chariots, horsemen, human figures, animals, and centaurs, are found at the village of Meigle. The death of Malcolm II. at Glaimis, is

represented

Twelve miles from Perth, the traveller arrives at the noted pass of Birnam wood, and must bid adieu, for a while, to verdant hills, extensive plains, and populous towns. The scene changes instantaneously to lofty mountains, covered with heath, or natural woods; to narrow vallies, winding streams, and extensive lakes. Wherever he directs his course in the Highlands, he is accompanied by wood and water.

represented on various stones near that castle. It had been generally supposed, that the hieroglyphic pillar at Forres on the Murray firth, was the last of that kind towards the north; but Mr. Cordiner's publications have opened a new field of antiquities, reaching to the extremities of the island.

Round Towers. These are supposed to be of Pictish or Danish construction, but their uses have not reached posterity. There are only two columns of this singular architecture in Britain, viz. one at Abernethy near Perth, whose height is 72 feet, and circumference at the bottom 47 feet. The other is at Brechin; its height is 103 feet, its circumference near the bottom 48 feet; the thickness of the wall at that part is seven feet two inches, and at the top, four feet six inches.

The *Palace of Scone.* Kenneth II. upon his conquest of the Picts in the ninth century, having made Scone his principal residence, delivered his laws, called the *Macalpine laws*, from a *tumulus*, named the *Mote Hill of Scone.* The same prince conveyed to this place, from Dunstaffnage, the coronation chair of his predecessors, and here it was used for that purpose by his successors, down to the year 1296, when Edward I. of England carried it to London, to the great mortification of the Scottish nation. Their kings, however, continued the practice of being crowned here till the reign of Charles II. the last monarch who honoured Scone with that ceremony.

Of the royal palace of Scone, the abbey, church, and other magnificent buildings, nothing now remains; they were completely destroyed in the year 1559, when there ensued, says Bishop Spottiswood, a pitiful devastation of churches, and church-buildings, throughout all parts of the kingdom.

Birnam Wood, and Dunsinane. The place called Birnam Wood is a lofty hill on the west side of the Tay, immediately on the entrance of the Highlands. Dunsinane is a small, but steep hill on the east side of the Tay, on the summit of which, Macbeth built and fortified his imaginary impregnable castle, as a place of security against the attacks of his rival, Malcolm III. No part of the building now remains; but the ditches which surround its area are still visible. The neighbourhood abounds in *tumuli* and other antiquities.

Every

Every valley, called in that country ſtrath or glen, hath its ſtream meandering from ſide to ſide, and dividing the whole into a number of little verdant peninſulas. The beds of theſe rivers, are ſand or pebbles, barely covered in ſummer, but which, during the autumnal and winter floods, ſeem ſcarcely ſufficient to contain the great body of water that rolls along with frightful impetuoſity. When, upon a thaw of ſnow, every mountain pours forth its tribute in numerous little caſcades, and every rill is ſwelled to a river, the inhabitants of the vallies ſee themſelves environed on every ſide, with impending danger to themſelves, their cattle, and their grain. Bridges, eſpecially thoſe of modern conſtruction, are thrown down, trees are torn away, and even ſtones of conſiderable weight yield to the preſſure of the torrent.

All the accumulating waters, from every direction, in a circuit of fifty miles, are received by the Tay; and this noble river, after collecting the various ſtreams of the centre of the kingdom, falls into the ſea below Perth. A river ſo conſiderable muſt, at proper ſeaſons, facilitate the floating of timber, from the glens, and interior parts of the Highlands; of this favourable circumſtance the gentlemen of thoſe parts ſeem now to be duly ſenſible. Its banks afford a rich proſpect of future wealth, ariſing, in many places, from grounds which could not otherwiſe be brought into uſe.

The Tay flows from the north, and receives at Dunkeld the river Bran, whoſe picturesque banks, improved by art, contribute greatly to the beauties around that elegant ſeat. The road northward exhibits on every ſide, an accumulating treaſure to the noble proprietor, and extremely pleaſant to the traveller. At Logyrait, eight miles above Dunkeld, the Tay and the Tumel unite their copious ſtreams. The natural beauties of this place are diſgraced

graced by a mean village, which, though the ſtation of two ferries, hath neither inn nor ſtable.

From Logyrait northward, the fine ſcenery of art and nature continues as far as Blair, a reſidence of the family of Athole during the hunting ſeaſon.

Thriving plantations, picturesque walks, cut with great labour, expence, and perſeverence, through rocks, and impending precipices, over glens darkened with timber; a ſeries of five natural caſcades, forming upon the whole near 200 feet in height, abundantly repay the traveller, whoſe curioſity leads him thus far into the Highlands.

From Blair northward, there are two roads; one leading to the pleaſant ſhire of Murray; the other to Fort Auguſtus, and Lochaber, now Fort William. Neither of theſe roads being convenient for carriages, travellers, whoſe buſineſs or curioſity leads them to the North of Scotland, generally go by the lower or eaſtern road, through Aberdeenſhire.

Blair, is therefore, the moſt northerly ſtage of *The Short Tour of Scotland*; the traveller hath no choice of returning by another road to Logyrait; nor will he, after a ſecond review of this romantic country, be ſorry for the diſappointment. Logyrait, ſituated at the conflux of the Tay and the Tumel, is alſo the centrical point where the roads from Dunkeld, Blair, Taymouth, and other parts of the Highlands, unite. From this place the traveller now proceeds weſtward, along the north ſide of the Tay, which winds, in conſiderable reaches, through a beautiful valley fifteen miles in length, called Strathtay, abounding in grain, meadows, and plantations. The water which glides through this fine tract receives on the north ſide, the river Lion, two miles below Taymouth, the ſeat of the earl of Braedalbane, already deſcribed, but all deſcription fails in the attempt to convey ſuitable ideas of its magnificence.

Here the Tay iſſues in a copious ſtream from Loch Tay, a lake fifteen miles in length, one in breadth, and from 50 to 100 fathoms in depth, furnished with salmon and other fish peculiar to the Scottish lakes. Its banks, on both sides, are fruitful and populous: the road westward, is finely diversified by the windings of the lake, and the various appearances of the mountains; some, impending in rugged precipices, others rising gradually, to a majestic height.

The west end of this lake exceeds, in the opinion of some persons, all the scenery of Dunkeld, Blair, or Taymouth. Here the Tay, and the Lochy, seem emulous in displaying their respective beauties, before they are blended with the lake.

The views of these rivers; of the lake, the islands, and the towering mountains, discover, every where, the patriotic hand of the late earl of Braedalbane; to whose munificence, the public are also indebted for the roads, the bridges, and the commodious inns of this extensive, but townless region.

Here, at Killin, the traveller may consider himself in the centre of Scotland, and nearly at the medium distance between Dunkeld and Loch Lomond, the two main openings into the Highlands, from the south. The road still leads westward, through Glendochart and Strathfillan, watered by the Tay, which hath its source amidst tremendous mountains, whereon stands the inn of Tyndrum, remarkable for being the most elevated habitable situation in the kingdom. The waters now take a western direction through the little vale of Glenurchie, till they are lost in Loch Awe, a narrow fresh water lake, 24 miles in length, partly shaded with wood, and ornamented with 12 small islands, whereon are the ruins of a convent, and two castles.

Since the publication of Mr. Pennant's and doctor Johnson's observations on the ecclesiastical remains at Icolmkill, and particularly since the discovery of the natural colonnades in the island of Staffa, several persons of distinction from different

parts

parts of Europe, have visited these curiosities; and it being probable that the number of strangers resorting thither will encrease, the following remarks may be found useful.

The waters of Loch Awe discharge themselves by a narrow rapide of 3 miles, into Loch Etive, a small branch of the sea. At the junction of these waters, called Bunawe, an English company have long carried on the smelting business, by means of the woods in that country, and highly beneficial to the poor natives, who find employment and good usage in the various departments of the works*. The verdant fields and other appearances on this little spot, plainly indicate the residence of Englishmen. Nor hath nature been sparing of her beauties, in the true Highland style: mountains, wood or water, are the inseparable attendants of those who choose to honour Loch Etive with a visit.

At Connel, some miles west of Bunawe, this lake being crossed almost from side to side, by a hidden rock, exhibits at half flood and half ebb, particularly the ebb of spring tides, a most furious cataract of about 10 feet high, called the Falls of Connel.

There are 2 roads from Loch Etive to Oban, viz. a horse road by Dunstaffnage, and a carriage road formed at a considerable expence across the moors, agreeable to the general practice of Scotland, when a trifle can be saved in distance, without reflecting that many travellers go thither, not to be chagrined, but amused. Persons of this description will prefer the horse road, however inconvenient, in order to view the remains of Dunstaffnage castle, a seat of

* One of the principal partners being informed by his clerk, that the work people had run in debt to the company to the amount of 1400l. this worthy man, whose name is justly revered over the whole country, enquired into their manner of living, and other particulars, and being informed of their sobriety, honesty, diligence, domestic qualities and numerous children, he ordered the whole debt to be immediately cancelled.

the Scottiſh kings, previous to the conqueſt of the Picts in 843, by Kenneth II. and where the coronation chair was kept till removed by that monarch to Scone *. This caſtle is built upon a rock at the mouth of Loch Etive, whoſe waters expand within, to a beautiful bay where ſhips may ſafely ride in all weather. Of this building, nothing remains except the outer walls, which, though rooſleſs, are ſtill in good order. The proprietors of the caſtle and contiguous lands, have erected ſome buildings within the walls, where the preſent laird reſides, and where the writer of theſe ſheets was hoſpitably entertained, and lodged undiſturbed by the rattling of arms, or the ſounding of the trumpet. At a ſhort diſtance is a ſmall, rooſleſs chapel, ſtruggling againſt time and weather, to accompany this ſeat of kings through ages yet to come. While a certain traveller was looking penſively at theſe poor remains, they opened their mouth, and ſaid, in a clear voice, " Mr. ——, your country is greatly obliged to you, I hope you will be rewarded in another world." In this manner, the

* Mr. Campbell the preſent proprietor, has a ſmall ivory image of a monarch ſitting in his chair, with a crown on his head, a book in his left hand; and, ſeemingly, in a contemplative mood, as if he was preparing to take the coronation oath. His beard is long and venerable; his dreſs, particularly his robe edged with fur or ermine, is diſtinctly repreſented. The figure was found among the ruins of Dunſtaffnage, and being conſequently engraved before the conqueſt of the Picts, it is to be conſidered as one of the greateſt curioſities now in the iſland. It corroborates the few remains of antient Scottiſh records; it repreſents the dreſs of thoſe early times; and it diſcovers a knowledge of the art of ſculpture, wherein the Scots ſeem to have made conſiderable proficiency, of which the before mentioned hiſtorical ſtones, are viſible proofs.

Some parts of an antient regalia, were preſerved at Dunſtaffnage, till within the preſent century, when they were embezzled by the ſervants of the keeper during his infirm years, probably for the ſilver with which the articles were ornamented, and nothing now remains excepting a battle-axe, 9 feet in length, of beautiful workmanſhip, and ornamented with ſilver. If Mr. Campbell ſhould be diſpoſed to preſent theſe curious remains of ages probably coeval with the Romans, to any of the Scottiſh univerſities, he would thereby merit the thanks of his country.

laird

laird of Dunstaffnage passes his jokes upon strangers; who, should they turn round abruptly, will perceive him speaking to a perpendicular rock, which hath the quality of conveying the words to the chapel, and thus between both, a stranger fancies himself amidst enchantments.

The situation of this regal seat, was calculated for pleasure, as well as strength; a proof that mankind, even in the rudest ages of society, are more or less governed by taste. The views of mountains, vallies, waters and islands, are delightful. On the north side of Loch Etive stood the town of Beregonium, supposed to have been the capital of the West Highlands. It seems, from certain mounds, excavations, and other appearances, to have been a strong fortress, to prevent invasion, or to secure a retreat, as occasions might require. The country abounds in Druidical, Danish, and other antient remains. At the distance of 2 miles from Dunstaffnage, is the bay of Oban, facing the island of Mull, and here travellers are furnished with small vessels, and necessaries for the voyage to Icolmkill and Staffa, which lie on the west side of Mull, in the Atlantic.

The traveller having thus crossed the kingdom from sea to sea, may return by the carriage road to Inverary, a day's journey from Oban, where, if furnished with recommendations, he will be amply rewarded for all his fatigues, and the inconveniencies of Highland inns *. This little capital is pleasantly situated on a small bay, formed by the junction of the river Aray with Lochfine, where the latter is a mile in width, and 60 fathoms in depth.

Inverary hath long been the principal residence of the antient and illustrious house of Argyle, descended from a line of kings; a family of distinguished war-

* In visits of this kind, particularly from mere strangers, it is usual to leave the servants, horses and carriages at the inns, while the company pay their respects to the noblemen or gentlemen in the neighbourhood.

riors, patriots, and ſtateſmen; the hereditary patrons of arts, ſcience and improvements; and whoſe hiſtory makes a conſpicuous figure in the annals of their country *. The preſent ſeat is a modern fabric, begun and completed by the late duke Archibald, who alſo formed the deſign of an entire new town, upon a commodious, elegant plan, becoming the dignity of the capital of Argyleſhire, a country moſt admirably ſituated for fiſheries and navigation. The town hath been rebuilt agreeable to the original deſign. The inhabitants are well lodged in houſes of ſtone, lime and ſlate. They are fully employed in arts and manufactures; plentifully ſupplied in the produce of ſea and land; and in every reſpect happy under the benevolent hand of the preſent proprietor. A noble example to the gentlemen of the Highlands, whoſe efforts, if aſſiſted by government, may do wonders in their hitherto uſeleſs country. We cannot quit this ſubject without remarking the comparatively happy ſituation of mankind, under the 3 noblemen, whoſe contiguous eſtates, occupy the greateſt part of a tract, extending from the borders of Aberdeenſhire, to the weſtern ocean. Emigration, ſo fatal to Britain, is ſcarcely known upon the eſtates of Argyle, Athol, and Braedalbane; an infallible proof of judicious meaſures, and humane uſage.

Reſpecting the planting around Inverary, it would be in vain to attempt even the outlines of deſcription. It is extenſive beyond conception, and admirably variegated.—Every crevice, glen, and mountain, diſplays taſte and good ſenſe.—Thouſands of the gloomy fir are weeded out, and trees pleaſing to the eye

* Agreeable to the traditional accounts of ſenachies and bards, their predeceſſors were in poſſeſſion of the lands of Loch Awe, before the departure of the Romans in the 5th century. Camden derives their origin from the antient kings of Argyle in the 6th century. The lineal deſcent of the family is traced from the reign of David I.

rise from the vale to the lofty summit, in all the sublime magnificence of nature.

This immense wood naturally suggests a conjecture into its value for the various purposes of bark, charcoal, forges, paling, furniture, house and ship building. Some of the beech are from 9 to 12 feet in circumference, and the pines from 6 to 9; but these being comparatively few, we shall state the medium girth of 2,000,000 trees planted within these last hundred years, at 3 feet, and the medium value at 4s. which produces 400,000l. and this for the most part, upon grounds unfit for the plow, being chiefly composed of hills and rock.*

Inverary is situated within a days journey of the Low Countries; but travellers, who incline to vary the scene, will make a previous excursion for a few days to the peninsula of Cantire. The road is carried along the banks of Lochfine, fringed in some parts with natural woods, which are successively devoured by a furnace, the property of an English company, for making charcoal. At the distance of 23 miles from Inverary is Loch Gilp, the proposed seat of a town and canal to the western ocean.

The gentlemen of the county have lately completed a new road from thence to East Tarbat, which affords most beautiful and romantic scenery. Lochfine is bounded at this place with lofty mountains, rising immediately from the edge of the water, whose bases of solid rock yielded to the force of gunpowder.

The road was completed at 100l. per mile, of which there are 14, to the Tarbat. It winds beautifully around the little head-lands, generally 40 to

* One of these hills rises immediately from the house a great height, in the form of a pyramid, and is cloathed to the summit with a thick wood of vigorous ornamental trees. On this summit, or point, Archibald duke of Argyle built a Gothic tower or observatory, where he sometimes amused himself. The ascent by the road seems to be half a mile, and the perpendicular height about 800 feet.

50 feet above the lake, now ſix miles broad, and of which it hath a commanding view. The appearances on the land ſide are tremendous and romantic. Impending cliffs, and frequently very large detached pieces of rock, produce a degree of terror in travellers unaccuſtomed to ſuch ſights. The aſcent is generally ſprinkled with young wood of oak, aſh, birch, and hazel, which is cut down every 20 years for the bark, and charcoal. Many of theſe trees grow out of the crevices of the rocks, and I have certainly perceived ſome growing from the large ſtones that lie upon the face of the precipices.

This whole ſcenery is greatly enlivened in wet weather, by a ſucceſſion of torrents pouring furiouſly from the ſummits, and frequently exhibiting beautiful caſcades.

The village of Tarbat, which terminates this agreeable ſtage, is the centrical paſs between Inverary and Campbeltown, being 37 miles from each. The little bay at this place is much encumbered with rocks at the entrance, but within, a number of ſhips may lie ſecure from all winds. An iſthmus of one mile in length ſeparates the bay from Weſt Loch Tarbat.

From this paſs a narrow peninſula, from 5 to 10 miles in width, and nearly 40 in length, called Cantire, ſtretches in a ſouthern direction, till it is almoſt in contact with Ireland.

Here the road takes a weſtern direction, from the banks of Lochfine to the weſt ſide of the peninſula, waſhed by the Atlantic, and in ſome parts protected from the great ſwell of that immenſe ocean by the Hebride iſlands, ſome of which, as Jura, Ilay, Giga, appear in full view.

Jura lies north-weſt from the road; its length is 20 miles, ſeemingly one continued mountain, riſing in ſome parts to the height of near 3000 feet. On the weſt is Ilay, ſeparated from Jura by a narrow but navigable ſtrait, called the ſound of Ilay.

The appearance of this iſland is the reverſe of

Jura,

Jura, being for the most part on a level with the surface of the ocean. It is 22 miles in length, nearly the same in width; and is reckoned the most improveable island in the Hebrides.

At a short distance from the road is Giga, nearly 5 miles in length, environed by lesser islands, which contribute to enrich the view.

Beyond these, on the south, is the island of Rathlin, near the Irish coast, of which there is an extensive view.

The ocean itself is a source of entertainment, whether in high winds or a dead calm, and in some parts the road is carried along declivities immediately above it. But the inns, if they may be so called, considerably diminish the pleasure of the journey, especially in seasons of scarcity, when oats cannot be procured at any price. Neither are the distances of these inns properly regulated.—They are thus: From Tarbat to the Whitehouse 5 miles; Whitehouse to Bar, 20 miles; Bar to Campbeltown 12 miles. But great allowances are to be made in these respects on a road newly opened, in a remote country, and seldom frequented. If health be an object worthy the attention of mankind, let them for a season quit the card table, with the other sedentary or frivolous amusements, to enjoy exercise, and the fresh air of the Atlantic.

The traveller being arrived at Campbeltown will perceive the good effects of the herring buss fishery, in the appearance of the town and harbour. The bay is beautiful, capacious, and safe, being landlocked on every side, and screened at the entrance by a lofty small island, which breaks the violence of the winds, and the force of the waves. The bay is 2 miles in length, half a mile in width, and hath from 5 to 9 fathoms water, with a good stiff clay bottom.

An antiquary will be surprized to find in this remote country, a cross of beautiful workmanship, and

and richly ornamented with foliage. It was brought from Icolmkill, from whose ecclesiastical remains the inhabitants of the continent have been pilfering for ages.

Respecting prospects, the main object with many travellers, and particularly those who visit Campbeltown, the surface of the country affords several principal situations. One of these rises from the south side of the bay of Campbeltown to a height which over-tops the neighbouring mountains; but to behold the grand expanse of land and water, to the greatest advantage, it will be necessary to ride to the lofty promontory called the mull of Cantire *, where no obstructions intercept those magnificent views of nature, comprehending the south Hebrides, the north coast of Ireland, separated from Cantire by a channel of 13 miles; the firth of Clyde; the islands of Sanda, Ailsa, and Arran; with the coast of Galloway and Airshire, at the distance of 30 miles.

Those who incline to visit the Giant's Causeway, on the opposite coast of Ireland, may, if the weather be settled, hire a wherry and four men at Campbeltown, which will convey them thither in a few hours; and should they choose to return by water to Inverary, the same vessel may be engaged at a trifling expence. This passage opens the firth of Clyde, and its islands, viz. Sanda, the craig of Ailsa, Arran, Bute, and the 2 Cumbras. Of these islands, Arran is the most considerable, being 14 miles in length, and generally 7 in width. It resembles Jura in soil, and yields to none of the Hebride islands in height. Bute is near 13 miles in length, and 5 where widest, tapering to a point at both ends. It is in general low and fertile, but totally abandoned by the earl to which it gives a title, who hath not vouchsafed to honour it

* The mull of Galloway, the most southern point of Scotland, lies in lat 54-44; the mull of Cantire in lat. 55-17; Malin-head, the most northern point of Ireland, in lat. 55-21.

with

with his presence, during these last 40 years, though he draws from thence 4000 guineas annually.

The narrow strait which separates Bute from the continent on the north, is called the Kyles of Bute, by which the voyage between Greenock and the Hebrides, through the proposed canal, will be shortened above 100 miles.

The opening upon the west side is the entrance of Lochfine, which with a brisk gale from the southerly points, may be navigated to Inverary in 4 or 5 hours; the whole voyage from Campbeltown may be performed with ease in one day, allowing sufficient time to dine at the Tarbat, or Loch Gilp.

The traveller, impressed with the unrivalled grandeur and vast expanse of the scenery he hath explored, will now behold the beauties of the little Highland capital with diminished rapture, and the rippling waves of Lochfine, with indifference. He will entertain his grace with the wonders he hath seen, the accidents and dangers he hath escaped, the keenness of his appetite, and the glow of his spirits; and now bidding adieu to Neptune, and his grace's claret, he sets out reluctantly from this hospitable and princely seat, upon his return to the south,

The first part of the stage lies close upon the edge of the lake, which gradually tapers to a point at Carindow, where it receives the river Fine, issuing from a glen of the same name. The tide flows as high as the bridge, and within a mile of which there is eighteen fathoms water. On the east side of the lake is the seat of Sir James Campbell of Ardkinless, a branch of the Argyle family.

After losing sight of the lake, the road affords nothing remarkable. It is carried unavoidably to the summit of a mountain, where the soldiers under general Wade erected a seat for weary travellers, to which they are invited by these words cut on the stone, "Rest and be thankful." From thence the descent is so precipitous, that travellers are glad

to

to quit their carriages, and walk near a mile, to a moſt gloomy and ſequeſtered valley, called Glencroe, bounded on each ſide by mountains which ſeem to vie with the Alps.

The various appearances of theſe mountains, their naked cliffs and ſummits in all manner of directions, and the clouds ſwimming underneath, ſerve to amuſe and to improve the contemplative mind.

The traveller, having emerged from this ſolitary ſpot, finds himſelf in view of Loch Long, a ſalt water lake, 10 miles in length, which communicates with the Clyde, facing Greenock. It reſembles Lochfine in its breadth, and hath 7 fathoms water, within half a mile of its head.

This lake, and a ſmall branch with which it communicates on the weſt, called Loch Goyl, abounds with ſeals, ſalmon, white fiſh and mackarel; of the latter, from 3 to 5000 are ſometimes taken at one haul. Theſe fiſheries afford plentiful ſupplies to Greenock, Paiſley, and Glaſgow, where they are ſold at moderate prices.

Gareloch, 6 miles in length, lies on the eaſt ſide of Loch Long, and abounds in ſalmon, though inceſſantly perſecuted by a voracious ſpecies of fiſh called pollacks, who are extremely prejudicial to the ſalmon fiſhing in the Clyde, and all the waters which communicate with it.

The ſmall diſtrict of improveable country round the head of Loch Long abounds in planting, and hath all the appearances of ſkilful agriculture. Here reſides the chief of the Macfarlanes, of venerable age, though wore down with misfortunes. This lake is the eaſtern boundary of Argyleſhire, a portion of which county, and of Perthſhire, includes the whole route of the traveller, ſince his departure from the eaſt coaſt at Dundee.

He now enters Dunbartonſhire; and at the diſtance of a mile, arrives at Eaſt Tarbat, ſituated amidſt natural woods, on an eminence, immediately above

Loch

Loch Lomond, and 10 miles from its head. This celebrated fresh-water lake is ornamented with 28 islands, some of them considerable in extent, and stocked with deer. It is 25 miles in length, and above five where widest. Its greatest depth is 720 feet, where it washes the base of Ben Lomond, a mountain which rises to the height of 3240 feet, above the surface of the water.

The elevation of the road from the Tarbat southward, contributes greatly to the pleasure of the traveller, especially after passing the point of Firkin, which instantaneously opens the whole expanse of the lake, and all the luxuriancy of its woody islands, and indented shores.

The lake is seen at best advantage from some high grounds above the village of Luss, 8 miles from the Tarbat, where there is a small inn and stabling. Travellers may also be furnished at this place with boats and watermen, ready at a minute's notice, to embark with their honours on a cruise amongst the islands, but without the conveniency of a canopy, which is frequently necessary, in rainy or hot weather. Here a London waterman, with his skuller "clean'd out so nice, and painted withal," would make his fortune.

On the edge of a small bay is the seat of Sir James Colhoun of Luss, who inherits, through a long series of ancestors, the greatest part of these picturesque domains.

The outlet of this lake forms the beautiful water of Leven, celebrated, in soft pathetic lines, by Dr. Smollet, to whose memory an obelisk hath been erected on its banks, near the place where that benevolent friend of mankind first drew breath.*

Here the manufacturers of Glasgow, induced by

* Too noble to cringe, fawn, or flatter; too just to oppress or cheat; too patriotic, liberal, and compassionate, he died a beggar, and left a widow to solicit, in the public newspapers, the means of subsistence.

the

the qualities of the water, have established the greatest printfields and bleacheries in that country; but the excises lately imposed upon these branches, with the high prices of provisions, and the boundless influx of India goods, will probably transfer these manufactures to foreign states. This is the sense and the language of every trader from one end of Britain to the other.

The Leven glides in a copious stream over a pebbly bottom, till it joins the Clyde, 5 miles below. It abounds in salmon and trout; and its branches form almost one continued wood, intermixed with villas, meadows and cornfields.

These appearances announce to the traveller his return to the Low Countries, to which Dunbarton, an antient royal borough, is the western entrance.

Here the Leven, navigable for vessels of 200 tons burden, falls into the Clyde, where the latter is a mile in breadth. At the point, or angle, formed by the junction of these rivers, a perpendicular double pointed rock rises from the level beach to a great height, and hath been occupied, from the earliest annals of the Scottish history, as a castle, or armory. A small tower on the summit is supposed to have been a Roman pharos or light-house. The situation of this castle, at the conflux of two considerable rivers, gives it a most extensive and variegated prospect over the shires of Renfrew and Dunbarton, which it fully commands; Cowal, in Argyleshire; the crowded summits of the Grampian mountains, in Perthshire; and the spires of Glasgow, at the distance of 14 miles, in Lanerkshire,

The road from Dunbarton to Glasgow, though mostly on a level, is uncommonly delightful. It is carried along the north shore of the Clyde, and hath throughout an extensive view of Renfrewshire, which forms the opposite shore. At the distance of a full mile from Dunbarton, commences a ridge of hills, which, under various names, extends in a north-east

4 direction,

direction, to Stirling. Of these hills Dunbuck is the western extremity. It rises immediately from the road, with such awful majesty, that romance itself cannot figure a nobler object. Eastward, the hills rise to a still greater height, and are cloathed, a short space, with oaks and other timber, which are cut down every 20 years, for the bark. At the distance of 3 miles from Dunbarton, where the hills dip into the Clyde, barely leaving a passage for travellers, was begun, or ended, by Agricola, the famous Roman wall, vulgarly called Graham's dike, from Graham, or Grimus, (governor of Scotland, during the minority of its prince,) who, upon the departure of the Romans, in the fifth century, broke through the northern barrier, assailed the wall between Newcastle and Carlisle, drove back the trembling Britons, and recovered the southern part of the kingdom, which the Romans had long usurped.

At the distance of half a mile eastward, the road, rising in a gentle ascent facing Erskine house, a seat of lord Blantyre, astonishes the traveller with the grandeur of its views. Here stands Kilpatric, or Cell Patric, so named from its being the birth-place of the famous St. Patric, a clergyman of this place, afterwards the apostle of Ireland. Every real or imaginary event of remote antiquity hath its tradition: St Patric, while fishing on a small rock in the Clyde, facing this place, was seized by Irish pirates, and carried to their country, where he became a great man. From this circumstance, the rock is called *Patric's Stane.** At Dunbarton, a fair held in March, is called, in honour of the saint, *Patric's Mass Fair.*

Hitherto the road displays a full view of the wide expanse of the Clyde; the picturesque intermixture

* Mr. Golbourne of Cheshire, who was lately employed by the merchants of Glasgow to deepen the Clyde, hath covered this little rock by a dyke run from the shore to the channel of the river near the key at Erskine ferry.

of hills, woods, ſeats and plantations. To the grandeur of this weſtern proſpect, a gentle elevation, after leaving Kilpatric, lays open the ſoft ſcenery of the Clyde towards Glaſgow, whoſe ſpires make a conſpicuous figure in the landſcape. South-eaſt, at the diſtance of five miles, is a full view of Paiſley, a large, irregular town, remarkable for its gauze manufactures, which adorn the heads of the Britiſh ladies, and even thoſe of Paris, as appears by the commiſſions ſent from that capital. From this hill to Glaſgow, the road is ſtraight and level; the villas are numerous; the farm-houſes ſmall but neat; the fields moſtly incloſed in the true ſtyle of judicious huſbandry. Theſe pleaſing objects denote the neighbourhood of a large commercial city, ſtriving to correſpond, in taſte and elegance, with the beauties of its environs.

Glaſgow owes the regularity of its ſtreets to a fire, which, in 1652, burnt one third of the city, including 80 warehouſes, and the habitations of 1000 families. This calamitous event is recorded in a letter from colonels Overton and Blackmore to Oliver Cromwell, and by which it appears that Glaſgow contained from 15 to 20,000 people, amongſt whom were ſome wealthy merchants.

Unfortunately for this, and all the towns in Scotland, the builders have copied the Gothic, unhealthy, and moſt inconvenient practice of France, inſtead of the clean, the decent, and commodious dwellings of England, where the whole building is occupied by one tenant only. From this error, in the rebuilding of Glaſgow, that city is at preſent a medley of beauty and deformity. The houſes have outwardly, an appearance of elegance; the ſtreets are moſtly ſtraight and wide; but the town is diſgraced by its narrow, unwholeſome lanes or cloſſes; by the inconveniencies of an over-crowded population, every houſe being inhabited by various families, and of various ranks in life. The builders had no conception of ſmall neat houſes, from 20 to 25 feet wide,

wide, containing a kitchen and cellars under ground; a ſhop, parlour, and yard; a firſt floor for letting out to occaſional lodgers; a ſecond and third floor for the family. Neither did they diſcover the utility of open airy courts, and back ſtreets, for the reſidence of clergymen, lawyers, and other profeſſions that do not require ſhops.

The principal inhabitants, ſenſible of the miſtakes of former times, and willing to repair them, have lately built ſeveral ſmall ſtreets compoſed of private houſes only. Theſe dwellings are commodious, ſubſtantial, and elegant; accommodated with gardens, offices, and all the conveniencies of a country ſeat. Perfection, however, is not the work of a day, or year, but of long obſervation, and gradual experience. While a ſtranger admires the elegance of theſe new buildings, he is greatly diſappointed in the appearance of the ſtreets. This is owing to the irregular poſition of the houſes, ſome being placed forwards; others a conſiderable way back. Neither hath any regard been paid to uniformity in the colour of the ſtone, every perſon conſulting his own fancy only, in the poſition of his houſe, and the materials of which it was to be compoſed: irreparable injuries to the elegance of the town, and will be regretted by poſterity. One ſtreet, however, hath hit, fortunately, upon ſymmetry and proportion, the good effects of which are perceivable at firſt ſight.

Nature hath been remarkably favourable in reſpect of ſituation, whereon to extend the preſent emporium and ornament of the north. The town is bounded ſouthward, by the Clyde; northward, by a gentle ridge of hills, lying in a parallel direction with that river. Theſe two natural boundaries ſcarcely admit of any miſtake in projecting new ſtreets; yet, if unaſſiſted by a ſpirited magiſtracy of taſte and judgment, miſtakes may, and will happen. Every builder will conſult his own convenience; and thus

 a ſpot,

a ſpot, formed by nature for health and ornament, will be obſcured and irretrievably loſt to the community. It would therefore be expedient to lay out, upon a regular plan, the whole front of the riſing ground from the High-ſtreet to Anderſton, and even beyond that village *. A city ſo diſtinguiſhed for the induſtry and ingenuity of its inhabitants, the variety of its manufactures, and the extent of its commerce, ſhould look forward with an invariable view to magnificence, and national honour.

The citizens have lately built by a tontine, one of the moſt extenſive and elegant coffee-rooms in Europe, to which is ſubjoined a ſuite of buildings for the purpoſes of a tavern and hotel, an aſſembly room, offices for notaries and under-writers. The deſign, and the execution of theſe buildings diſplay great judgment, and an excellent taſte. The expence did not amount to 7000l.

The Clyde hath 5 feet water at Glaſgow, and admits of a number of ſmall craft from Greenock, Port Glaſgow, and the Highlands. The walks on the banks of this river have a rural ſimplicity, and are extremely pleaſing.

The great ornament of Glaſgow is its very reſpectable and much-frequented univerſity, whoſe profeſſors have long been eminent in the various branches of ſcience, and claſſic education. This ſeminary ſtands on a riſing ground, cloſe upon the country, and is poſſeſſed of a large garden for the conveniency of the ſtudents; adjoining to which is a botanic garden, an obſervatory, and a handſome well-furniſhed library.

When the Romans raiſed the well-known northern barrier againſt the Caledonians, commonly named

* It might be proper, for the information and conveniency of the inhabitants, to publiſh on copper-plate a handſome plan of the town, including the propoſed additions, and the weſtern environs, as far as the Kelvin, a river which, in leſs than half a century, may become the boundary on that ſide.

Graham's

Graham's dike, they erected stones with inscriptions, which denote that certain parts of the work were made by detachments of such and such legions. These stones have been collected by the university, together with altars, and other monuments of Roman greatness, which are highly entertaining to the antiquary*.

About thirty years ago, a son of the family, which is the head of the clan Macfarlane, made a valuable present of astronomical instruments to this university.

* Near the western extremity of this wall, at Duntocher, a countryman, in digging a trench upon the declivity of a hill, turned up several uncommon tiles, which exciting the curiosity of the peasantry in that neighbourhood, they broke in upon an entire subterraneous building, from which they dug out a cart load of excellent tiles. Being then, 1775, upon my return from the Highlands, and hearing of the circumstance, I repaired immediately to the place, and by threats and promises put a stop to all further proceedings, in the hope that some public spirited gentlemen would take off the surface, and explore the whole plan of the building, without demolishing it. The tiles were of 7 different sizes, the smallest being 7, and the largest 21 inches square. They were from 2 to 3 inches in thickness, of a reddish colour, and in perfect sound condition. The lesser ones composed several rows of pillars, which formed a labyrinth of passages, of about 18 inches high, and the same in width; the largest tiles being laid over these pillars, served as a roof to support the earth on the surface, which was two feet deep, and had been plowed through time immemorial. The building was surrounded by a subterraneous wall of hewn stone. Some professors in the university of Glasgow, and other gentlemen, having unroofed the whole, discovered the appearances of a Roman hot-bath. The passages formed by rows of pillars were strowed with the bones and teeth of animals, and a sooty kind of earth; in the bath was placed the figure of a woman cut in stone, which, with a set of the tiles, and other curiosities found in this place, is deposited in the university.

On the summit of the hill stood the Roman fort or castella, of which Mr. Gordon hath given a drawing. The foundation was lately erased by a clerk, or overseer of an iron manufactory in that neighbourhood, who was, however, disappointed in his expectations of finding treasure. The same Goth expressed a strong desire to erase a fine remain of the Roman wall, which is carried along the base of the hill, but he hath not succeeded in his wishes, and it rests with the

sity. And, in 1783, Dr. Hunter, late physician to the queen, bequeathed to it his famous anatomical preparations, library, and museum, which will be a benefit and ornament not only to this place, but to the whole kingdom.

The editions of the classics which were printed under the inspection of the professors, with the types of the ingenious Mr. Wilson, and by the celebrated Messrs. Foulis, are held in such esteem abroad as to sell nearly at the price of antient manuscripts. His present majesty, when prince of Wales, Archibald duke of Argyle, and many other persons of taste and learning, patronised these elegant editions.

Nor must I, as a well-wisher to science, and useful arts, forget to mention the apparatus for natural philosophy in this university, it being unanimously esteemed the most extensive and most useful in these kingdoms. It was brought to that perfection at the expence, and by the unremitting labour of Mr. Anderson, who not only gives lectures on the mathematical and scientific parts of natural philosophy, to those who are designed for learned professions, but who likewise gives separate lectures to artists and manufacturers, in the most simple and engaging manner.

At the north extremity of Glasgow stands its magnificent cathedral, the only entire building of that description now in Scotland. It owes its preservation to the spirit and good sense of the tradesmen, who, in 1579, upon hearing the beat of drum, for collecting the workmen appointed to demolish this venerable edifice, flew to arms, and declared, that

family of Blantyre to prevent such practices in future, upon grounds of which they are the superiors. "The houses in the village," says Mr. Pennant, "appear to have been formed out of the ruins of these erections, for many of the stones are smoothed on the side, and on one is the word *Nero* very legible." Which stone, with another, on which is the word *Lucius*; also some of the Roman tiles, &c. hath found the way to Richmond.

the

the first man who pulled down a single stone should that moment be buried under it. No monument hath been erected to the memory of those virtuous citizens.

There are two main roads leading from this city to Edinburgh; the south road, consisting of 44 miles, and the north road, which, though 50 miles in length, is generally preferred, on account of its views, and the towns through which it passes, or which are contiguous.

The distance by this road to Stirling is 28 miles, through a broken, rough country, very little indebted to modern improvements. A lofty verdant ridge, called the Campsie hills, bounds the northern view. On the south, the road is enlivened by the navigation of the great canal, formerly described.

At a short distance beyond Kilsyth, the road to Stirling takes a northern direction, and gradually opens a view of the Forth, which, from the Queen's ferry to Alloa hath all the appearances of an extensive inland lake.

Stirling is built upon a hill environed with rich plains; and rises, like Edinburgh, of which it is the miniature, in a gentle ascent westward, where it is bounded by a perpendicular, lofty rock, called the Castle, once the seat of kings, and the national councils. The royal palace serves at present as barracks to a few invalids; the parliament house, their lumber room. This building is 120 feet in length, and of proportionable height. It hath been stripped, in the true Scottish manner, of its ornaments and galleries; the roof, unassisted by the public, is mouldering away; and of the royal gardens, some few vestiges only can now be traced.

The views which claim the preference, in Scotland, are those from Galloway, Cantire, Arthur's seat, and Stirling castle; the first, as the reader will perceive by the map, are of kingdoms, islands, seas, promontories, and far distant shores. Those

 from

from Stirling are purely inland, displaying all the beauties and softness of an Italian landscape, agreeably intermixed with waters, plantations, and lofty downs or sheep-walks. Amidst this scenery, the river Forth winds, in a most picturesque manner, to Alloa, forming, in the short tract of 6 miles by land, a navigation of 24 miles or upwards. Above Stirling, the landscape is equally engaging, if not more so. Here the windings of the Forth are less frequent, but more extensive, This western view is bounded by Ben-Lomond, and the Grampian mountains, whose summits are perceived from every direction throughout the centre of the kingdom.

The distance from Stirling to Edinburgh by the Queen's ferry is 36 miles. The first stage to Falkirk commands an extensive view of both sides of the Forth; the rich plain called the Carse of Falkirk, the Carron manufactory, famous for its cannon, and an endless variety of tools and furniture in cast iron. Near Falkirk the traveller passes under the aqueduct bridge formerly mentioned; where the canal is raised above 100 feet in the course of a mile, by means of ten locks, and at the expence of 18,000l. one of the most extraordinary works of art in these kingdoms, and which nothing but ocular demonstration could convince of its reality. A most delightful journey upon the south banks of the Forth, where that river is above three miles wide, leads to the elevated and magnificent seat of the earl of Hopeton, situated above the narrow strait at the Queen's ferry, and commanding a compleat view of the river and its islands, from the sea to Stirling,

A short and pleasant stage, through a well-inclosed country, carries the traveller to the base of Edinburgh castle, which, though he hath lately traversed the Grampian mountains, will command his admiration.

Travellers, who entered Scotland by the eastern roads, through Berwic or Kelso, generally return by the

the west, through Carlisle. The first stage from Edinburgh rises gradually to a considerable elevation above that city, and affords, at the distance of ten miles southward, a most extensive view of the Forth, the Lothians, and the county of Fife, overtopped by the summits of far distant mountains.

Here the traveller takes a final leave of the northern Caledonia; and having passed the narrow ridge of hills which crosses that part of the kingdom from sea to sea, he is carried many miles through a pastoral country, amidst verdant downs, rural streams, and long winding solitary vales *.

In passing these extensive tracts, he will have sufficient leisure to contemplate the works of God, as having been exhibited to his view, in a boundless variety of forms and appearances, and all designed for valuable purposes, which it is the business of man to discover and improve. This will bring to mind what hath been done, and what remains to be done; the vast tracts of country yet in a state of nature; the many thousands of sober, well-disposed people, who are thereby lost to themselves, their families and the state. He will perceive that the kingdom through which he hath passed, its vallies, seas, lakes, and islands, is a great store yet in reserve for the aid of a dismembered empire, in strength, in commerce, and national consequence, whenever government shall be disposed to call forth and improve these important sources.

Of the Famine; the Failure of the Fisheries; and the Hurricanes of 1782.

While I was engaged in the preceding pages, an event of the most calamitous nature, befel the inhospitable regions which I had been describing. The year 1782 proved remarkably cold and wet, the crops over great part of Europe were more or less

* The property of the duke of Buccleugh, a nobleman equally distinguished for his public and private virtues.

 injured,

injured, and the northern climates experienced a ſcarcity, amounting to a famine. The ſcanty crops in the Highlands of Scotland were green in October, when a fall of ſnow, attended with froſt, prevented every ſpecies of grain from arriving at maturity. The labour, the ſeed, and the ſtraw were loſt. Potatoes, which in bad ſeaſons had provided a ſubſtitute for grain, were this year froſt-bitten, and rendered entirely uſeleſs. Thus the earth withheld its bounty for the ſupport of man and beaſt. During this diſtreſs at home, no relief could be obtained from abroad. Ireland, the granary of the Hebrides and the weſtern ſhores of Scotland, ſhut its ports againſt the exportation of grain; thoſe of the Clyde were unable to give any aſſiſtance; while on the eaſtern ſide of the kingdom, the hazards of enemies cut off the neceſſary ſupplies from Germany, the Baltic, and in a great meaſure from England.

Thus deprived of every reſource, by the double calamity of war and ſcarcity, many hundred perſons languiſhed and died through the want of ſubſiſtence. The huſband and the parent, unable to behold theſe ſcenes of diſtreſs, without endeavouring to relieve them, ſet out, amidſt froſt and ſnow, upon the long and almoſt impracticable journey to Inverneſs, where they expected to purchaſe a little grain, with the produce of their cloaths or furniture, which they had previouſly ſold, in the diſtricts where they reſided. Several of thoſe who had engaged in this generous enterprize, fell a ſacrifice to hunger and cold, in their way to the market. They were found dead on the road, in caverns, and amongſt thickets, where they had taken ſhelter from the inclemencies of the weather, while the ſmall, emaciated horſes, the companions of their diſtreſs, could ſcarcely ſtand or walk.

Such was the dreadful ſituation of the main land, and the iſlands, during the winter and ſpring; and though expreſſes were diſpatched to the Lowlands, by the clergy and others, imploring immediate relief for a periſhing people, it doth not appear that application had been made to government, for that purpoſe, before the beginning of the ſummer 1783, when a generous ſupply was readily granted.

Let us now ſuppoſe that a few ſmall harbours and granaries were eſtabliſhed at proper diſtances, along theſe weſtern ſhores, and that the communications to the Lowlands were ſhortened by means of inland navigation; ſuch calamities, if not in a great degree prevented, might be ſo far mitigated, as to ſave many lives, beſides obviating the neceſſity of occaſional calls upon the Treaſury for the relief of thoſe parts.

The year 1782 furniſhes another argument in favour of theſe propoſals. The annual arrival of the herrings in the Weſt Highlands had never been known to fail, almoſt completely, till this remarkable year, when theſe little viſitors ſeemed to conſpire with the ſeaſons, in order to rouſe the notice of government towards thoſe diſtant ſhores. While the elements kept back or deſtroyed the regular produce of the earth, the herrings abandoned their well-known lakes, directed their courſe towards the Iriſh channel, or ſtopt there, after their uſual progreſs round Lands End; and here the Highlanders, not being provided with proper veſſels, were unable to follow them.

This was not all. While thoſe people were deprived of grain, roots, milk, vegetables and herrings, their uſual food in good ſeaſons; an almoſt uninterrupted ſucceſſion of ſtorms, ſuch as had not happened within the memory of man, prevented them from attempting the white fiſhery; neither could they, had the weather been moderate, go to ſea, without the means of ſupport. Here therefore was a double famine, the cup of affliction and diſtreſs, ariſing from every poſſible cauſe, was now full. From this *ne plus ultra* of human depreſſion, we entertain a hope

hope that matters will revert into a contrary direction, under the auspices of a benevolent sovereign and parliament, to whose humane, as well as political attention, that country and people are most humbly recommended.

The temporary relief granted by parliament on the above melancholy occasion, had not the desired effect. The first supply consisted of a single peck, or 8 pounds of meal to each family, barely sufficient to keep them alive 2 or 3 days. The second supply did not arrive till August or September, during which interval the distress was unspeakably great. The quality of the meal also afforded matter of complaint. It was a mixture of oat, barley, and pease-meal, in such bad condition, that persons who had any means of subsistence, loathed the sight or taste of it. This is not to be imputed to the persons who had the management and distribution of the meal, but to unavoidable necessity, arising from the extreme scarcity of that article. It may be supposed, that meal of the worst quality was the last upon sale, and that the managers had no alternative.

Voyage from Ireland to the West Highlands—Distresses of 300 Emigrants cast amongst the Rocks of the Irish Coast—Further Remarks on the present State of the Highlands.

To the sterility of soil, the cold, watry climate, the avarice of certain proprietors of lands, the want of towns, and inland communications, it hath been observed, is owing that spirit of emigration and adventure, so prevalent, of late years, in the Highlands of Scotland, and which neither remonstrances, shipwreck, nor hardships of any kind can check, as appears from the following relation.

Being desirous to obtain full information relative to the European fisheries, and particularly those of Ireland, now flourishing through the wisdom and munificence of its parliament, I made a circuitous journey in September 1784, to the West Highlands, by the way of Dublin and the North of Ireland, the seat of the Irish fisheries.

From the increase of Dublin in the space of 10 or 12 years, the elegance of the new streets, the number, magnificence and solidity of the public edifices, lately completed or now erecting, a stranger, unacquainted with the present state of Europe, would conclude that Dublin was the metropolis of a mighty kingdom, whose revenues were boundless: that the spirit and taste of the Greeks and Romans had been transplanted thither, to enliven and ornament the Atlantic.

The country from Dublin to Drogheda, (24 miles) and from thence to Dundalk, (16 miles) consists chiefly of gentle risings, like Devonshire, and produces excellent crops*. A spirit for inclosing with hedge-rows, lined with trees, is now become fashionable in Ireland, but it hath not yet become general in this part of the kingdom.

The majority of the people as far as Dundalk, are of the catholic persuasion, and seem very poor. From Dundalk northwards, appearances change greatly for the better. In this extensive district, usually called the North of Ireland, the people are mostly of Scots descent, industrious, enterprising, and mercantile. The inclosures are numerous, the country is highly improved, and the inhabitants are comfortably lodged in neat houses, whitened with lime. It is hardly necessary to observe, that this is the seat of the great linen manufacture; besides a variety of

* I was informed by an inhabitant of Drogheda, that the exports of grain and meal from that port to Scotland, amounted, upon an average of 7 years, to 100,000l. annually. He said that the millers had lost the manufacture of grinding the oats of late years, through their own avarice, by the practice of mixing sand and lime with the meal, sold there by weight; which discovery had induced the Scots to purchase grain instead of meal.

other

other branches lately eſtabliſhed, for the ſupply of the kingdom, as well as America and the Weſt Indies; in which branches, the inhabitants are greatly favoured by the cheapneſs of proviſions, and the exemption from injudicious exciſes impoſed in Britain, on ſoap, candles, coals, ſalt, leather; articles on which the labouring man expends a principal part of his hard-earned pittance.

The ports in the North of Ireland are numerous; all of them are engaged more or leſs in the herring fiſheries, and moſt of them, as Belfaſt, Newry, and Londonderry, have a briſk trade beyond the Atlantic. The coaſt, from Belfaſt loch northward, is precipitous, lofty, and when leeward, extremely dangerous to ſhipping, on account of the violent winds and counter tides of the Atlantic and the channels which communicate with it.

Having arrived at Larne, a ſmall commodious port within 30 miles of the mull of Cantire, from whence the Scots are ſupplied with excellent limeſtone, I began to make inquiries reſpecting the voyage acroſs the channel, and had the good fortune to meet with a genteel family, who were to ſail next morning for Cantire, in a light ſloop, properly manned and equipped for the paſſage. The idea of the ſcenery which the voyage would afford, was a luxury of the imagination, too great to be realized. Next morning, Wedneſday, September 15, though fine, proved hazy. The coaſt of Galloway, Cantire, the craig of Ailſa, and the Hebride iſles, which are diſtinctly ſeen in clear weather, were now wrapped up in impenetrable obſcurity.

The ſame miſt deprived us of a ſight equally ſingular and diſtreſſing; a large ſhip, with 300 emigrants from the North of Scotland, had been that morning driven upon Rathlin iſland, which we paſſed at a ſhort diſtance. A freſh breeze afforded reaſon to hope that the vapour would vaniſh, and gradually open the grand views on every ſide; but great

was

was our ſurpriſe and diſappointment, as well as danger, when by the increaſing fog, we perceived ourſelves amidſt darkneſs itſelf, totally deprived of the ſight of land, though within a few miles of the lofty rocks at the extremity of Cantire. We kept, however, in the ſame direction, expecting every minute to ſee that cape, which, by our reckoning, muſt be very near; but the cape, as if diſpleaſed with the unfavourable character I had lately given of the coaſt, was ſulky, and would not be ſeen by the naked eye, or the teleſcope. An uncommon rolling of the veſſel, gave the firſt intelligence of our ſituation. This aroſe from the jarring currents of the countertides near the mull of Cantire, which occaſion a ſwell, reſembling the bay of Biſcay.

Our ſituation under a briſk gale, amidſt darkneſs, ſtrong currents, rocks, breakers and iſlands, became ſomewhat alarming. At length the cape appeared, like a dark cloud, at the diſtance of 2 miles, on the weſt, and the iſland of Sanda directly a-head, where, not daring to make the main land, we caſt anchor in a ſmall, but ſafe bay, with 2 fathoms water almoſt to the edge of the rocks. This bay or channel, gives ſhelter to many veſſels, and the poor Highland boats, in dangerous weather, but it hath neither key nor inn.

We were, however, amongſt hoſpitable Highlanders, furniſhed with tea, eggs, butter and fiſh; but the beds and bedchambers were not very inviting; the company were indiſpoſed, and reſt was neceſſary. It was therefore reſolved to attempt a landing on Cantire, which, with much difficulty we accompliſhed. If a ſtout, light veſſel, met with ſuch hazards in the month of September, the ſituation of loaded buſſes and Highland boats, croſſing theſe ſeas in the long tempeſtuous nights of winter, muſt be undeſcribable*.

After

* Of which I have been a witneſs more than once, when the noiſe of the rigging, winds and waves, reſembled the loudeſt thunder,

After ſpending ſome time at Campbeltown, on the ſubject of the fiſheries, I propoſed leaving that place on the morning of the 18th of September, at which time ſeveral of the inhabitants favoured me with their company, and by whom I was informed that a number of ſhipwrecked emigrants had juſt entered the town, and were begging money to carry them back to Greenock, to which place a large ſhip had been ſeen ſteering, without her mainmaſt; which, at that ſeaſon was an uncommon ſight. It immediately occurred, that ſome uſeful information might be collected from theſe unhappy people, reſpecting the cauſes of their emigration, and other particulars. With this view I ſent for ſuch of them as were in the neighbourhood, and 3 men immediately appeared. My friends being moſtly in the magiſtracy, and 2 of them juſtices of the peace, it was at firſt propoſed to examine theſe 3 men officially, upon their affidavits, to which they readily agreed; but it was at laſt reſolved, that the town-clerk ſhould only take their ſimple declaration, which was as follows:

" At Campbeltown, the 18th day of September, 1784,

" In preſence of Dugald Campbell, eſq. chamberlain of Cantire, and Ronald Campbell, eſq. collector of the cuſtoms at Campbeltown, two of his majeſty's juſtices of the peace for the county of Argyle, appeared George Smith, Simon Frazer, and Alexander Calder; who being judicially examined, declare, That upon the firſt day of September current, they ſailed from Greenock, on board of the ſhip   of Greenock,   commander, at which time there were on board about

der, and that for many hours without intermiſſion; but the greateſt apprehenſions were from a lee-ſhore, which, in theſe narrow ſeas, is not eaſily avoided. Having thus experienced the inconveniencies to navigation by this channel, I reſolved to examine the banks of Lochfine, relative to a ſhorter paſſage, the reſult of which inquiry hath been fully ſtated.

300 passengers, including a number of children, bound for America. That after several days storm, their mainmast was carried away on Monday the 6th current, about 4 o'clock in the afternoon, and many leagues to the westward of Ireland. That immediately after losing their mainmast, the master and crew resolved to return with the ship to Greenock, and having put about for that purpose, and continued their course accordingly, they found themselves upon Tuesday evening, the 14th, between the island of Rathlin and the coast of Cantire. That upon Wednesday morning thereafter, about 5 o'clock, the morning clear, and fine calm weather, with a small breeze, they found themselves close upon the rocks of Rathlin, and before any effectual efforts were made to get clear, the ship struck upon the rocks. That after the ship struck, all endeavours were used to get her off, without effect, upon which about 100 souls were landed upon the island, without any necessaries whatever, but their cloaths. That about one hour after the passengers were landed, the ship got clear off the rocks, and for two hours thereafter, continued safe at anchor, when they cut their cables and set sail, the weather being still fine, and the above-mentioned passengers on shore. That after they (the passengers) saw the ship under sail, they followed her about a mile and a half along shore, making signals for taking them on board, but to no purpose, although at this time the master might have taken them on board with the greatest ease and safety to the ship, which was then very near. That the passengers being thus left upon the island without provisions or any other necessaries, they found themselves under the necessity of applying to the rector of the island for assistance, when, after remaining there 2 days and 2 nights, the declarants, and about 20 other passengers, were furnished with the rector's boat, and landed yesterday forenoon, near the mull of Cantire, and came this morning

to

to Campbeltown, leaving the other passengers at Rathlin. That in consequence of a contribution from the well-disposed inhabitants of Campbeltown, the declarants and their companions have hired a boat to carry them to Greenock. Declare, that the night before the ship struck, as aforesaid, the commander went down among the passengers with an open knife in his hand, and threatened with that knife any person that should oppose him in any thing he then intended to do; upon which he deprived them of their chests and provision-boxes, and put them all into the hold of the ship, which deprived them of the power of carrying any necessaries on shore with them, when they were landed at Rathlin. And being asked why they were leaving this kingdom, they declare, "That their doing so, is altogether owing to their wanting bread at home, and high rents, joined with several successive bad seasons;" and several of the other passengers having appeared in course of this examination, they confirm the above declarations, and are hereto subscribing, all which they declare to be truth."

The paper was signed by 9 persons, mostly farmers and labourers, and also by the above-mentioned justices of the peace, and delivered into my custody, where it now remains. While the clerk was taking the evidence in writing, we examined a seemingly intelligent farmer, relative to his rent, the quantity of grain sowed, the produce of that grain, the number of horses, black cattle and sheep on his farm; when it appeared, that upon a medium of years, the whole produce of the farm, in grain, cattle, sheep, &c. did not amount to the rent which he was bound to pay; thus as the farm did not pay itself, he was giving his labour for nothing, and his family must have been supported by friends, or the petty industry of the women and children in spinning and knitting. He said that many poor men were in the same situation, labouring and toiling, not for themselves,

but

but for others, who were never satisfied; and this was affirmed by his companions in the same line of life. Other particulars came out, which I forbear to mention; I shall only observe, in general terms, that they confirm, were it necessary, the representations formerly stated in the course of this work. One of the gentlemen present, who hath an estate and several tenants, exclaimed in a kind of triumph, upon hearing these circumstances, "Thank God, we have no such doings in Argyleshire."

The people discovered the most resolute determination not to remain in Scotland, even supposing the owners of the ship should refuse to take them on board upon their arrival at Greenock.

The case of these poor wanderers was remarkably singular and distressing. After a wretched existence, devoted year after year, to fruitless toil and drudgery, they set out almost pennyless, with their wives and 60 children, on a journey of near 200 miles to Greenock; they pay 5 guineas each for their passage; sail on the 1st of September, upon a voyage of 3000 miles; meet with storms till the 6th, when, at the distance of some hundred miles, they lose their mainmast, and dare not venture across the Atlantic. They return for the port from whence they set out; are driven against rocks, and left upon a strange island, without friends, money or change of apparel, in the view of their wives and children, whose situation, thus deprived of their only dependence, is still more distressing.

The consideration of what the women must suffer, gives additional poignancy to the feelings of the men. They are now 100 miles from Greenock; seas must be crossed; a boat must be hired; they have no money to pay for it: Mr. More, a humane clergyman, sees their distress, lends them his boat, and gives them a certificate, stating the particulars of their case*. They land near the mull of Cantire; beg

* The boatmen of Rathlin extorted 1s. or upwards from each of the persons carried on shore, when the ship struck, though the distance.

their way to Campbeltown; where they raiſe a ſmall ſum of which 1l. 5s. is paid down for a boat to Greenock, a voyage of 60 miles or upwards; from whence, the ſhip being refitted, they again embark for the long wiſhed for land, though to certain ſlavery or ſervitude for life.

Being thus furniſhed with the authentic documents of theſe ſcenes, which happened almoſt in my own view, I hope the narrative will prove a leſſon to both maſters and tenants. I had formerly ſaid ſo much upon the bad policy of raiſing rents ſo greatly beyond their value in the preſent ſtate of that country, that the ſubject ſeemed to be exhauſted; but the ſtriking circumſtances of this event, and the cauſes of it, oblige me, reluctantly, to reſume the diſagreeable topic.

I ſhall not, as heretofore, waſte paper upon arguments which, with ſome minds, paſs as tinkling ſounds. Since neither the precepts of chriſtianity, nor philoſophy, can make any impreſſion; ſince humanity and avarice never can aſſimilate, we muſt change our ground, and trace the ſubject to its origin. The earth which we inhabit, was given for the general ſupport and benefit of all mankind, by a Being who is incapable of partiality or diſtinction; and though in the arrangements of ſociety, the earth is divided into very unequal proportions, and theſe confined to a few individuals, whilſt the great body of the people are totally cut off, this diſtribution doth not give the poſſeſſors a ſhadow of right, to deprive mankind of the fruits of their labour. The earth is the property of him by whom it was called into exiſtence; and, ſtrictly ſpeaking, no perſon hath an excluſive right to any part of it, who cannot ſhew a charter or deed handed down from the original and only proprietor of all nature; if other-

diſtance was not many yards. It is to be hoped that Mr. More will take notice of this ungenerous conduct.

wiſe,

wise, they hold their possessions upon usage only. Grants of lands were made by princes to their champions, friends, and favourites, and these have been handed down from father to son, or by them transferred to new possessors; but where are the original charters from the Author of nature, to those monarchs? In vain may we search the archives of nations from one extreme of the globe to the other. If so, and who can controvert it? the man who toils at the plow, from 5 o'clock in the morning, to sun-set, and who sows the seed, hath undoubtedly a right to the produce thereof, preferably to the lounger, who lies in bed till 10, spends the remainder of the day in idleness, extravagance, and frivolous or vicious pursuits. The tenure of the former is held from God, founded upon the eternal law of justice; the claim of the latter is from man, held in virtue of the revolutions, and casual events of nations.

He, therefore, who denies his fellow-creatures the just earnings of their labour, counteracts the benevolent intention of the Deity, deprives his king and country of an industrious and useful body of the community, whom he drives from starvation at home, to slavery abroad, ought to be considered as an avowed enemy of society; particularly the man who can take the cow from the aged widow, and afterwards, the bed, the kettle and the chair; thus turning out the decrepid at fourscore, to wander from door to door, till infirmities and grief close the scene of tribulation.

Since human laws do not reach such persons, while petty rogues are cut off, in dozens, their names ought to be published in every newspaper within these kingdoms, and themselves excluded from any place of honour or profit, civil or military.

It is such men who bring an odium upon the whole body of the landed gentlemen in the Highlands, and its neighbourhood. Those who, by their

 universal

universal benevolence, have the fairest and best of all titles to their possessions, are censured indiscriminately with men who hold their lives only through the defect of human laws; it is therefore proper to draw the line, and to rescue the innocent or the meritorious from a stigma which, upon the strictest inquiries, seems ill-directed, if not unjust.

When lands began to rise in the more southern parts of the island, the gentlemen of the north, who drew a mere pittance from extensive districts, considered themselves as having an equal right to an increase of rents, but without duly attending to the circumstances of soil and climate, the want of towns, manufactures, and capital.

The tenants, accustomed from age to age, to possess hundreds of acres, for the value of a few pounds, were thunderstruck on finding their rents doubled; and in many places trebled; while all the feudal services, some few estates excepted, remained in full force. The consequence of this premature increase of rents need not be repeated; many gentlemen now see their error, and are taking measures for their own relief and that of the tenants; but it is too evident, that, from the natural circumstances of the country, no expedients can be effectual, unless assisted, in the first instance, by the public. The proprietors may in some parts, improve the soil, but they cannot improve the climate. Herein lies the great barrier to agriculture in the Highlands; on which account, the greatest part of the vallies, as well as hills, would have been turned into pasture-grounds, for the raising of cattle and sheep, had not humanity and patriotism stepped forth in the generous breast, and said, *by turning these lands into grazing parks, you will depopulate your country, and deprive the state of* 200,000 *inhabitants.* Gentlemen recoiled at the thought, and at this moment submit to all the inconveniencies of a numerous tenantry, whose rents on some estates are from 2 to 10l. per annum;

annum; on others, from 10 to 20l. each, which is thought high, though much more could be gained by letting out large districts to opulent graziers, and without risk or trouble.

There is something generous in this self-denial, which merits not only the public applause, but the thanks of government.

Address to the lower Ranks of People in the Highlands.

Having always found you inquisitive after news, and particularly respecting North America, and the encouragements to poor men in that country, I shall give you such lights as have come to my knowledge, and on which you may rely.

While America remained under the protecting and fostering hand of Great Britain, (by which you are to understand England and Scotland) the people were happy and flourishing, beyond any example on record; every year increased their commerce, shipping, and towns, and rolled in new sources of wealth. They were protected at the expence of this country, against all enemies; liberal bounties were granted by Parliament for the encouragement of their natural produce; they were allowed a free trade with our sugar colonies, by which they supplanted the mother country, to a great amount annually, without contributing in men, ships, or money, to the defence of these islands; they had the monopoly of ship-building, and Britain was the principal market, while many of our own ports were neglected, choaked up, or in ruins; they traded on the capital of British merchants and manufacturers to the amount of 4 or 5,000,000l. and were supplied with British and India goods, free of those burdens which the native subjects paid; with other benefits, exemptions and privileges, too numerous to recapitulate, and which would have been further heaped upon them,

 had

had they been actuated more by political wisdom than the machinations * of restless factious minds in both countries, aided by foreign powers, jealous of an empire, which in time might have held the balance in Europe.

The consequence of the war, was an intire separation of those colonies from Britain, and instead of a great and happy line of coast extending 1500 miles in length, it is now split into 13 different states, loaded with debts and taxes; distracted in their councils; without public virtue; shut out from the West India islands; their commerce reduced; their ship-building abridged, and their specie completely drained away.

In a period of such distraction, perplexity, and personal aversion to the natives of Great-Britain, it is not advisable in any man to go thither as an indented servant, much less so, to drag his family to a country where they will be insulted, and doomed to bondage with negroes, under the rod of a master who hath an uncontroulable power over their persons and services.

More powerful arguments against emigration remain to be mentioned. The soil of those states is in general very productive; but it is well known, that the sudden transitions from extreme heat, to extreme cold; the long fogs, extensive marshes, and excessive rains, produce a train of diseases

* During the last war it was the practice of certain evil-disposed persons of the capital, to print inflammatory hand-bills, which they sent by thousands to America; where, with others of American manufacture, they were distributed amongst the revolted colonies. Seafaring people frequently brought some of these papers to London, as curiosities; one of which acquainted the good people of America, "That the king of Great Britain was besieged in his castle of Windsor, by 20,000 Londoners; and that the queen, a bigotted Roman catholic, had sent her jewels to Venice, where she was going to reside." Great pains were taken, both in England and America, to represent the king in colours the very reverse to his rule of government, which hath been regulated by the spirit of the English constitution, and of universal equity towards all his subjects, of whatever country, religion or complexion.

very

very fatal to British constitutions, particularly fevers and agues, to which almost every man is subject who is exposed to daily drudgery without doors, or in the woods; besides the tormenting, and almost pestilent stings of musketoes and other virulent insects, from which labouring people cannot escape; insomuch that their legs are frequently ulcerated, and their life becomes completely burdensome.

The only provinces exempted from taxation, are Canada and Nova Scotia, which still compose a part of the British empire, enjoying all the benefits of its protection, commerce, laws, and constitution; but these countries are covered with frost and snow from November till April, which oblige the inhabitants to dress in skins and furs, and cut off all communication between Canada and Europe during 7 months in the year. Whoever, therefore, prefers America to the temperate, wholesome climate of Great Britain, will find themselves greatly disappointed; and even the Highlands of Scotland may, with a little assistance, be rendered a more desirable place of residence to its natives, than any part of the American hemisphere.

Such being the natural and political state of that country, which many of you considered as a desirable asylum from your present wretchedness, you have no alternative in the choice of your future residence, unless in the season of anguish and despair, you take the desperate resolution of plunging yourselves from bad to worse. Though this account may probably deprive you of those hopes, which, from nature, and the circumstances of the times, will be found delusive, it is a duty to state the truth, that you may no longer remain in suspense on that head.

Supposing therefore, all the golden prospects of a country flowing with milk and honey, to vanish from your imagination, and that the anguish of your minds, thus deprived of the only remaining prop, is become almoſt inſupportable, it would be in vain; whatever may be ſaid on the contrary, to preſcribe what are uſually called ſpiritual comforts. A mind overwhelmed with afflictions, too great for human nature to ſuſtain, and without the hope of ſeeing better times, is incapable of thoſe ſenſations which reflection and contemplation affords, in the days of eaſe, health or proſperity.

Yet hope ought not to be totally precluded. Nations, as well as individuals, are often reduced, by a concurrence of circumſtances, to apparent, and ſeemingly irretrievable ruin; but it is evident, that this humiliating ſtate frequently proves the termination of their difficulties; that after ſuch a day, or year, their diſtreſſes gradually vaniſh. Heaven, the diſpenſer of all things, prepares a train of circumſtances, all co-operating in their favour, and which lead infallibly to the vertical point, preſcribed by Divine wiſdom.

The loſs of America, which in ſome reſpects is a national misfortune, will, in others, prove a national benefit, by diſpoſing the public to look towards a country, which, in days of great proſperity, was totally diſregarded. Secondary circumſtances, as the famine in 1782, may alſo contribute to enforce and haſten this deſirable work; nor ſhould the diſtreſſes of your countrymen on the coaſt of Ireland, though at a favourable ſeaſon, paſs unnoticed; their determined reſolution, after theſe diſaſters, to hazard another voyage, affords the cleareſt evidence that the country requires relief.

In order to ſtrengthen your faith in what is likely to happen, let me call to your remembrance the following events, which have actually taken place during theſe laſt 3 years, viz.

1. The liberty to reſume the dreſs of your anceſtors.

2. The reſtoration of the forfeited eſtates, which, though the benefits extend to a few individuals only, ſhews

shews the confidence which the king reposes in his Highland subjects.

3. The liberal supply voted by the house of commons, for your relief during the season of scarcity.

4. A generous subscription for the relief of the Orkney islands, first opened in the northern counties of England.

5. The late cruise of his majesty's son, upon your coasts; his honouring Stronaway with a visit, and his minute inquiries respecting the fisheries.

These are happy omens of the good disposition of the king and people towards you, and may be considered as preludes to an extensive chain of measures for your relief in all cases that shall be found expedient and practicable; the principal of which will be enumerated in the subsequent chapter. And I may further add, that the major part of the nobility and gentry, both on the continent and the islands, are resolved to take an active share in the generous designs.

These favours or indulgencies from the public, and your chiefs, require a grateful return on your part to God the first cause, and to your king and country, as the means. The benefits between the public and you must be reciprocal; this is what the nation have a just right to expect in return for the expenditure of public money, at a period when the subjects are born down with the weight of unavoidable taxes, to which you contribute nothing, and from which it is probable you will be legally exempted, when the circumstances of your country shall be investigated by the senate.

The departments wherein you are to act in the grand machine of national polity, relate to the army, the navy, and the fisheries.

Of the army department little need be said: you have ever shewn a manly readiness to rise, when called upon, in your country's defence, and an inflexible adherence to your engagements. You have been

been essentially serviceable in every part of the empire, when surrounded with an host of foes, and it is expected that the same spirit, courage and firmness will characterise Highlandmen, in all future ages. I have calculated the quota of intrepid, stout, and bold young men ready and qualified to serve during a subsequent war, at 20,000. If towns shall be built, by which men, women, and bairns may be encouraged to remain on their native soil, I conjecture that, upon any great emergency, you will be able to send out double the above number, to give the Monsieurs and the Dons a warm salute, wherever the young chiels can get within musket-shot of them.

But the main strength, and grand efforts of Britain, are from the navy; which, when properly commanded, hath always proved invincible against combined nations, and let every Highlandman wish that it may long maintain that superiority. As France is now copying Great Britain in her naval equipments, and exerting every nerve to surpass the latter, both in the number and magnitude of her ships, we must be always ready to meet that potent nation, at least with equal force. Within the memory of some men in the Highlands, the number of seamen voted for the war establishment was 45,000; the number hath been increased every succeeding war, and in 1782, it amounted to 110,000; the next war will probably require 130,000, to raise whom we shall be brussen enough, for ye ken fu well, with what difficulty we raised a smaller number in the last struggle. Now, it is evident, that all the other nurseries for seamen united fall short of the fishery nursery, both in number and hardiness, and if government shall be pleased to put the west coast in a way of employing 500 busses, and 4000 large boats, or wherries, which would engage 31,000 seamen, they must lend a hand to the royal navy, when called upon by his honour's highness prince William Henry, and take a spell of what's going on against the Monsieurs; for it would be a sin and a shame, thence, to lay the whole burden of fighting, as well as of building ships, upon England.

The great aim of government in supporting the fishery business, is the aid which that branch may be able to afford the nation, when attacked by restless neighbours; and if the public, after laying out thousands, and tens of thousands of guineas, in the Highlands, shall rely upon your honour and faith, in the seasons of difficulty, gratitude as well as justice, should animate your breasts on those occasions, so as to overcome all feelings, or mercenary considerations. The lads must not skulk or run away, when called upon, but enter freely, and with a good grace, upon his majesty's bounty. Besides, they will be benefited by seeing a little of the world, and though there is a great deal of swearing aboard a man of war, no man is under a necessity of conforming to other people's nonsense. Some officers of distinguished bravery, both by sea and land, have scarcely ever been known to utter an oath, which at best, is a paltry low habit, unworthy a man of sense, education, or delicacy.

Neither should the lads suffer their manners to be corrupted in any shape whatever; advise them, with all your eloquence, to retain their original sobriety, temperance, and modesty; qualities which do not pass unobserved by the officers, and on which account the Highland seamen are highly valued in the navy.

The third capacity required of you is of a civil nature, and will benefit yourselves as well as the community. The greatest part of those who reside on the shores and lakes will, it is hoped, be encouraged to direct their attention to all the branches of the fisheries throughout the whole year, by means of bounties to boats, as well as busses, with permission to sell their herrings to strangers. For these and other particulars, I refer you to the next chapter.—If matters shall be put into the train therein stated, your country will become respectable, new fields will be opened

opened for induſtry, and ſtrangers will reſort to your infant towns, from all parts of the kingdom; a complete revolution will pervade the whole Highlands, to the aſtoniſhment of the old and the young, all of whom will find employment adapted to their age, capacity, and abilities. But while your condition will be thus mended, and your wants ſupplied in all things requiſite for human exiſtence, dangers of a ſerious nature are to be apprehended, and guarded againſt. When the trading world ſhall break in upon you with all its vicious habits, and when you ſhall begin to aſſimilate with that world, it will be difficult to reſiſt the force of example, and the alluring temptations that will appear in a thouſand different forms, all of them tending to eradicate your native virtues, and to ſubſtitute inſtead thereof the long train of vices which degrade human nature, and are ſooner or later their own puniſhment. Vice admits of two diſtinctions, very different from each other in their effects upon ſociety; viz. Thoſe of the ſenſes, and thoſe of the heart. The firſt are natural or conſtitutional vices, operating more or leſs upon the whole human race, and therefore the life of every conſcientious perſon is a continued ſtruggle between reaſon and the paſſions. From perſons of this deſcription, you have little to fear in ſocial intercourſe. You will generally find them fair and open in their dealings, ſincere in their profeſſions, and warm in their friendſhips.

Very different are thoſe whoſe crimes flow from the heart; as envy, malignity, double dealing, hypocriſy, cruelty, boundleſs ambition, and inſatiable avarice. Theſe are the perſons who diſturb the peace of individuals, of families, and communities; who overthrow empires, deſtroy millions, and keep the world in continual fermentation.

Such, you may be aſſured, will be the imports, as ſoon as your ſhores ſhall hold forth inducements for the reſort of ſtrangers. The thoughtleſs being, who is

no

no-one's enemy but his own, is a rock appearing always above water, which you may easily avoid; but the man of the world, whose ideas continually centre in one object; whose mind is ever on the stretch, devising by what new means he may supplant his neighbour, is a rock which only appears at low tides; while, to close the simile, the designing, the dark, and the ambiguous hypocrite, is a rock always under cover, fatal to thousands, whose inexperience or credulity leads them in that direction. The religious impostor being particularly tenacious of his reputation, is consequently more artful and refined in his designs than other persons, and from the same cause, more unrelenting in his resentments against the objects whom he hath injured.

Such, with some exceptions, is the world, and, if you doubt the truth of this representation, let me remind you of the words of Solomon, founded upon experience, and a general knowledge of mankind. He found *one man*, that is, a man of integrity, in a thousand. Charles II. of England, who was equally conversant with mankind, and equally penetrating into the human heart, used to say, in his humorous way, that "There were two kinds of rogues in the world, all those who wore wigs, and all those who wore their own hair." Mankind in all ages have given nearly the same character of their own species, and a personage, with whose life you are well acquainted, was particularly pointed against human depravity, especially those of high pretensions. The love of splendour, honours, and wealth, having become the ruling passion amongst men of all ranks and persuasions in these kingdoms, it is highly requisite, that you be guarded not only against their artful devices to obtain these gratifications, but also against imbibing the poisonous infection. I have often ruminated upon this head, whether it would not be better to remain in your present state, uncontaminated with the world, though almost ready to sink under the weight of many evils; or to be placed above these distresses, at the hazard of your morals. In the day of battle, you stand firm and invulnerable against all dangers, however numerous your opponents. Will your fortitude be equally proof against an army of vices, in all their tempting shapes? Be not too confident of your own strength. Cannon and muskets are trifling in the comparison to what you must encounter, from the moment after you first drink out of the same cup with Lowlandmen, Englishmen and Irishmen. I know your answer before-hand; the wetness of the present harvest, by which your crops will be partly lost, and the dreadful prospect of a new famine, leave no room to hesitate. Give us employment, by which we may purchase from others what our own miserable climate does not afford, is your ardent supplication; in which policy, humanity, and moral justice are your advocates. As your request must sooner or later be granted, it will be essentially necessary to assist you at the same time, in the struggle between your consciences on the one side, and the world on the other; for this purpose, an additional number of intelligent clergymen may be settled among you, who would not only attend to matters of spiritual concern, but also assist you with their counsel, in such temporal affairs as might require their aid, in the proposed new line of action.

But as, from the great extent of country, there will still be a deficiency of clergymen for ages to come, you may in some degree supply this defect, by means of a small assortment of well-chosen books; and in order that neither your time nor money may be misapplied, I would advise you to reject all books upon religious controversy, and religious intolerance; or which affirm that the people of such a church or such a sect, and they only, can be saved. This is presumption with a witness! and if all such books were collected together and set on fire, with severe penalties on those by whom they were reprinted, it would be doing mankind an essential service. Such writers have the assurance to dictate to the Almighty, to measure out his goodness by square and rule, or by pounds and ounces, which they claim, forsooth, as the exclusive right of themselves, and those of the same persuasion. The books I mean to recommend are such as will not puzzle or distract, but aid the devout mind; as Scougal's Life of God in the Soul of Man; Doddridge's Rise and Progress of Religion in the Soul; Beveridge's private Thoughts; Mrs. Rowe's devout Exercises of the Heart. These books, to well-disposed minds, will prove a never-failing source of comfort; till at length the person, thus disposed, will perceive his own heart to be a church, and that all nature are the preachers. You will discover that every object within your view, from the blade of grass to the mighty oak; from the smallest insect to the elephant, and from the most minute inhabitant of the boundless ocean, to the monsters which sometimes visit your shores, is of itself a perfect system, complete in all its parts, and governed by unerring laws, peculiar to its nature, in its formation, growth, maturity, and decline. Could you extend your contemplations beyond the objects immediately before your eyes, new sources of wonder and admiration would present themselves without end: the globe which we inhabit would, in the comparison with the works of God, appear as a drop of water to the boundless ocean; a mere particle in the wide expanse of the universe, and which, were it burnt to nothing by a planet, would scarcely cause a blank in the great machinery, formed and regulated by Omnipotence.

The same wisdom and power that you see displayed in the little circle which you inhabit, is seen and felt throughout innumerable worlds, whose existence,

tence, the ingenuity and diſcoveries of man have fully confirmed.

By frequently exerciſing the mind on ſuch objects you will begin to make the important diſcovery, that there are other ſources, beſides gold or ſilver, more ſatisfactory in their operation, and more permanent in the tenure. If there be any real felicity in this world, it is ſurely in the correſpondence between the ſoul and its Creator; it is alſo that kind of riches which accumulate, in proportion to a man's ſincerity and integrity. You have therefore greater wealth in ſtore, than many of you are at preſent aware of; and thus poſſeſſed of increaſing ſterling treaſure, you will lament the extreme folly of thoſe who ſacrifice every valuable conſideration of this world and the next, for paltry tinſel, by which their avarice may be gratified, and the pitiful object, vanity, may be flattered.

Induſtry is both a commendable and a neceſſary duty, when its object is merely to procure the neceſſaries, or even the innocent gratifications of life, and the ability to aſſiſt, in a proportionate degree, the aged or the helpleſs, whoſe merit may claim your notice.

So far you may proſecute buſineſs with a good conſcience, void of offence; but, beyond that line, danger is near, both to yourſelves and thoſe with whom you may be connected, in the concerns of life.

In proportion as the love of money predominates in the mind, conſcience loſes its force, till at length it ceaſes to operate, when the deluded being gives full ſway to all his deſires, breaks through all laws, divine and human; becomes a falſe friend, a double dealer, and in all reſpects a dangerous neighbour; thus laying up one ſum after another, till cruel, unrelenting death, drags him reluctantly from the ill-gotten acres, bonds and mortgages, frequently without allowing him time to aſſign the diſpoſal of his imaginary riches.

Beſides the above-mentioned books, every family on the ſhores of the Highlands ſhould be provided with a dictionary spelling book, a small dictionary, a book on practical arithmetic, ditto on practical navigation, a copy book, and a compendious treatise on diseases and cures. These, from the scarcity of school-masters, and surgeons or doctors, are positively necessary; the expence of the whole, including a Bible, and Confession of Faith, will not exceed 1l. 4s. a sum which, though beyond your abilities to advance at any one period of time, may be laid out occasionally in shillings or half crowns, till your library shall be completed.

Every family should also be provided with a copy of the fishery laws and custom-house fees; and every man ought to conform strictly and religiously to those laws in all cases whatever, conducting himself in an orderly and decent manner, without injury or offence to those engaged in the same employ; and he who is detected in maliciously cutting his neighbour's nets, or obstructing him in any shape whatever, should be for ever expelled from the fisheries, and the company of all honest men.

Address to the Convention of the Royal Boroughs in Scotland.

GENTLEMEN,

It is universally acknowledged that the fisheries of Great Britain have a strong claim to the particular attention of the legislature,

1. As a nursery of ship-carpenters, who may be ready, when their country demands their assistance, to serve in the royal dock-yards, and facilitate the equipment of our navies.

2. As the primary nursery of hardy seamen to man those navies.

3. As furnishing, if properly encouraged, a considerable article of commerce, giving freights to shipping, and drawing hither from the various mar-

kets of Europe and the Weſt Indies, in ſpecie and goods, to the amount of 750,000l. annually.

4. In ſupplying the labouring people with cheap and wholeſome food, to the amount of 1,000,000l. annually.

5. In giving employment to half a million of people of both ſexes, and of all ages; as coopers, blackſmiths, joiners, block-makers, painters, hecklers, ſpinners, net-makers, rope-makers, ſail-cloth-manufacturers, and ſail-makers, tanners, ſalt-makers and labourers.

6. As opening inexhauſtible ſources of wealth amongſt a numerous body of people in both kingdoms, thereby contributing to the extenſion of manufactures, and the increaſe of revenue.

7. As contributing particularly to the improvement of that hitherto loſt country, the Highlands of Scotland, and furniſhing 3 or 400,000 people with a competency of the neceſſaries of life, whereby emigrations would ceaſe, and a numerous colony of ſoldiers, ſeamen, and fiſhers would be ſoon eſtabliſhed.

8. As raiſing the value of natural woods, and conſequently barren lands.

To ſum up the whole, as giving vigour to the centre of empire, rendering us leſs dependant on foreign countries and foreign connections, at all times expenſive and precarious.

Such are the gifts that Heaven hath beſtowed upon our ſhores, of which ſtrangers have hitherto reaped the fruits, as ſtated in the foregoing hiſtory of the fiſheries, down to the beginning of the preſent year.

The following particulars will enable you to form ſome concluſion reſpecting the preſent meaſures of government, for the recovery of that national ſtaple.

The remarks which I had ventured to bring into public view reſpecting the fiſheries, being generally approved of by the inhabitants of England

land as well as Scotland, brought forward that Herculean foe to the buss-fishery, Dr. Adam Smith, commissioner of the customs in Scotland, whose specious writings on that subject, have had too much influence over the minds of men not sufficiently informed to judge for themselves, or to discover the virulency of the author, when he writes on that head.

But the evil doth not rest here. It is greatly to be feared that the unfair statements and conclusions of this writer have also influenced administration and many senators respecting the formation of new laws. If so, we may bid adieu to the Scottish fisheries. But let us not meanly give up the cause of our country without a struggle in its defence. Now is the critical moment, when every practical fisher and well-informed person, ought to take his stand in the best of all causes, the natural rights of mankind, and the relief of distress. It is a cause wherein the Author of Nature, if I may so express myself, is a party concerned. He bestowed those fisheries upon your country, as an equivalent for its barren soil, and shall the inhabitants spurn at the benevolent gift? Shall the prejudices, the dogmatical decrees, and baneful insinuations of a board of customs, be permitted to counteract the beneficent intentions of the Deity. Your ancestors, during the reigns of the 5 James's, enacted laws, enforcing the buss-fishery, as the mode which was best suited to the Scottish seas; they even compelled the nobility, principal gentry, and royal boroughs, to fit out decked vessels proportioned to their abilities, for exploring the boisterous ocean; while boats or wherries were busily employed in the firths and bays. The distractions of subsequent ages, and particularly the capture of the sea vessels, by Cromwell or his officers, annihilated the buss-fishery on the east coast. It was again resumed during the reign of his late

 majesty,

majesty, and carried on with great spirit from the western ports, encouraged by the demands for the West Indies; and again it hath been almost suppressed; not by civil commotions, or foreign invasion, but by the machinations of your countrymen, co-operating with various discouraging circumstances, formerly enumerated.

A committee of the house of commons was appointed in March last, to inquire into the present state of the British fisheries, and into the most effectual means for their improvement and extension. Evidences were examined from both kingdoms; several valuable papers, transmitted to different members, were read, arranged, and printed, for the inspection of the parliament. The season was now too far advanced for entering upon the subject of bounties, but it was proposed to bring in a bill for removing certain impediments, and unnecessary restrictions, as a preliminary to the main objects in reserve for future discussion.

The sense of the Committee was as follows:

From the Facts which are stated in their present, or contained in their former Report, Your Committee have unanimously agreed upon the following Resolutions; viz.

Resolved, That it is the opinion of this committee, that every buss or other fishing vessel, properly fitted out and furnished as by law required for vessels entered for the bounty, should be allowed to clear out of any port of Great Britain, at any time between the 1st day of June and the 1st day of October, and to proceed immediately to her fishing station, and to cast her nets, without being obliged to rendezvous at any other port or place—*Agreed to by Parliament.*

Resolved, That it is the opinion of this committee, That the masters of busses and other vessels employed in in the herring fishery should be at liberty to purchase fresh herrings of the boat fishers (being British subjects) and to ship the herrings which they shall take, or which they shall purchase as aforesaid, on board any attendant British vessel, with permission to land the same, under proper regulations, in any of the ports of Great Britain, upon oath being made, by the master of the smaller vessel so landing them as aforesaid, or by the owner of the fish, that the fish were, to the best of his knowledge and belief, caught by British subjects; provided that, if the attendant vessel which shall sail with such fish, shall land them at any other port than that from which the principal vessel cleared out, a proper certificate of the number of barrels of salted fish so landed, shall be obtained from the principal officer of the customs at such port, before the bond for the duties on the salt taken on board the principal vessel shall be discharged; and provided also, that no buss or vessel, returning to port within the space of twelve weeks after her clearance outwards, unless with a full cargo, the whole of which shall have been taken, and cured or salted, by such buss or vessel, should be intitled to a bounty.—*Agreed to in part.*

Resolved, That it is the opinion of this committee, That for reviving and encouraging the cod fishery in the North Seas, and in Iceland, the owner of any vessel employed therein should be at liberty to use in the said fishery British-made salt, duty-free, and to warehouse, under the key of the officer, any surplus salt remaining in such vessel, upon her return to the place of her outfit, under the like rules and regulations as are provided for surplus salt brought back in vessels employed in the herring fishery.——*Agreed to.*

Resolved, That it is the opinion of this committee, That all busses, and other fishing vessels, should, in future, be permitted to be entered for the bounty, without any limitation of their burden or tonnage;

except that no veſſel of leſs than 20 tons ſhould be intitled to any bounty, and except that no buſs or other veſſel ſhould be intitled to the bounty for more than 80 tons, although of a larger burden.—*Agreed to.*

Reſolved, That it is the opinion of this committee, That all buſſes and veſſels employed in the herring fiſheries, ſhould be at liberty, during the time of their continuance at ſea, to catch and cure cod, ling, and hake, as well as herrings, and ſhould be ſubject to the ſame regulations, and have the ſame privilege of curing the ſaid other ſpecies of fiſh with ſalt duty-free, as in the caſe of herrings; but that no bounty ſhould be allowed on the exportation of the ſaid other ſpecies of fiſh; and therefore, that ſuch other fiſh ſhould be marked by cutting their tails, in the manner preſcribed for marking fiſh cured for home conſumption.—*Ditto.*

Reſolved, That it is the opinion of this committee, That the duties payable upon fiſh caught and cured by Britiſh ſubjects (ſuch fiſh being entered and landed as by law required for fiſh cured for home conſumption) ſhould ceaſe and be diſcontinued.

I am ſorry to obſerve, that the new laws, though they aboliſh ſome impediments, are, in other reſpects, diſcouraging to the Scottiſh herring and white fiſheries, which will undoubtedly give your rivals of Ireland and the continent, a decided advantage over you in both.

Firſt, reſpecting the herring fiſhery: by the former laws, veſſels were to remain at ſea 3 months after their departure from port, unleſs they ſhould ſooner have completed their loading. By the new law, they are to remain at ſea 3 months, not from the time of ſailing, as formerly enacted, but "from "the day upon which ſuch owners or maſters re-"ſpectively, firſt ſhot or wetted their nets." Now,

k

it too frequently happens, that vessels do not fall in with the herrings for several weeks, sometimes 2 months after their departure from port: consequently, every owner must engage men, and lay in provisions and stores for 5 months, instead of 3. It may indeed be supposed that there is a loop-hole, as it is called, by which the law may be evaded, viz. by wetting the nets immediately on sailing out of port. Setting this aside, what chance have the Scottish fishers with their neighbours of Ireland, who are under no restrictions whatever respecting the time of sailing or arrival between the first of May, and the first of February, whether loaded, half loaded, or empty. You will also perceive that the inland duty is continued upon herrings, though "the annual produce of this duty, as appears by "a report transmitted to the committee from the "salt office, upon an average of the two last years, "scarcely exceeds 1,400l."

This trifle requires the same attention and entries as a revenue of 100 times the amount; and is equally troublesome to the merchant or agent.

Secondly, respecting white fish: By the former laws, all white fish exported was entitled to the following bounties, viz.

	£.	s.	d.
On every cwt. of dried white fish, —	0	3	0
On every barrel of 32 gallons of wet do.	0	2	0

By the new laws these bounties are withdrawn on British fish, while the Irish merchant is allowed,

	£.	s.	d.
On every score of ling or cod taken on the coast of Ireland, — —	0	5	0
On every score of hake, haddock, or cod fish, and conger eel, — —	0	3	0
On every tierce, containing 41 gallons, of cured wet fish — — —	0	4	3

What chance have the British fishers at foreign markets, against these bounties; or with the Norwegians, who frequent the northern ſeas at half the expence of our people, in proviſions, wages, and the equipment of veſſels?

This, gentlemen, is a ſpecimen of what may be expected as the "moſt effectual means for the im-"provement and extenſion of the Britiſh fiſheries," whilſt the friends of thoſe fiſheries vainly imagine, that this moſt important of all national buſineſs can be permanently eſtabliſhed with little or no public aid; in which deluſion they are encouraged by fawning ſycophants, who have recourſe to ſuch flatteries, as the readieſt means of retaining or procuring miniſterial favour, though at the expence of the public welfare, and individual ſubſiſtence.

It is not to be ſuppoſed that perſons in the higher ranks of life have given any particular attention to the ſubject of fiſheries, excepting thoſe immediately concerned therein, by profeſſion, or local ſituation, of which the number is extremely few*; it is therefore highly expedient, that perſons of practical experience

* That the importance of the fiſheries is not properly comprehended, appears evident from the oppoſition made by Mr. Eden, one of the moſt intelligent members of the houſe of commons, to the remiſſion of the inland duties on herrings, which Mr. Beaufoy ſtated at no more than 1400l. This trifling ſource of revenue alſo attracted the attention of the miniſter, who moved that the clauſe might be poſtponed for the preſent.

The debates on this ſubject alſo afford a convincing proof, that the ſubject of the fiſheries is little underſtood. Mr. Eden "made "no ſcruple to acknowledge that he was not ſufficiently maſter "of the ſubject to pronounce upon it with certainty. He ſaid, "he had no other information reſpecting it, but what he had ob-"tained from peruſing the ſecond report, and from conſulting "2 or 3 volumes of the ſtatute books upon the table, ſince he "came into the houſe, and he would venture to ſay, without "dread of being thought guilty of any affront to the committee, "that very few of the thirty members preſent were better ac-"quainted with the ſubject than himſelf." Mr. Eden's obſervation on this head is fully confirmed in the third and principal report, where the gentlemen who methodized the ſame, fairly confeſs themſelves enveloped in myſtery and darkneſs. It is not to be wondered that this ſhould be the caſe, when perſons, whoſe ſituation

perience should ſtep forth to reſcue the fiſheries from the hands of ignorant adviſers, and conſequently from aliens, by which means they will be effectually ſecured to the native ſubjects.

With this view, I ſignified to ſeveral members of parliament, an intention to draw up a ſet of propoſitions for the peruſal of the traders and fiſhers in Scotland, as a ground-work, on which the convention of the royal boroughs may compoſe and prepare a body of fiſhery regulations, ſuited to all caſes and circumſtances; which, when completed, may be tranſmitted to government.

Beſides my own obſervations and enquiries reſpecting the Britiſh and European fiſheries, I have been furniſhed with remarks, in the form of memorials, ſigned by the reſpective magiſtrates, merchants, and principal fiſhers on the weſt coaſt. I have alſo received much uſeful information from the epiſtolary communications of individuals in different parts of the kingdom, who are engaged in that branch, as well as thoſe who have relinquiſhed the buſineſs, as an unprofitable, or a ruinous purſuit.

By means of theſe materials, I have been enabled to proceed, ſo far, on ſure grounds, as you will perceive in the preceding chapters, where each ſubject is ſeparately ſtated; but as theſe communications are confined to 15 or 20 heads, I have ventured, alone and unſupported, to branch out this great ſubject to the various caſes which occur at preſent to my memory

ſituation in life gives them a claim to a hearing, advance falſe ſtatements, as Dr. Smith, who in the eſtimates of the herrings taken by the Scottiſh buſſes, includes only thoſe caught in the firſt, or what is called the bounty voyage, whereas "the buſſes often make a ſecond, and ſometimes a third; and as, one year with another, the herrings taken in theſe voyages are believed to equal thoſe taken on the bounty voyage, it follows that the quantity taken by the buſſes is double what they are ſtated," conſequently Dr. Smith's main argument falls to the ground.

memory, the outlines of which I submit, with due deference, to your consideration.

1. As the Scottish seas abound with fish throughout the whole year, besides an annual reinforcement from the great northern ocean, in a compact body, equal in extent to the British kingdoms, it is the duty of the natives to avail themselves of this heaven-directed bounty, to the fullest extent, without ceasing.

2. That the restraining laws enacted from time to time militate against the benevolent intentions of Providence, and have contributed to throw that valuable branch into the hands of aliens, thereby depriving the natives of their birthright.

3. That an unlimited discretionary power should be given to all persons concerned in the herring fisheries, respecting the time of sailing and return, between the months of May and February.

4. That the busses may be allowed to fish, to purchase from the natives, or do both; and in every respect to act as circumstances may dictate for their own benefit, provided, however, that all fresh herrings so purchased shall have been taken on the preceding night, and not before.

5. That the British and Irish seas and fisheries may be common to the natives of either country, subject to the same laws and regulations.

6. That vessels may be allowed to send their captures to the ports from whence they sailed, by means of carrying vessels, when, and as often as they shall judge it expedient.

7. That Ireland, formerly a market for Scottish herrings, hath not only supplied herself, of late, but also become a rival at the West India market, through the wisdom, liberality, and unwearied exertions of their parliament, particularly in bounties, which, by the first laws, amounted to 20s. per ton to all vessels carrying between 20 and 100 tons burden; and is now raised to 30s. besides 1s. 3d. per barrel on all herrings cured after the

Dutch

Dutch manner; also 2s. per barrel on all herrings exported.

8. That Sweden, also a market for Scottish herrings, so late as the year 1750, now supplies herself, the Baltic, &c. to the amount of 200,000 barrels annually, upon an average of years, at from 8 to 10s. per barrel. That the herrings being taken at, or near the mercantile city of Gottenburgh, by means of large nets, in the manner of the salmon fishery, no extraordinary expence is requisite, which circumstance, with the cheapness of the casks, operates as a large bounty, by which the Swedes are enabled to undersell all other nations *.

9. That

* The following table of exports from Gottenburgh may be useful to persons concerned in the fisheries.

	1775	1776	1777	1779	1780	178[illegible]
To Cork and other Irish ports,	25,836	56,400	19,267	7,313	12,[illegible]	
Madeira and the West Indies,	6,07[illegible]	7,437	9,826	20,[illegible]	9,18[illegible]	[illegible]
Dantzic,	5,69[illegible]	4,381	3,716	755	538	1,120
Stettin,	2,967	74[illegible]	1,485	2,4[illegible]	1,77[illegible]	6,6[illegible]
Koningsberg,	4,670	4,970	6,590	740	1,60[illegible]	1,[illegible]
Riga,	1,365	3,798	7,337	2,414	2,[illegible]	9,534
Petersburgh,	2,175	4,198	7,507	6,265	2,182	3,198
Wolgest,	1,96[illegible]	2,209	2,458	3,901	9,1[illegible]	8,38[illegible]
Different ports in the east Sea,	20,72[illegible]	16,930	35,370	41,397	31,[illegible]	50,170
France and the Mediterranean,	300	4,267	5,413	8,369	11,614	24,215
Barrels of 32 gal. 900 her. in each,	73,964	105,195	94,971	94,60[illegible]	77,[illegible]	107,[illegible]
Different ports in Sweden.	20,607	23,272	17,0[illegible]	40,[illegible]	28,[illegible]	49,3[illegible]
Total,	94,578	128,467	132,[illegible]	135,[illegible]	[illegible]	[illegible]

The sale of Swedish herrings hath lately been very considerable in the Dutch island of Eustatia.

When the herrings first returned to the Swedish coast, in the year 1752, they appeared in July and August; they have gradually fallen in with that coast at a later season, and are now seldom seen before the beginning of November, neither are the fish so fat as when they appeared early.

The herrings, as soon as gutted, are regularly laid into the casks or barrels, with salt; after standing 10 or 12 days, they reckon

9. That of late years there is alſo a conſiderable herring fiſhery on the coaſt of Norway, taken and cured at little expence.

10. That under the diſcouraging circumſtances of rivalſhip, and reſtrictions at home, added to the diſproportionate expence of out-fits, &c. the Scottiſh fiſheries have declined, are declining, and will in all probability be reduced to the mere ſupply of the kingdom, unleſs they ſhall be placed on a footing with thoſe of Ireland, Sweden, and Norway.

11. That the patriots of Ireland have declared their intention to advertiſe in the Scottiſh newſpapers, for experienced fiſhermen and traders of the latter kingdom, to ſettle in the towns now erecting upon the north-weſt coaſt of Ireland.

12. That ſome of the moſt experienced fiſhers and traders of the weſt of Scotland have declared to the author of theſe ſheets, their determined reſolution to remove with their families, veſſels, and property to the coaſt of Ireland, unleſs the Britiſh government ſhall place the Scottiſh fiſheries and all ſalt duties upon an equal footing with thoſe of the former country.

13. That theſe uſeful men have often ſtated their caſe to government, with little or no effect, owing, it is ſuppoſed, to the ſecret influence of their enemies. That they lately renewed their humble appli-

reckon them ready for ſhipping, when the barrels are well daunted, and filled up. The herrings that are ſalted yield no oil, it is extracted only by boiling them in boilers that contain from 10 to 20 barrels. On an average 18 barrels of herrings yield a caſk of oil, nearly 32 gallons meaſure. In 1781, the Swedes exported 14,542 barrels of this oil, not having conſumption or demand for the herrings which lay on their ſhores. The markets for herring oil are the Baltic, Holland, and Spain. The average price is about 2l. 7s. per barrel. The quality is greatly inferior to whale oil, and even to liver oil; having this inconveniency, that in cold weather there is no keeping it from congealing to a conſiſtence ſomething like honey. *Mr. Meaſon's Anſwers to Mr. Byres's Queries concerning the Herring Fiſhing on the Coaſt of Sweden; inſerted in the third Report of the Committee on the Britiſh Fiſheries.*

in

cations, in a clear and circumstantial deduction of facts, founded upon the experience of former as well as the present times.

14. That the schemes suggested by Dr. Smith and Dr. Anderson, for carrying on the Scottish fisheries by means of boats, without the support of the public, or by premiums during a limited time, are totally inadequate to the nature of those fisheries, and the hazards of the Scottish seas.

15. That all schemes calculated for that important end, upon a contracted plan of œconomy, will prove delusive to the state, as well as individuals.

16. That to enable us to meet foreigners at the European and West India markets, on equal terms, certain aids, suited to the nature and modes of each respective fishery are unavoidably necessary.

17. That to render those fisheries subservient to the great purposes of naval strength, the extension of commerce, and the employment of the people, it will be expedient to encourage the same by means of decked vessels, for the floating fishery in the open seas, and by wherries, for the coasts and inlets.

18. That nothing less than a general bounty, extending to vessels of every size, and to fisheries of every denomination, will be found effectual upon the experiment; neither can any plan be adopted, so simple in its operation, or less subject to frauds, jobs, collusion, or imposition.

19. That the mode of encouraging the herring fishery, at the time of the Union, by means of high premiums on fish exported, opened a door for perjury, and the abuse of the public money, the barrels being frequently entered a second time upon the bounty, while the iniquitous practices of the traders, in exporting fish unproperly cured, and sometimes filling the barrels in part with stones, or lumber, lost to these kingdoms the confidence of foreigners,

foreigners, and the ſale of herrings at the European markets.

20. That nature hath been ſingularly favourable to the Iriſh fiſheries, by confining them to a narrow point on the coaſt of Donegal, while the ſtation of the Scottiſh fiſheries, that of Shetland excepted, is at all times uncertain, and requires much time and patience, beſides expence, before the herrings are diſcovered.

21. That the parliament of Ireland having lately granted, in further aid of their fiſheries, a bounty of 30s. per ton, on all veſſels carrying from 20 to 100 tons, beſides ſmall premiums per barrel, it is eſſentially requiſite that the Scottiſh fiſheries be put on an equal footing, which, allowing for the certainty and facility of the former, and the uncertainty, expence, and hazards of the latter, will require at the leaſt, a tonnage bounty of 40s. extending to all veſſels from 20 to 100 tons, beſides premiums on herrings exported, ſimilar to thoſe granted by Ireland.

22. That the adventurers be permitted to build veſſels on ſuch conſtructions as experience hath proved beſt adapted to the reſpective ſeas, ſhores, and modes of fiſhing, agreeable to a plan to be drawn up by the convention.

23. That all veſſels built and equipped after the Dutch manner, which ſhall clear out for the Shetland fiſhery in the proper ſeaſon, and which ſhall take and cure after the Dutch method, the rich high-flavoured herrings, for the European markets; and alſo follow the ſhoals without ceaſing in their emigrations ſouthward, and which ſhall continue the floating fiſhery without boats, from the 24th day of June (or ſooner if it ſhall be found expedient by the convention) to the 24th day of Auguſt, be intitled to an additional bounty of 20s. or 3l. per ton.

24. That all veſſels which ſhall engage to proſecute the herring and white fiſheries alternately through the whole year, be intitled to 3l. per ton.

25. That all bounties be immediately paid to the respective claimants, or their order, on producing satisfactory vouchers or proofs of their having conformed, in all respects, to the intent and spirit of the law.

26. That all custom-house fees, in whatever relates to fisheries, be abolished under a penalty.

27. That all boats or wherries properly equipped, and carrying 5 men and 1 or 2 boys or apprentices, which shall prosecute the floating and ground fishery during the usual continuance of the herrings on their respective shores, be intitled to an annual bounty of 15l. per boat, upon producing vouchers as above stated.

28. That all such boats or wherries, which shall prosecute the herring and white fisheries alternately through the whole year, and whose crew shall not jointly or severally occupy any lands beyond acres each; and shall not exercise any profession or trade unconnected with the fisheries, be intitled to an annual bounty of 20l.

29. In order to facilitate business, as well as to bring offenders more speedily to justice, the owners of a fishing vessel shall cause the name of such vessel, and the port to which she belongs, to be cut in characters at least 5 inches long, and one quarter of an inch deep, on the stern of the said vessel, the same to be painted with white lead and oil; as also on all boats and buoys belonging to the said vessel. And the collector shall cause a number to be added to such names, which number shall be inserted in the entry, and painted in like manner on the vessel, and on the boats and buoys.

30. That the name of the skipper or master of each boat or wherry on the bounty, be cut, or painted in large characters, with white lead and oil, on the stern of said boats, and the initial letters cut or painted on her oars and buoys.

31. That

31. That no veſſel frequenting the fiſheries, be permitted to moor or ſhoot her nets at the entrance of the bays and creeks, thereby preventing the herrings from entering ſuch bays or openings; nor ſhould any perſon be allowed to lay long lines for taking of cod and ling acroſs the entrance of theſe bays.

33. No nets ſhould be ſhot or wet for taking herrings in the day-time.

32. A certain portion of the coaſt or beach ſhould be allotted for the various purpoſes of the herring and white fiſheries, exempted from all claims or ſhore dues whatever.

34. That a ſet of regulations, ſuch as are expedient and practicable, be drawn up by the convention, reſpecting the beſt modes of curing, packing, and marking, ſuited to each reſpective ſeaſon of the year, particularly the early Shetland fiſhery, in which the convention will be conſiderably aſſiſted by the Dutch laws. *See page* 257, *&c. alſo page* 391.

35. That the practice of curing in bulk, and the preſent mode of daunting, be cloſely inveſtigated, and the propriety or impropriety thereof, be clearly defined.

36. That the thickneſs of the barrels for the reſpective ſeaſons be determined; the age and quality of the wood ſpecified; and the duty upon European ſtaves remitted.

37. That the growth of willows be encouraged on fenny grounds, near water-carriage.

38. That as the preſent townleſs ſtate of the Weſt Highlands, renders the natives of that great ſeat of fiſheries utterly unable to conform to laws and regulations reſpecting ſalt; and as theſe laws, however mild or indulgent, will ever prove a barrier againſt the extenſion of the national fiſheries in general, it is ſubmitted to the convention whether it would not be expedient to ſubſtitute another object of revenue

equivalent to the 13,000l. raised at present from salt, which in this case might be abolished.

39. That the Scots, hitherto denied the use of English rock salt, though free to other nations, be allowed to import the same, on equal terms with Ireland.

40. That the convention be particularly attentive to the salt regulations, specifying such and such kinds and qualities of salt, for such and such herrings and white fish, as on this depends in a great measure, the reputation of the Scottish fish, and the extension of the sale at the European markets. The Dutch regulations on this head, as before stated, may be found useful.

41. The size and qualities of the nets, with the dimensions of the meshes, also merit particular attention.

42. The duty upon herrings for inland sale in both kingdoms, though the net revenue arising therefrom is little more than a name, operates as a check to that branch, enhances the price double-fold to the labouring part of the community, and ought to be abolished.

43. To the above particulars, I have to add various objects, which, though of a general nature, will contribute essentially to the prosperity of the fisheries in all their varieties. They are matters of considerable expence, and can only be executed by means of the public revenue, or properly speaking, by a loan from the public stock, which will be repaid in due time with ample interest. The first of these, is the proposed communication between the Low Countries and the West Highlands, by means of a canal from Lochfine to Loch Crinan, of a sufficient depth for the largest busses when loaded, and drawing 12 feet water. *See page* 410.

44. Secondly, a navigable communication between Inverness and Fort William in the North

Highlands, of the ſame depth, and for the ſame purpoſes. *See page* 422.

45. A line of 8 market-towns, built on the weſt coaſt of the main land, to ſerve as ſtorehouſes and marts, where the natives may buy and ſell, and enjoy all the privileges of Britiſh ſubjects.

46. Opening ſundry carriage-roads in Roſs-ſhire, from ſea to ſea, which may be done by the military at no great expence.

47. Erecting lighthouſes from the mull of Galloway along the whole weſtern coaſt to cape Wrath; from thence along the coaſt of the Pentland firth; at North Ronalſha, in the Orkneys, and Kinnaird's head, at the entrance of the Murray firth*. Beacons ſhould alſo be erected, and buoys fixed in the moſt neceſſary ſituations.

48. It would be expedient to ſtation 2 or more revenue cutters annually, on or before the beginning of June, at the Shetland iſles, furniſhed with fiſhing nets in order to attend the 2 diviſions of the herrings in their ſouthern progreſs along both ſides of the kingdom, to obſerve all their motions by ſinking the nets, and to give notice thereof to the inhabitants or fiſhers, that the buſſes may not be under the neceſſity, as heretofore, of wandering from place to place, to find out the ſhoals, by which much valuable time is loſt, and frequently the foreign markets. That ſuch veſſels ought to have ſignals for the purpoſe of giving notice, when met at ſea, of the direction the ſhoal is taking, its magnitude, and other particulars. That the ſaid veſſels make ſoundings and obſervations upon the coaſts, ſearch for fiſhing banks, and examine thoſe already diſcovered, in order to aſcertain the beſt fiſhing grounds†.

49. It

* The two laſt were recommended to the committee on the fiſheries, by that experienced navigator, Captain Kyd, commander of one of his majeſty's cutters on the northern ſtation.

† "It is to be remarked," ſays Mr. Travis of Scarborough, "that the fiſhermen ſeldom find any cod, fry, or other round fiſh, upon

49. It would be expedient to authorise those cutters to board any vessel, or boat, upon the bounty, whether fishing in the open sea or at anchor, with powers to examine into the number of men, and other particulars, of which an account might be transmitted annually to the commissioners of the customs.

50. The cutters should also be empowered to maintain good order amongst the fishers, to enforce the laws, take cognisance of trespasses, whereby delinquents may be brought to justice, and expelled from the bounty fishery.

I shall close this list of propositions, by recommending to your notice a subject on which the prosperity of the fisheries greatly depends, though hitherto overlooked by political writers.

It is a melancholy truth, that two-thirds of the harbours, and consequently many of the towns in Scotland, have fallen into decay.

That most of the inhabitants, instead of prosecuting fisheries and coasting trade with the vigour and perseverance of their ancestors, have sunk into a state of sloth and indigence, become mere drones in society, subsisting upon a precarious illicit traffic in teas*, spirits

upon the Dogger-bank itself, but upon the sloping edges and hollows contiguous to it. The top of the bank is covered with a barren shifting sand, which affords them no subsistence, and the water on it, from its shallowness, is continually so agitated and broken, as to allow them no time to rest. The flat-fish do not suffer the same inconvenience there; for when disturbed by the motion of the sea, they shelter themselves in the sand, and find variety of suitable food. It is true, the Dutch fish upon the Dogger-bank; but it is also true, they take little except soles, skates, thornbacks, plaise, &c. It is in the hollows between the Dogger and the Well-bank, that the cod are taken, which supply London market."

This important information should stimulate cutters as well as fishing vessels to explore the edges of the Long-forty's, Marr's bank, and the whole chain of banks on the western coast.

* Tea is subject to a duty of 18 per cent. to which, if we add the expence of carriage and insurance from London, with commission

ſpirits, tobacco—and the equally pernicious trade of receiving bribes, at the expiration of every 7 years, by which they are enabled to pay off old ſcores, and to drag through a miſerable exiſtence, unprofitable to their families and their country. I have made ſome progreſs on the ſubject of harbours, and I expect, in a ſhort time, to be poſſeſſed of the preſent ſtate of every harbour in the kingdom, with eſtimates of the expence in cleanſing, deepening, repairing or enlarging, where neceſſary.

Such, gentlemen, is the field in the maritime line, which demands attention. Your eſtabliſhment is amongſt the moſt antient in Europe; the powers delegated to you by the ſtates of the nation, ſince the middle of the 12th century, are almoſt unlimited in all matters relating to commerce, navigation, and fiſheries, of which you are the hereditary guardians. Though your eſtabliſhment ſunk to little more than a name under the depreſſion of your country, during theſe laſt 150 years, its invigorating powers ſtill exiſt, and may be called into action at the very firſt meeting of the convention. Your late ſpirited conduct relative to the enormous cuſtom-houſe fees, had a good effect; your memorial relative to the privilege of fiſhing on the coaſts of Ireland and the iſle of Man, brought the commiſſioners to their ſenſes, and humbled their pride, as appears by their late circular letter amongſt the fiſhers; but this ſelf-raiſed tribunal, this terror of ſlaves, ſeems ſtill inclined to diſpute every inch of ground with the antient and only legal commercial court of the nation. Though its pretenſions are ſpurious, its influence is great, and there lies the danger. It is evident, from re-

miſſion or profit laid upon it by the London agent or merchant; the whole will probably amount to 30 per cent. above the price paid to ſmugglers; but were the Eaſt India company diſpoſed to eſtabliſh warehouſes in Scotland, where teas might be ſold to ſhopkeepers at or near the London prices, they would thereby cruſh ſmuggling effectually.

cent

cent publications, that the ideas of these men respecting the fisheries, are incompatible with the true interest of the British nation, which consists in establishing permanent extensive fisheries, by means of liberal bounties, to be renewed from time to time, as circumstances shall require. This would immediately diffuse a spirit of exertion and adventure upon every coast, firth, and lake of the kingdom. Boats and vessels of every size, from 5 to 120 tons, would be immediately put on the stocks, while the old and the young would again resume the various branches of net and canvas making. These observations, gentlemen, are not the effusions of idle speculation; they are founded upon long observation, and ocular demonstration. Eradicate, therefore, any impressions which specious, florid and artful declamation may have made on your minds, and let reason and humanity supply their place.

In order that your decisions on this important business may contain the sense of the nation, it will be necessary to deviate in one instance, from the strict rules of your constitution. Your body is composed of delegates from the royal boroughs, and none else. The revolutions that have happened since this regulation was framed, have greatly altered the face of the country, and the state of the boroughs, in particular. Some ports are so greatly reduced, that they have scarcely a single vessel at sea; while places which 100 years ago scarcely deserved the name of villages, now carry on the principal fisheries of the kingdom, as Greenock and Port Glasgow. Other towns, as Salcoats, Eymouth, Peterhead, and Cromarty, have also a claim to notice. It is therefore submitted to your consideration, whether to admit delegates from these places, with the liberty of voting on such propositions as shall come before you. It is also submitted to your consideration, whether to admit representatives from the West Highlands, and Hebride isles, which, though townless, are the principal seats of the fisheries, and consequently the natives have a natural right to be heard on subjects wherein they are so immediately concerned. If this indulgence should be granted, a representative from Oban on the main land, might be appointed; and also from Mull, Ilay, and Sky, nominated by the principal proprietor of each respective island.

This conduct would discover such moderation and liberality of sentiment, as could not fail of contributing to the success of your applications to the legislature. Moreover, the subject of the fisheries will be found more extensive and perplexing in the discussion, than you at present foresee, which renders the assistance of these men essentially necessary.

The impediments now existing, and the most eligible mode of granting public aid, being stated or settled, other objects will appear to your view, branching out from one another in a seeming endless chain of regulations, which must be adapted to the various seasons and modes of each respective fishery. Many of these being new to Scotsmen, it will be necessary to appropriate one or two seasons in experiments, the result of which will enable the convention to proceed on sure ground in the framing a practicable system of fishery laws, whereby their country will gradually rise from its ruins, and again become respectable in Europe.

Extracts from a Petition and Memorial to the Right Honourable the Lords Commissioners of His Majesty's Treasury, from the General Convention of the Royal Boroughs of Scotland, September 1783; in Answer to a Petition of certain Officers of the Customs, and a Report of the Board of Customs at Edinburgh and their Inspector, in June 1782. With Remarks.

"IN the port of Leith," says the Memorial, "which, with a few exceptions, is the most moderate in Scotland, the fees upon coals within the firth are now triple of the board's regulations in 1730. There are at that port also, besides other variations, about 15 or 20 additional high fees established for clerks, that were not known in in 1742. Nor was the illegal and incredible oppression of bonds and cockets, upon small quantities of goods passing within the river, even under 5l. value, and at times by ferry-boats, practised there till very lately.

"At Borrowstounness, the fee for a cocket on coals was only 2d. as stated in a table of fees, signed by the collector and comptroller of that port, and transmitted to the board of customs anno 1742. But this fee of 2d. is now raised to the extraordinary sum of about 5s. exclusive of stamps, and 3 or 4 shillings more for sufferances, coast-waiter, &c. Bonds and cockets, with high fees, have also been exacted on goods passing on the river Forth, down to the value of 30 or 40 shillings, though, by law, no fee at all can be taken on goods under 5l.

"A small boat of 8 tons burden, carrying under 35 shillings value of coals for a few miles, in the same custom-house district, within the river, was illegally subjected to bonds and cockets, for 34 trips in one year, 1780; the fees for which, with stamp-paper, amounted to about 20 per cent. of all the value of the coals she carried, and nearly to the whole freight which the boat earned. Nay, such is the rage for fees on the river Forth, and the indiscretion of the officers, who it seems have been long without any controul in this respect, that in the 2 districts on the head of the Forth, 50 miles above open sea, they have ventured, without the least shadow of lawful authority, to extort bonds and cockets, with high fees, even upon rafts of foreign wood, just after the duties on them were paid, for passing a few miles on or across the river, to enter the canal for Glasgow. And what may seem altogether incredible, one of these raft-bonds, for want of a certificate, was sent to be put in suit in the Exchequer.

"Wool, that great raw material of our manufacture, which passes free in all rivers and firths, and even at many turnpikes in England, is loaded with excessive fees in passing at the upper ferries of the river; and what can scarcely be believed, at the narrow passage of Queen's ferry, about 20 miles above open sea, these fees seem of late to be farmed to the innkeepers at the water side. They, without any dispatch being given, levy a tax for the officers, at 8d. on each small pack of 12 stone weight of wool, equal to the exorbitant sum of about 6s. a ton, or 30l. on a single 100 tons of this raw material. Even poor men and women, unable to hire horses, have been compelled to pay a share of this gross imposition for each load of wool carried on their backs."

These, and other impositions, of which endless instances might be given, are contrary to the laws of Scotland, and decisions of the courts, which positively say that all ferries are considered as high roads, and all goods passing the Forth in boats, are to be free, of which wool is particularly mentioned.

"At Aberdeen," says the memorial, "the fee on landing goods, from general vessels coastways, was, by their own table in 1742, scarcely one farthing per barrel, which was itself unreasonably high, but is now raised to a full penny sterling, or 8d.

per ton, amounting annually to a sum equal to the whole land-tax of the city and its liberties. There is also at this port, an additional fee of about 18d. a ton on raw wool brought coastways. At Montrose, Thurso, and other small ports, the fees are in general still higher than at Aberdeen.

" Reports on small vessels from abroad in ballast, are not exacted at some great English ports, particularly at London and Yarmouth; and at some other ports, 6d. only is taken for such reports; while in the firth of Forth the fees amount to 7, 10, and 16 shillings; and at some distant ports they are even higher. The fees also on reports of vessels outwards, in the two countries, especially with coals and corn, differ nearly in the same proportion.

" By the table annexed to the book of rates, the following article is twice narrated, under the head of Subsidy Outwards: '*For making and entering a transire or let-pass, from port to port in Great Britain, 6d.*' and, under the head of Fees for Searchers and Waiters, '*Transires for the coast free.*' But at many of our ports, 1s. 6d. and in some places, 3s. and 5s. is exacted for such transires, besides a large fee to the shipping officer, or waiter, though prohibited, as above, and this upon trifling parcels of goods of small value, within rivers; and 2 shillings is taken even on lime.

" *By the book of rates, coast sufferance is to be given without fee*; and accordingly none is taken at London, and other English ports, whatever the value of the goods may be; but at Leith 6d. is taken for each sufferance, and sometimes to the number of 10 to 20 of them on a single coasting vessel. At other ports, 1s. 1s. 6d. and sometimes more, is exacted on each sufferance.

" The fees for coals shipped here for London, are three times higher than what they are at Newcastle, on vessels of far greater burden, and five or six times as high as what they are in England upon their exportation. Nay, there are instances, where the fees on small vessels with coals exported to Ireland, have equalled, and even sometimes exceeded the king's duties.

" The fees on the exportation of corn also, by small vessels, amount, at several of our ports, to six times what the same business costs at Yarmouth, and other great ports of England. Regular high fees are also taken at some or all of our ports, upon fish and salt, and on corn exported on bounties and on debentures, though directly prohibited by law.

" At the port of Dunbar near Edinburgh, in particular, the officers not only take high fees on fish, but have been known to force the same merchant into many different entries, cockets and debentures, upon single ladings of corn exported on bounty; and, in defiance of law, to exact 5s. for each, upon paying, or certifying these debentures: so that the expence, besides incredible trouble and delay, amounted to twenty times what the same business would have cost at many English ports.

" In England the firths or navigable rivers are as free as high roads for every kind of home or foreign goods, and so were the

Scottish

Scottish firths and rivers for some time after the union; but the officers have of late years, for their own gain, tax all our rivers, with the exception of a small part of the upper Clyde, considered as open sea up to their first bridges, even where the rivers are not half a quarter of a mile broad, and in the case of the Forth, 60 miles above the real open sea. Small parcels of home goods cannot pass across, or up and down such rivers, for a mile or two; nor between the Glasgow canal and the Forth, without an expence of 8, 10, 15s. or more, nearly the same as if they were full-trading ships going round the island; and many cases have happened, where persons have been forced to carry small parcels of goods, such as coals and meal corn, by land, and could not use the river or canal navigation with it, even in vessels, unless they submitted to pay 30, 40, or 50 per cent. of the value in fees.

"The great articles of coals and culm, which pass free of fees in English rivers, is most illegally subjected on the river Forth, to an expence of about 10 per cent. on their original cost, for fees; and in the lower Clyde, where the craft are smaller, (many of them poor Highland boats of 5 or 6 tons) to 10 or 15 per cent. besides an incredible delay and waste of time to the mariners and lightermen.—Of all these facts the convention has undoubted evidence. Indeed, the illegal oppression upon coals carried within the firth of Forth especially, is put beyond all doubt, by accounts recently delivered in by the officers themselves, to the honourable house of commons. From these it appears, that the single fees of the collector of Borrowstounness, amount, on an average of three years, to 709l. annually, while those of the collector, 2 customers, comptroller, 5 land-waiters, and of all the other officers of every denomination together, at the great port of Newcastle, including Howden Pans and North Shields, amount only to 795l. 6s. annually; although at the same time, the quantity of coals shipped in Newcastle district, is probably 90 times of that in Borrowstounness. At Seatoun Sluice, and Blythe Nook, where perhaps near as many coals are shipped as at Borrowstounness, the fees of the collector, and all the other officers together, amount only to 90l. 6s. annually. The fees of the collector of the little port of Borrowstounness, also (arising chiefly from the illegal imposition on coals) amount, by the same accounts laid before the house of commons, to 53l. annually more than those of the collectors of the 3 great Scottish ports of Port Glasgow, Leith, and Dundee, put together. Those of the collector of the small port of Alloa, where there is little trade but in coals, amount also annually to more than the collectors at Newcastle, and to near as much as the collectors at Port Glasgow and Leith separately draw in fees."

The revenue officers made a stout defence in a counter petition to the lords of the treasury, supported by the board of commissioners of the customs at Edinburgh, who modestly report to their lordships, "That the fees now taken at the different ports of "Scotland, are sufficiently established by usage, and that no imposition has been made in the time of any officer now employed "in the service of the revenue under their management." (Though the then collector of the port of Leith, had been in office 40 years, the period in which most of these impositions had been made on the public) "That they have no information of inconvenience "arising from the continuation of the former practice."

"It appears," answered the convention, "from what has already been said, that these assertions are founded on misrepresentation, to give them no worse name; and what the board here recommends, is not only highly improper, but also illegal, and directly contrary to the statute 8th of queen Anne, above recited. The subjecting the trade of the inland navigation with the river Forth, to bonds and cockets, seems to have proceeded from the board itself,—at least an order for it was some years ago signed by their inspector, to the officers at Glasgow."

It also appears that the commissioners and the officers lately drew up a new table of fees for Scotland, and transmitted the same to the lords of the treasury for their sanction and approbation; on which table the convention make the following remarks.

"With regard to this *very singular table*; it may be observed in general, that were it adopted, the present rates of fees on the great foreign trade of Glasgow and Leith, would be nearly quadrupled; and the great river trade of Glasgow, between that city and Greenock, would be subjected to a very heavy new expence; besides an incredible delay and inconvenience.

"In several particulars the fees would be triple, and in some instances ten times as much as are paid in England for similar business; and in a great many instances, high fees would be payable on goods, which in the like situation are not charged with any at all in South Britain. But still more, this table proposes a variety of fees to be taken on different articles, which are particularly exempted from any, by positive statutes.

"The book of rates contains the following article, under the head of Rules for the Ports in general, '*Fish by British, or British shipping or vessels, inwards or outwards, or along the coasts to pay no fees*;' and the same are prohibited on salt and corn, exported on bounty, by different statutes. But this table contains regular articles for fees on salmon and herrings exported, and salt used in curing them; not satisfied with this, a let-pass to England with salmon is stated by the officers in the table at 7s. 6d. though the book of rates has an article 'for making and entering 'a transpire, or let-pass, from port to port in Great Britain, 6d.' So these officers would not only have a fee on fish, though directly prohibited by law, but would have fifteen times as much for a salmon let-pass, or transire, as the law allows for one upon other goods really subject to fees.

"Again, a transire for coals, under 15 tons, within the river Forth, is stated at 1s. 6d. which is not only three times the legal rate upon other goods subject to fees upon the open coast, but is also directly against law; because 15 tons of coals are not, at a medium, worth above 3l. and the law expressly prohibits any fees

on

on goods under the value of 5l. not only by the statutes establishing fees, but by a particular article in the book of rates, under the head of Rules for the Ports in general, as follows: '*All goods under the value of 5l. in the book of rates, paying subsidy the sum of 5s. or less, shall pass, without payment of any fees.*'

The convention, after stating other articles to the same purport, observe, that "it would be endless to enter into the particular absurdities of this table, in making out of which, the officers have shewn either *the greatest ignorance of, or disregard to the laws*, the orders of the sovereign, of the house of commons, and of the former boards of treasury. The convention cannot again avoid expressing their astonishment at these officers having the assurance to desire your lordships sanction to a table, in almost every article against law, and subversive of the treaty of union [which enacts, that all regulations 'for *navigation, and carrying goods coast-ways*,' shall be the same in Scotland as in England; and that the merchants and other persons '*entitled to any benefits, allowances, advantages or remedies, touching, or concerning any the customs in Scotland, shall have and enjoy the same in Scotland, as fully and amply, to all intents and purposes, as they may, or might, if the same were or arose in England.*' And the officers of the customs in Scotland are required to make and allow the same accordingly.] and that the assistant-secretary, and the inspector of the customs here should have ventured to sign such a table, which would never have been submitted to in this country. They are still more surprised, that this has been countenanced by the commissioners of the customs. Upon the whole the memorialists submit the consideration of this extraordinary business to your lordships wisdom, without further comment, and they return to their other requisition, founded on the treaty of union, and subsequent statutes." Next follows the plan or out-lines of a new table of custom-house fees, with other regulations, founded upon the laws now existing; which if complied with, will at once put an end to this iniquitous business, and rescue that oppressed nation from the hands of unexampled avarice, and the illegal mandates of a self-created legislature.

The convention, among other tables, and comparative statements of fees, have inserted the following particular account, which we shall give verbatim, as a curiosity for the amusement of the reader.

[Copy of an account sent from Dunmore harbour.]

Fees at the little Port of Alloa on Coal Barks passing within the Firth, or even crossing the Firth, 40 computed Miles above the Mouth, or Isle of May.

N. B. *The river at Alloa is no wider than the Thames above Westminster bridge.*

	£.	s.	d.
Sufferance to load, — — —	0	1	0
Sending for ditto, and ferry to pay, — —	0	0	8
Bond, — — —	0	4	3
Docket, — — —	0	3	0
Carried over	0	8	11

Brought over	0	8	11
Charges going to clear, and ferry,	0	1	2
Boatmen,	0	0	6
Shipping officer at Dunmore,	0	1	0
Total in Alloa district,	0	11	7
Sufferance to unload at Borowstounness, 10 miles distant on the same river,	0	1	6
Certificate there, and return of bond,	0	1	6
Sending for ditto two expresses from Carron,	0	1	0
Land-waiter at Carron,	0	1	0
	0	16	7
Given on return at Alloa,	0	0	6
	0	17	1
N. B. If a boat of 10 tons, with best great coal of 5s per ton, the cargo is worth	2	10	0
If with chow coals, ditto	1	3	0
If with pan-wood, or culm, ditto	1	0	0
	4	13	0
The freight of 10 tons to Carron,	0	11	8
The average value of 10 tons,	1	11	0

So that the fees are above 150 per cent. of the freight, and 50 per cent. of the value of the cargo, and in all probability they would have been gradually raised to the full value of the cargo, in less than 20 years, notwithstanding any tables to the contrary, had not the convention stepped forth in the cause of justice as well as humanity; and it is the universal wish of the kingdom, that this commercial court may persevere with firmness, in procuring a new table of fees, agreeable to the laws of the realm, with penalties annexed to each trespass, by bribes, connivance, or collusion.

As the board of commissioners, instead of suppressing this obstruction to inland commerce, seem to have taken an active part in favour of the persons whom they have appointed to these offices, it is not to be wondered, if suspicions unfavourable to that board should be entertained by the public, though possibly, there may be no just grounds for the same. Had the custom-house-officers observed any degree of moderation in their demands upon inland and coasting trade, they might have exacted their contributions with facility, and lived comfortably, with the good-will of their neighbours; but they knew not when to set bounds to their extortions; they lost sight of equity, and consequently became hardened against shame; the result of all which is this; that by grasping after too much, they will probably lose the greatest part of those excessive encroachments which they have too long enjoyed.

At

At the ſame time, it is neceſſary to obſerve that, in Scotland, the ſalaries appointed for this claſs of men are inadequate to their [illegible], to the duties of their office, and inſufficient for the ſupport of their families, even with the greateſt economy. Many of them, eſpecially the collectors, are perſons of genteel families, liberal education, and rank with gentlemen; yet, ſtrange as it may ſeem, the general ſalaries allowed the collectors is only from 30 to 60l. per annum; and to the comptrollers from 20 to 40l.

Beſides the pernicious effects of this ill-judged economy, as before ſtated, the neceſſities of the revenue-officers [illegible], in many of the inferior ports, render them dependent for a livelihood on the very perſons, whoſe illicit practices they are officially bound to watch. Under ſuch circumſtances, it can be no matter of ſurpriſe, if bribery, colluſion and fraud ſhould frequently happen to the great injury of the revenue and the fair trader. Nor ſhould cuſtom-houſe officers be conſidered as ſingularly culpable for ſuch conduct. Place any other claſs of men in the ſame ſtations, under ſimilar circumſtances, and they will tread in the ſteps of their predeceſſors, with little or no variation: mankind of every ſtation of life being nearly alike, and governed by one ruling principle, *ſelf*, to which all other conſiderations are ſubſervient.

Reſpecting the ſpecific fees paid by perſons engaged in the weſtern herring fiſheries, the reader is referred to page 124 of this work; and underneath are the particulars of charges at Inverneſs on ſhipping a ſmall cargo of ſalmon, at the little port of Findhorn, on the Murray firth, copied from the third report of the committee of the houſe of commons on the fiſheries. Page 311, viz.

	£.	s.	d.
Report, &c. outwards, ——— ——	1	6	0
Surveyor, and indorſing cocket, ——— ——	0	5	0
Land-ſurveyors and land-waiters fees, at 1d. each per barrel, ——— ——— ——	2	10	0
Their riding charge from Inverneſs to Findhorn, the place of ſhipping cargo, ——— ——	3	3	0
Entertainment when there——An article we dare not queſtion, without incurring their diſpleaſure, and of courſe trouble, —— —— ——	3	3	9
Tide-waiter at Findhorn, ——— ——	0	5	0
Collector's, comptroller's fees for the debenture at 1½d. per barrel, with 5s. to the clerk, ——	8	8	6
	20	14	3

Copy of expence on ſhipping one ton of ling fiſh and two barrels of ſalmon for Cadiz, March, 1784

Fees at loading coaſtways from Stornaway, ——	0	5	0
Entry, cocket, land-waiter, and ſurveyor, ——	0	10	6
Collector and comptroller on being paid the debenture,	0	2	6
Land-waiter, ——— —— ——	0	2	6
	1	4	6

Charges

Charges on 24 barrels of herrings, value 27l. 12s. ſhipped at the weſt end of the Glaſgow canal, for Borrowſtounneſs at the eaſt end, viz.

Bond 9s. ſurveyors 2s. 6d.	0	11	6
Cuſtom-houſe fees at Borrowſtounneſs,	0	4	0
Cancelling the bond,	0	0	6
	0	16	0

Remarks on ſundry Paſſages in Dr. Anderſon's Report to the Lords of the Treaſury, and his ſubſequent Evidence and Diſſertations before the Committee on the Britiſh Fiſheries, May 1785.

Having ſince Nov. 1784, applied with more than ordinary aſſiduity to the various ſubjects contained in this bulky volume, I perceived ſome relaxation to be indiſpenſibly neceſſary, previous to which however, a moſt diſagreeable, though not different buſineſs was to be diſcuſſed.—A ſtatement of Dr. Anderſon's poſitions, relative to the fiſheries, propoſed towns, canals, and other matters which more immediately concern the northern part of the iſland; with remarks thereon, by which the public will be better enabled to form concluſions on ſubjects of very conſiderable importance to the ſtrength and proſperity of theſe kingdoms.

The doctor embarked on a voyage to the Hebrides Aug. 22, 1784, and ſays, "The lateneſs of the ſeaſon prevented him from accom-"pliſhing one half of the neceſſary circuit." The doctor might have added to the lateneſs of the ſeaſon his own neglect. He embarked at Ilay, and made for the long Iſland, the main portion of which is called Lewis, accommodated with the excellent port of Stronaway, and the only town amongſt the Hebrides. Lewis is equal in extent to Cheſhire, or Derbyſhire, contains 15,000 people, and its ſhores are one continued fiſhery; yet, though time, at that late ſeaſon was precious, the doctor ſpent the greateſt part of it at the Long Iſland only; at Stronaway in particular, he ſtaid 6 or 7 days, without waiting upon the proprietor of the greateſt part of the iſland, a member of the houſe of commons, and diſtinguiſhed for his exertions, in whatever relates to the improvement of the town and country, as well as the fiſheries. This gentleman condeſcended to invite the doctor to his ſeat, but receiving no anſwer, he wrote a ſecond time, to which the doctor paid not the leaſt regard. He ſerved Mr. Mackenzie's ſteward with the ſame neglect *, neither did he attempt to examine the iſland, or any

* Very different was the conduct of prince William Henry towards this gentleman, and the principal inhabitants, to whom he behaved with the greateſt affability and condeſcenſion, expreſſing at the ſame time, a ſtrong deſire for information in every particular worthy of notice. Equally inquiſitive and diligent were Mr. Pennant, Mr. Boſwell, Dr. Johnſon, and other travellers through theſe iſlands, though at their own expence.

part of it, beyond the vicinity of the town. While the doctor [illegible] particularly [illegible] of the waste, as he calls it, of the public money, and of jobbing, his conduct as above stated affords room to suspect a job, in the fullest sense of the word.

Respecting the main land of Scotland on the opposite coast, the great islands of Sky, Mull, and Jura, his conduct was equally superficial; and the same neglect of the principal proprietors of these shores hath been complained of, which contributes to strengthen the unfavourable suspicion of a job.

Having thus neglected the means of information which his situation afforded, both from conversation and ocular observation, we must consider his report as containing little more than gleanings from the late worthy but credulous Dr. Campbell, who copied from Martin, Buchanan, and other writers, still more credulous. But as the doctor's writings have a manifest tendency to puzzle gentlemen in their investigations respecting the measures to be adopted for the improvement of the Highlands, and the extension of the fisheries, it becomes a duty to undeceive the public respecting his very singular positions, or what may be called his *Originals*, wherein others have no share of the merit.

"Among the Hebrides he found many large and fair islands, "containing extensive fields of land, naturally endued with an "uncommon degree of fertility."—And adds, "That the cli-"mate in these islands is more favourable for bringing corn to "maturity, and that the harvest is for the most part earlier than "on the parallel coast of Scotland."—These are new discoveries, unknown to the above-mentioned gentlemen, who examined them with uncommon minuteness, and to whose descriptions the reader who wishes to ascertain the truth, is referred.—See also page 15[illegible] of this work. Were further evidences necessary, we might observe that the distance between the main body of the islands and the continent is far too short, to allow any difference in the climate.

The distance is thus:

Between Islay and the continent	—	—	15 miles
——— Jura and ditto	———	—	4½ ———
——— Mull and ditto	———	—	1 ———
——— Sky and ditto	———	—	½ ———

Two thirds of the lesser islands of the Hebrides lie contiguous to these, and many of them within a mile of the continent. In fact, these islands, as well as the continent, are so subject to autumnal floods, that humanity alone prevents some of the proprietors from turning their estates entirely into pasture lands.

"Except in the summer season," says Mr. Pennant in his description of the Hebrides, "there is scarcely a week of fair wea-"ther: the summers themselves are generally wet, and seldom "warm. What is properly called the rainy season commences "in "in August: the rains begin with moderate winds; which grow "stronger and stronger till the autumnal equinox, when they "rage with incredible fury. The husbandman then sighs over "the ruins of his vernal labours: sees his crops feel the injury "of the climate: some laid prostrate; the more ripe corn shed by "the violence of the elements. The poor foresee famine, and conse- "quently disease.—Poverty prevents him from making experiments "in rural œconomy: the ill success of a few, made by the more "opulent, determines him to follow the old tract, as attended with "more certainty, unwilling, like the dog in the fable, to grasp at "the shadow and lose the substance. The produce of the crops "very rarely are in any degree proportioned to the wants of the "inhabitants: golden seasons have happened, when they have "had superfluity, but the years of famine are as two to one— "The proper product of all the Hebrides are men and cattle."

"Their weather," says Dr. Johnson, "is not pleasing: half "the year is deluged with rain. From the autumnal to the vernal "equinox, a dry day is hardly known, except when the showers "are suspended by a tempest. Under such skies can be expected "no great exuberance of vegetation. Their winter overtakes "their summer, and their harvest lies upon the ground drenched "with rain. They gather a little hay, but the grass is mown "late; and is so often almost dry, and again very wet, before it "is housed, that it becomes a collection of withered stalks, "without taste or fragrance; it must be eaten by cattle that have "nothing else, but by most English farmers would be thrown "away. The barns of Sky I never saw. That which Macleod "of Raasay had erected near his house was so contrived, because "the harvest is seldom brought home dry, as by perpetual per- "flation to prevent the mow from heating.—In the penury of "these malignant regions nothing is left that can be converted to "food."

"Unless it be the island of Arran," says our romancer, "which "is very mountainous, *all the other islands are in general low "grounds*, for the most part pretty level and capable of cultiva- "tion." No other answer need be given to an assertion so noto- riously false, than the doctor's own words in another part of the report.—"The western parts of the Highlands of Scotland are "for the most part extremely steep, rugged, and mountainous, "*and the same may be said of many of the islands*, forming healthy "pasture for sheep."—"The islands," continues he, "which "are at present possessed of a breed of sheep carrying *finer wool "than any in Europe*, and which could be easily there preserved "without debasement, or even improved so as to yield *great quan- "tities of wool, of a quality superior to any that is yet known*, "would in many cases yield a return, if stocked with such sheep, "perhaps tenfold greater than if pastured with cattle."—Happy discovery for Scotland, and which eluded all the minute investiga- tion of a Pennant and Johnson! What will become of Spain and poor old England, when the Hebrides shall pour forth their un- equalled [illegible] fleeces in great quantities among the manufacturing towns of Europe and America?

[illegible] not England be cast down by Scotch.——"The goats of "the Hebrides," says Dr. Johnson, "are like others; nor did I "hear any thing of their sheep to be particularly remarked." Mr. Pennant is totally silent respecting the quantity and quality of wool in the Hebrides, though he was particularly inquisitive on that subject. He only observes that the sheep sell at 5s. each, wool included. Great pains have of late years been taken by the proprietors of those watery deserts, and, though they have improved the breed, and also the wool, they acknowledge the [illegible] of the climate for ever bringing the wool to an equality with the second kinds in England. Many English sheep have been carried to the West Highlands at a great expence, and put upon the best pastures in the country, but the breed degenerates as well as the wool.

Respecting the general appearance of the Hebrides, which Dr. Anderson says, "are in general low grounds; for the most part "pretty level, and capable of cultivation," hear Dr. Johnson's observations on that head, who travelled amongst them on horseback, and saw more of the interior part than Dr. Anderson. "In "the islands there are no roads, nor any marks by which a stran-"ger may find his way. The horseman has always at his side a "native of the place, who, by pursuing game, or tending cattle, "or being often employed in messages, or conduct, has learned "where the ridge of the hill has breadth sufficient to allow a horse "and his rider a passage, and where the moss or bog is hard "enough to bear them. The bogs are avoided as toilsome at "least, if not unsafe, and therefore the journey is made generally "from precipice to precipice; from which if the eye ventures to "look down, it sees below a gloomy cavity, whence the rush of "water is sometimes heard. The Highlander walks carefully "before, and the horse, accustomed to the ground, follows him "with little deviation. Sometimes the hill is too steep for the "horseman to keep his seat, and sometimes the moss is too tre-"mulous to bear the double weight of horse and man. The "rider then dismounts, and all shift as they can."

Mr. Pennant having mounted one of the highest elevations in the Hebrides, thus describes the great island on which he stood, as well as others within his view. "The prospect to the west was "that of desolation itself; a savage series of rude mountains, "discoloured, black and red, as if by the rage of fire.

"The view to the north-east and south-west is not less amazing: "a sea sprinkled over with various isles, and the long extent of "coast [illegible] into all the forms of Alpine wildness."

Dr. Anderson is more happy in his statement of the mineral produce of the Hebrides, these being fully described by Martin and Campbell; but why tell the public that "the lead mines of "Islay have never been thoroughly worked, but which will be "opened next summer?" Mr. Pennant speaks of them thus: "Vast "the mines carried on under the direction of Mr. Freebairn, since "the year 1763, (viz. 11 years) the ore is of lead, much "mixed with copper, which occasions expence and trouble in the "separation: the veins rise to the surface, have been worked at "intervals for ages, and probably in the time of the Norwegians, "a nation of miners." So very opposite, in every particular, are these writers; the one fabulous, the other authentic and instructive. These mines have been thoroughly wrought, and the last company, of whom Mr. Freebairn was the acting partner, were thereby thoroughly ruined.

Our reporter, speaking of the behaviour of the Highland lairds towards the people of the Highlands, whom he states at near 500,000, says that "Contumely is added to oppression, and the "poor people are cruelly insulted and abused, instead of being "tenderly sympathized with, and kindly supported and che- "rished." The doctor, in the subsequent examination before the committee on the fisheries, being asked by one of the northern members, "Whether he imagined that the proprietors in the "islands, and western coasts of Scotland, behold, with indifference, "the poverty of the lower orders of people on their estates? or, "whether they do not rather make exertions to free them from "that distressful poverty which he described in his report?" He answered, "That he imagined that the proprietors of the western "coasts of Scotland in general, shew a spirit of lenity to their "tenants, and the lower order of people under them, equal, at "least, to that discovered by the gentlemen of any other part of "Britain that he is acquainted with." This recantation appears to have been only *pro tempore*; a most virulent invective against the gentlemen of the Highlands, was afterwards delivered in by the doctor to be printed with the report, which was, however, prudently suppressed.

Having given a specimen of the doctor's descriptive powers, we shall now consider him as an improver, a politician, and financier. We had, in a former publication, urged the expediency of public aid, and that with a liberal hand, for the improvement of the Highlands, by means of fisheries, inland communications, and small towns, situated at convenient distances, upon a line of coast extending 150 miles in length.

These propositions met with that kind of approbation which frequently stimulates envy, bordering on resentment, in persons of illiberal dispositions. They were well received in both kingdoms, and the plan of towns hath been partly adopted by the Irish legislature, on the western and more barren coasts of that kingdom: a country resembling the Highlands of Scotland in its rugged appearance, and where the fisheries are in greatest plenty*. After conversing with all degrees of people in the Highlands, as well as

* For this purpose 20,000l. was voted last sessions, and the business is actually begun upon the coast of Donegal.

the

the Low Countries, on those subjects, I was strongly encouraged to express and defend the propositions, as the only practicable measures that can be adopted with mutual benefit to the public and individuals. In the mean time, Dr. Anderson, who never saw the West Highlands before August 1784, adopts the popular subjects above-mentioned, and borrows the thoughts, but from the ambition of being considered original, he artfully conceals his obligations by striking out new modes, which, though mostly impracticable, in many instances unnecessary, and usually inefficacious, he transmitted and recommended to the lords of the Treasury, as the best system of policy that can be offered respecting the country. But it is conjectured that the doctor was only a tool in this business, and it would seem, by his descriptions, his visionary, impracticable schemes, and thorough ignorance of these subjects, that he is unqualified for any department of a serious nature.

The doctor speaking of the canal between Inverness and Fort William *, says, in a note, "he should be extremely cautious "about advising any undertaking of great public expence, where "it did not appear to be absolutely necessary at the very moment. "And though he thinks the canal now in question, would be a "work of the greatest national utility that could be proposed, yet "as the want of it would be more felt some time hence, *should* "*these regions be more improved*, than at present, he is of opinion "that *then* would be the proper time to carry it into effect." Government are much obliged to the doctor for his friendly advice upon every occasion respecting the public money, and for suggesting the impropriety of granting that northern country any assistance till the barren rocks thereof shall be improved, and "*full* "of people, manufactures and commerce."

The great objects proposed by this canal, seem totally to have escaped the doctor's notice; they do not relate to the improvement of the incorrigible wilds, lying immediately in the tract of the canal, but to the general benefit of the whole North of Scotland, by opening a communication between the two seas, whereby the half-starved inhabitants of Lochaber and the western shores, would be readily supplied with grain, and at a small expence of carriage, from the fertile coast of the Murray firth, on the east side; while the people of that coast, and Aberdeenshire, who are expert fishermen, would be conveyed with safety and expedition to the great herring and white fisheries of the west. These are the objects of mutual benefit, on which men of trade and knowledge ground their arguments in favour of this northern navigation; besides the utility to the general commerce of these kingdoms, by thus avoiding the tedious and hazardous navigation on either side of the Orkneys. *See page* 422.

"From this grand canal," says the Doctor, "would branch off "several others of lesser note, which would carry the navigation "to many places in the most internal parts of the country. The

* A map of Scotland will assist the reader on these subjects.

 "most

“ moſt conſiderable of theſe branches is that which goes from Fort “ William, through Loch Shiel, and enters the weſtern ſea at “ Loch Moidart. This communication is ſo nearly open at pre- “ ſent, and would be immediately attended with ſuch benefit to “ the country, and could be executed at an expence ſo very ſmall, “ that it ſeems to be one of thoſe leſſer undertakings which is per- “ fectly adapted to the preſent ſtate of the country, and therefore “ might be accompliſhed with *profit to the undertakers.*”—“ This “ canal” ſays the doctor in his notes, “ would be of very great “ benefit to that country in a double reſpect. In the firſt place, “ were it finiſhed, it would open a direct communication between all “ the countries round Loch Yell (the doctor means Loch Eil) and “ Lochaber, and the ſea at Loch Moidart, near which are found “ abundant beds of ſhelly ſand, which could thus be carried in boats “ to many *extenſive fields in Lochaber*, which by that means could be “ highly improved, and rendered of *great value* to the proprietors, “ at a ſmall expence, but which never can be improved at a mode- “ rate expence, in any other way, that has yet been diſcovered. On “ the other hand, the woods that come down from Loch Lochi, “ which are ſo much wanted in the Weſtern Iſlands, but which “ cannot be carried thither at preſent, ſave by *a long* navigation “ round Ardnamurchan, through the ſound of Mull, could be “ carried down by the return of theſe boats, at a ſmall expence, “ to the very near neighbourhood of Skye, and other iſlands in “ that part of the country. This would tend much to facilitate “ the improvement of theſe parts.”

It muſt be acknowledged that the doctor hath great merit in dreſſing out fictions with ſuch ſeeming plauſibility, that perſons unacquainted with his manner, and the ſubjects on which he exerciſes his talents, muſt be diffident to an extreme degree, who do not give implicit belief to his reaſoning.

But theſe tales, however they may miſlead the Engliſh readers, ſerve only to excite laughter in a country where, as may be ſuppoſed, the inhabitants are better informed. Inſtead of extenſive fields in Lochaber, that country is univerſally allowed to be one of the moſt barren unimproveable diſtricts in the Highlands. “ Fort William, ſays Mr. Pennant, “ is ſurrounded by vaſt moun- “ tains, which occaſion almoſt perpetual rain.—The great pro- “ duce of Lochaber is cattle: that diſtrict ſends out annually 3000 “ head; but if a portion of Inverneſs is included, of which this “ properly is part, the number is 10,000. There are alſo a few “ horſes bred here, and a few ſheep; but of late ſeveral have “ been imported. *Scarce any arable land*, for the exceſſive wet “ which reigns here, almoſt totally prevents the growth of corn, “ and *what little there is fit for tillage*, lets at 10s. an acre. The “ inhabitants of this diſtrict are therefore obliged, for their ſup- “ port, to import 6000 boles of oatmeal annually, which coſt “ about 4000l.; the rents are about 3000l. per annum; the re- “ turn for their cattle is about 7000l. the horſes may produce “ ſome trifle; ſo that the tenants muſt content themſelves with a

“ very

"very scanty subsistence, without the prospect of saving the least against misfortune or accidents."

Dr. Johnson, in his remarks upon these wilds, says, "what is not heath is nakedness, a little diversified by now and then a stream rushing down the steep. An eye accustomed to flowery pastures and waving harvests, is astonished and repelled by this wide extent of hopeless sterility. The appearance is that of matter incapable of form or usefulness, dismissed by Nature from her care, and disinherited of her favours, left in its original elemental state, or quickened only with one sullen power of useless vegetation."

On doctor Anderson's second position respecting the carriage of wood from Loch Lochi to Skye, it may be remarked that this island abounds in turf, that the opposite coast of the main land abounds in natural woods, as the banks of Loch Urn, Knoydart, the peninsula of Ardnamurchan, &c. consequently, the idea of carrying firewood from a distant inland country, by means of a canal burdened with tonnage dues, is ridiculous. Besides, the woods of Loch Lochi being preserved for the bark, till they arrive at the age of 20 or 25 years, the supply from thence would be only 4 or 5 times in a century.

Thus the many extensive fields of Lochaber seem to exist only in the doctor's brain, and the supplies of wood from Loch Lochi vanish like a dream. Here therefore an expensive work is proposed without an object, but which, if we may rely on the doctor's assertion, may be accomplished *with profit to the undertakers*. Of what use is the opening a canal from one ridge of rock and stones to another? To whom would the benefit accrue? From what source would the undertakers be repaid with profits?

The doctor also informs us, that this communication could be opened from Fort William, through Loch Shiel and Loch Moidart, to the West Sea, at a small expence. The truth is, that nature hath placed an insuperable barrier against a communication by this channel, at any expence. The water called Loch Shiel, which falls into the ocean through Loch Moidart, and which the doctor supposes to be a navigable lake, is in one place a river only, and cannot be made navigable, on account of rocks and declivities, one of which is called the Salmon Leap.

In order to assist the doctor in these points, we shall reverse, or as the printers term it, transpose his propositions. First, complete the main line of the grand canal from Lochaber or Fort William to the East Sea at Inverness: and secondly, open such collateral branches as shall appear practicable and necessary, but neither the one nor the other can ever be effected by private undertakers.

The only public benefit that can arise from a cut through the peninsula of Ardnamurchan, relates to the fisheries, of which the doctor says not a word. When the communication shall be opened from Inverness to Fort William, a canal at this place would facilitate the paſſage of the fiſhing veſſels to and from Loch Broom or King George's channel, being ſome miles ſhorter than the natural paſſage by the Linnhe Loch. The late Sir Alexander Murray, proprietor of the peninſula of Ardnamurchan, perceiving the impoſſibility of forming an opening through Loch Shiel and Loch Moidart, as propoſed by Dr. Anderſon, was at the expence of an engraved drawing or plan of another line of communication. This drawing, together with his papers on that and other ſubjects, for the improvement of the country, is in the hands of Sir James Riddel, his ſucceſſor, by whom I was favoured with the peruſal of them. The plan is practicable, but it cannot be of public utility until the main cut ſhall be finiſhed.

We now come to the ſouthern navigation, whereon the doctor uſes many words to little purpoſe. "The Loch Crinan navigation he conceives to be one of thoſe *leſſer undertakings* that are "perfectly adapted to the preſent ſtate of the country, which "might be *now undertaken with a certainty of indemnification to* "*the undertakers*."

Not ſatisfied with one canal between Lochfine and the Weſt Sea, as propoſed in the former editions of this work, and now further elucidated, (*ſee page* 410) the doctor propoſes *another* at the Tarbat, diſtant only 12 or 14 miles from the former.— "Both theſe canals, he has no doubt, were proper acts of parliament obtained for that purpoſe, to give a reaſonable ſecurity to "thoſe concerned, might be executed by private hands, with "very little, if any, public aid."

Speaking in another place of the Crinan canal, we have the following remarks; which, if they do not edify the people of that country, will, at leaſt, afford ample matter of comment. "It muſt be adverted to," ſays he, "that this canal will ſerve to "join two ſeas of conſiderable extent; (he means Lochfine from "1 to 6 miles, and the Atlantic 3000 miles wide) and there are "no maſſes of *bulky or weighty commodities* immediately in that "neighbourhood, that would require to be carried through it to "market; of courſe, all the commodities that would paſs through "it, would be brought from a diſtance in ſhips. In the next "place, as the goods to be carried through that canal, would be "*always* intended for a *more diſtant market together*, &c."

The traffic and navigation of this canal being fully ſtated in the chapter on that head, beginning with page 410 before mentioned, we ſhall in this place only obſerve, that the immediate traffic of the canal and its neighbourhood, will chiefly conſiſt in empty caſks outward and homeward; pickled and dried fiſh, ſkins, oil, timber, coals, manure, limeſtone, ſlate, &c. ſo that, to underſtand the doctor, we muſt again reverſe his language, as thus; there are no goods immediately in that neighbourhood that would require to be carried through the canal, but ſuch as are bulky or weighty.

"With regard," ſays he, "to the ſecond queſtion, whether "ſhould

"should this canal be executed at the public expence, or by "private individuals? I would, in the first place, observe, that "I should consider it as an unreasonable demand, to ask the pub-"lic funds for forwarding any work tending to promote the trade "and prosperity of a particular district, without stipulating a "return for that aid, unless where the trade of that particular "district could not afford to pay for it, without being loaded "beyond what it could possibly bear. But the present case does "not come within that description, as there cannot be a doubt "but that a very *moderate* tonnage on vessels passing this way, "would do *much more* than afford a reasonable interest for the "money that would be required for executing this canal——From "these considerations I should wish to see this work undertaken "by individuals; not from any public-spirited view, or under the "semblance of charitable contributions, *but* merely as a *gainful* "*project*, as a profitable way of employing their money."

The reader, if a native of the West of Scotland, and acquainted with the nature of the proposed navigation, will conclude upon reading this nonsense, that our reporter is completely qualified for the strait waistcoat. In answer to these strange reveries, we shall give the estimates of the expence of both canals proposed by the doctor, as stated by Mr. Watt, the engineer, by whom the grounds were surveyed, viz.

To making a thorough cut at Tarbet of 12 feet water	73,849
To ditto at Crinan of 10 feet water 48,405 l; but as 12 feet will be absolutely necessary, I have stated the expence in page 419, at 60,000 l. though it is probable that 10,000 l. more will be called for, in winding up the account.	60,000
	£133,849

Supposing that these canals had a probability in their favour of producing 7½ per cent. on the capital, the annual tonnage to be raised will be thus:

Interest at 7½ per cent. on 133,849 l. sunk —	10,038
Annual expences of both canals in repairs, cleansing, collecting the tonnage, &c. — —	1,000
	£11038

A pretty large sum to be raised annually from a navigation purely local, on which the whole traffic will be chiefly confined to fish, timber, &c. between the Clyde and the West Highlands; the utmost tonnage will not exceed 500 l. annually without injuring the fisheries, or forcing the vessels to go round by the mull of Cantire; which sum will be little more than sufficient to keep one canal in good order. However flattering the doctor's language may appear upon a superficial view, to government, or to gentlemen who wish to embark in these navigations, either from public spirit, or the view of *a gainful project*, the whole representation, as stated by the doctor, is a gross affront on the understandings of mankind, to whose animadversions we shall submit the subject.

"Many other canals," says the doctor, "equally easy to be "executed, and extremely beneficial if made, might here be "pointed out—but these would come to be discovered, and carried "into effect, as the rising commerce of the country called for "them. To launch out into a multiplicity of undertakings of "that sort at present, would only exhaust that stock which might "more profitably be otherwise employed. When wealth is gra-"dually acquiring, these communications will come to be suc-"cessively opened, as the want of them comes to be felt. More, "therefore, needs not now be said on that head." Very true, doctor, and if you had said nothing on *that head*, you would not have exposed your ignorance in the geography of your country. Except the works just mentioned, and the removal of some fords in the Tweed between Berwic and Kelso, and also in the Forth, above Sterling, or carrying canals near the banks of these rivers, works of trifling expence, nature admits of no artificial openings whatever in that kingdom. The doctor may impose upon the treasury, to whom this false report is addressed, but he cannot impose on those who know more of the country than himself.

The doctor's plan of towns in the Highlands comes next under consideration, a subject on which he seems to have given full scope to the flights of his imagination. I had proposed the coast of the main land between Loch Crinan and Cape Wrath, as the most eligible station whereon to lay the foundation of 8 towns or ports, and that the same should be at the public expence; for this very obvious reason, that, unless the business shall be taken up by government, the Highlands must remain in their present helpless state. But the doctor, who pretends to befriend that country, instead of countenancing a proposal to which the public expressed, as with one voice, a hearty concurrence, labours, we hope ineffectually, to dissuade government from a measure indispensibly necessary for the general benefit of the island; and which would soon repay the state, with interest, as stated in the chapter on that head, page 433, and other parts of the volume, to which the reader is referred. "To attempt," says he, "to give houses, as "*some will propose*, he conceives would give rise to jobbs and frauds of various sorts, which would exhaust much treasure, and benefit the poor people very little. By the sentence, *as some would propose*, the doctor affects to be ignorant of the plan communicated in the first edition of this volume, while, at the same time, his insidious condemnation of the measure, plainly indicates his having seen the book, or the newspaper extracts on that head. Instead, therefore, of affecting to alledge, as some *will propose*, it would have been more candid to have said at once, as some *have proposed*.

He hath made ample amends, however, for this little finesse, at [illegible] of the report, where he [illegible] acknowledges his [illegible] the pamphlet. While passing a great many encomiums on himself, and the superiority of his proposals to all others, he observes to their lordships, in the ardour of his zeal for the [illegible] of the national welfare; "nor are they calculated, [illegible] brilliant proposals, that announce expensive and glaring undertakings, to please the taste of the populace, who judge of the importance of any object merely by its show, and the parade with which it is introduced to their notice." The doctor having thus taken off the mask, we shall take a short review of those measures which he hath recommended as the best of all political systems; and may not only be executed at little or no expence to government, but also prove "the only true and unequivocable mode of augmenting the national revenue with which the reporter is acquainted."—"The prosperity of the country, were the measures proposed adopted, the reporter conceives would be certain and unavoidable."

The doctor's plan is in substance this:

A number of towns, consisting of 1000 houses each, are to rise, as it were, by magic, and to increase rapidly, till they become general emporiums of trade, and the resort of shipping from all parts of these kingdoms. "The expenditure on the part of government, is 1,750l. for each 1000 houses or families, for which the public are to receive in return a clear revenue of 10,000l. a year." "This surely," says the doctor, "will be allowed to be a most advantageous bargain. It is impossible here to avoid drawing a short comparison between the effects of money laid out thus, and for other purposes on which the national treasure is usually expended. We have all known 20 guineas given to raise a single recruit to the army, who, instead of yielding any revenue, only helps to exhaust it—whereas, an equal sum, thus applied, would purchase a perpetual annuity (I should say a perpetual increasing annuity) of 110l. sterling. It is thus, and thus only, I mean by putting the people into such a situation as gives room for effective industry, *that even the national revenue can be effectually advanced*. All other systems of finance are but *the [illegible] workings of little minds*, which occasion much trouble, and end in vexation and disappointment."

Ye statesmen, senators, and other little minds, be of good cheer, and let these kingdoms rejoice at the happy discovery. To the Highlands of Scotland we are to look not only for brave soldiers and intrepid hardy seamen, which is universally admitted, but for new, productive, and boundless sources of revenue accumulating *ad infinitum*.

"By the mode proposed above," says he, "many large villages (of 1000 houses each) might be *quickly founded*, which would gradually attain the size of towns. But something more is

wanted

"wanted to give a vivacious ſtimulus at the beginning, to put the "whole machine in motion. A vigorous puſh ſhould be made to "eſtabliſh at the beginning, at leaſt, one large town, which "ſhould ſerve as a centre of trade, as a general market for all "the adjacent places; and which ſhould be endued with higher "privileges than thoſe already mentioned, and be exalted to a "degree of pre-eminence becoming the dignified part ſhe ſhould "have to act among the ſurrounding leſſer communities."

The doctor hath given a very minute plan of a municipal town or city; it is to be divided into ſtreets, wards, and diſtricts, properly adapted for giving effect to the ſeveral neceſſary regulations of police, with other edifying particulars which need not in this place be repeated. The doctor, in a long diſſertation in favour of large cities, wherein he ſtates the ſuperior preference in the preſent caſe, to ſmall towns or villages, argues thus in his notes.—"In ſuch a ſituation too alone, the ſallies of wit, and productions "of genius find encouragement; for it is there alone that mental "efforts can be brought to market. There alſo it is that printers "and news-writers, pamphleteers, reviewers, magazine makers,* "with all their numerous dependents, find employment; none "of which could ever have been called into exiſtence, but by the "influence of large towns."

"I judged it neceſſary," ſays he, "to explain on this occaſion, "ſome of thoſe circumſtances which give to large towns ſuch a "decided ſuperiority over ſmall places in regard to commerce, "arts, manufactures, and agriculture, to ſerve as an apology for "that predilection I have expreſſed for them in the *Report*. "Many ſpeculative men, who have not attentively conſidered this "ſubject, think they perceive numberleſs objections to large cities, "and expreſs a predilection in favour of villages and hamlets."

The doctor hath at leaſt ſpoke truth for once. Theſe viſionary projects are the ſubjects of ridicule and contempt wherever they are mentioned. We were informed in the Highlands, that the doctor talked largely of his propoſed cities, comparing them in magnitude to Edinburgh and Glaſgow.

In a ſubſequent note, he propoſes 5 cities to be immediately raiſed, and hath alſo ſpecified the moſt eligible ſituations agreeable to his ideas, viz, Dunvegan, in the Iſle of Skye; Stronaway, in Lewis; Loch Boiſdale, in South Uiſt; Tobermory, in Mull; and Bowmore in Iſlay. I had propoſed the coaſt of the main land, for the ſeat of 8 market towns and ports; becauſe, lying in the centre between an extenſive back country upon the eaſt, and the Hebrides directly in front on the weſt, the benefits of this line of ports, would pervade the whole internal diſtricts of the conti-

* Some years ago the doctor attempted to eſtabliſh a weekly magazine in London; but, ſuch was the want of taſte and diſcernment in the metropolis, that the ſale did not defray the expence, and the deſign was relinquiſhed. The plan may, however, be reſumed with better ſucceſs amongſt the Hebridean cities.

nent,

towns, at the distance of 50 or 60 miles; and in the north Highlands from sea to sea, as soon as carriage roads shall be formed. While, at the same time, similar effects would be felt among the Hebride islands lying in front. If these towns would diffuse such blessings amongst the interior districts, and the islands, we may easily conceive the still greater benefits to the cultivated line and coast on which they shall be immediately placed. But Dr. Anderson, with his usual propensity to counteract every proposal, however well adapted to nature and circumstances, places his Utopian cities, not upon the coast of the main land, but on the islands; consequently, the greater territory would depend on the lesser, and the back country be totally deprived of any benefit whatever from such erections; particularly the city of Boisdale upon South-Uist, a small island lying in the main Atlantic, 50 miles distant from the continent. But though this city would be of little service to the kingdom of Scotland, the inhabitants might carry on a great trade with the Esquimaux Indians on the coast of Labradore, and other Americans inhabiting the parallel latitude of that region. These Esquimaux would, no doubt, embark every summer on board their canoes, with cargoes of skins for the city of Boisdale, taking back whisky, the only produce of the island, in exchange; a circumstance wholly omitted by the doctor in his dissertation upon cities in the Highlands.

Unfortunately for these schemes, a most unpropitious circumstance remains to be mentioned, viz. That though the greatest exertions were made by the late earl of Seaforth, to raise a respectable town at the fine harbour of Stronaway, universally acknowledged to be well situated for fisheries, and on which account several Dutch families resided there in the last century; yet, with all those advantages, the present proprietor, who inherits the public spirit of his predecessor, is obliged to advertise in the English and Scottish news-papers, for a tanner to settle there, which is no great proof of the progress of Stronaway, since the year 1606, when it was made a royal borough. And it may be further observed, that to induce persons to build and settle in this place, the quit rent for 36 feet in front and 120 feet deep, is only [illegible] annually. I have also to observe, that Inverary, the capital of an extensive county, situated on an arm of the sea, frequently the seat of herring fisheries, and the residence of one of the most persevering liberal patriots in these kingdoms, hath not had an increase of ten houses, within the same number of years. Another proprietor attempted to raise a small village on the north-west coast, and gave it every support consistent with his abilities, but without effect. It is therefore the height of wantonness, folly, and presumption, to put such fallacious schemes into the hands of administration.

The system which the doctor labours to subvert, is briefly this; Since neither the proprietors of lands, the traders or fishers can accomplish the erecting a single town, however necessary, on that extensive

extensive coast, and as no valuable purpose can be effected without towns or marts, a plan was sketched out upon principles adapted to the circumstances of the country, and the situation of its inhabitants, suggesting the expediency of public aid in the first instance, as the only radical measure by which these important fisheries might be placed upon a permanent footing, and the whole region of the Highlands put into a train of improvement for their own as well as the public benefit. With this view it was proposed to erect 8 port towns in the most eligible situations of that coast, at the undermentioned places, all of them the occasional resort of the herrings, viz.

1. Upon the banks of the proposed opening into that coast, at Loch Crinan.

2. At Oban, a fine bay facing the south end of the island of Mull, lying also at the south entrance of the Linnhe Loch, a branch of the sea which penetrates inland as far as Fort William in Lochaber.

4. At Loch Sunart, a lake 12 miles in length, whose banks abound in extensive roads, and valuable lead mines; but still more important from its situation opposite Tobirmoire bay, near the north end of Mull.

4. At Bernera, within a mile of the great isle of Skie; altered in the present edition upon the representation of lord Macdonald and other competent judges, to Loch Urn, five miles to the southward; a well-sheltered arm of the sea, frequently crowded with herrings, and its banks adorned with extensive woods.

5. At Gareloch, a capacious and secure bay, facing the south end of the great fishing bank, which stretches as far as Cape Wrath; and frequently the resort of herrings.

6. At Loch Ewe, a large well sheltered bay of easy access, which penetrates 6 miles into the country, where it receives, through a narrow channel, the waters of Loch Maree, a fresh-water lake, 12 miles in length.

7. At Loch Broom, a large and safe arm of the sea, 12 miles in length, the greatest resort of herrings on that coast, and the general station of the busses from the south.

8. Towards Cape Wrath, principally for the benefit of a harbour for the safety of the British and Irish shipping, in their passage to and from the Baltic. In the new edition, Loch Laxford is specified as the best station on that very remote coast, being a capacious fine bay, well sheltered, and the ground good.

"The plan of these towns was,

1. A key or breast,

2. A range of warehouses for the various purposes of the fishing business, and serving also as stores or granaries.

3. Sheds for gutting, salting, curing, &c.

4. A small market place.

5. A corn mill.

6. A small church, and house for the minister.

2 7. A house

7. A house for a school.

8. A public inn.

9. Premiums or bounty lands to be given gratis on certain conditions to coopers, carpenters, net makers, and persons of other professions connected with the fisheries. To which, in the new edition, I have added,

A house and shop for an apothecary and surgeon.

A house for a superintendent of the fisheries.

A piece of ground for a common.

These are what may be called public works, all of which will be found indispensably necessary at the first outset. There are other objects to which a council appointed to superintend the business must pay particular regard. First, the manner of inducing strangers to build; and, secondly, the means whereby these strangers and their families may be supported through a winter of six months continuance, and often longer.

Though it may be necessary for the encouragement of the first settlers in these inhospitable and barren shores, not only to accommodate them with offices, garden-ground and three small fields rent free, but also with houses ready built and completely finished; those who shall arrive at late periods, having the benefit of society, and of granaries, stores, &c. cannot expect to be indulged to the same extent as the first settlers; the bountiful aid of government will be gradually withdrawn, but not to cease, in each respective village until 200 houses shall be built, which may be considered as the second stage of the business. The place will then assume the appearance of a town and port; men will begin to embark in the various fisheries of the northern seas; while others will find employment in the numerous mechanical branches depending thereon; magistrates will be appointed, and a regular police established.

For the speedy and effectual accomplishment of these desirable events, a portion of ground equal to a quarter of an acre, might be given in perpetuity, to every person, their heirs and executors, who shall erect a house thereon, agreeable to a plan for the regulation of the buildings; provided also, that the expenditure on each house shall not be under 25l. exclusive of offices, walls, and other conveniencies.

The prospect of comfortable lodging, plentiful supplies of fish, roots, vegetables, and principally the possession of a decent warm dwelling, increasing in its value proportioned to the increase of trade, and the number of inhabitants, would induce both strangers and natives to co-operate with government in raising these towns, and to prosecute the fisheries with unwearied perseverance. A town composed of 200 fishers, traders and mechanics, besides resident and occasional labourers, would, upon the plan of fisheries, soon become possessed of decked vessels, wherries and boats; a place of traffic for all the varieties of fish peculiar to these seas; for oil, kelp, salt, coals, timber, bark, grain, meal, cattle, sheep, &c.,

skins, poultry, and the lesser articles of husbandry, the produce of the main land and the contiguous islands; where, to sum up the whole, the inhabitants of the town and country, the fisherman, the coaster, and the merchant, would mutually supply and be supplied, in the productions of sea and land.

The expence to the public in raising and endowing each town, is calculated at 20,000l. or 160,000l. for the whole; and when we take into the account the ground to be purchased, and the buildings to be erected with stone, lime and slate; also a stipend to 8 resident clergymen, salaries to 8 schoolmasters, and the same number of superintendants of the fisheries, every disinterested sensible person, will coincide both in the propriety of the plan, and the moderation of the estimates.

Here is no waste, no unnecessary expence, or room for jobbing. Every expenditure hath a valuable object in view, and forming part of a machine which once set in motion, will act through future ages by its own powers, without further aid, repaying a hundred fold, the expenditures of its infant state.

Now let us contrast this simple, practicable, and popular sketch, of colonizing the Highlands at the expence of 160,000l. with that proposed by Dr. Anderson at little or no expence to government.

He speaks with great confidence of raising many towns or villages, consisting at the first set out, of 1000 houses each; to connect which towns or villages, he proposes five large cities to be built upon the Hebride isles. The proportion of the villages to the five cities cannot, agreeable to the doctor's ideas, be stated under 40 or 50, the expence of which and the cities, supposing the houses to be built of stone, lime and slate, with sash windows and other conveniencies in the modern style, could not be less than 5 millions sterling; now as the doctor almost entirely exempts government from any part of this immense sum, and as the persons who may happen to go thither, will be composed of pennyless, speculative adventurers, with others possessed of some capital, which they will wish to employ not upon building, but in fisheries and trade, it may be supposed, that the doctor among the vast schemes of his fertile brain, hath an eye to an embassy to the moon, there to negociate with the emperor of those regions, for half a million of his highness's subjects, and a sum equal to 5 millions British money, whereby to build and people the 5 cities and 40 villages at Boisdale, and elsewhere in the Highlands of Scotland; and, as a security for the money so advanced, the doctor might mortgage the said 5 cities and 40 villages, till the whole sum should be paid with interest. The doctor in order to facilitate the business of his commission, might display in lively colours and a strict regard to truth, the excellency of the climate, the richness of the soil, and the extent of the fields, naturally endowed with an uncommon degree of fertility, in the many large and fair islands of the Hebrides. He might expatiate from one full moon to another, on the prodigious abundance of minerals and metals, the transcendant excellency of the

the cattle, far superior to any yet discovered, and which has been searched for in vain by the others; but, above all, the immense quantity of eiderdown and wool in these islands, possessing a peculiar silky softness, and elasticity, that is not to be equalled by any other wool yet known. The latter subjects interested and greatly affected by the report of facts thus faithfully stated, and of observations founded on these facts, would draw upon the treasury at sight, and send the doctor joyfully home.

The fisheries come next under consideration, a subject on which the doctor is remarkably copious. Being asked by the committee, whether, till of late years, the best fishing on the north-west of Scotland was not always in November and December? and whether the herrings caught at that time of the year, do not find a preference at market before the summer fish, on account of their size? He said in his answer, that "he did not know that the size of the "fish is in any respect connected with the season of the year in "which they are caught." Very strange indeed, after having spent 6 weeks at the public charge, in order to investigate whatever relates to fish and fisheries! Had the committee put the same question to any cabbin boy from that coast, they would have received an immediate satisfactory answer. It argues an uncommon degree of presumption in a person so unacquainted with the subject, to lay down schemes and systems, as the best and most efficacious measures that can be adopted by the state.

Being asked, whether it is not possible, in the months of November and December, to fish for herrings in the deep sea; and whether a winter fishery must not always be a loch fishery? he said, "If by deep sea, it is understood those seas that lie between "the Long island and the main land, usually called the Minch, "he does not think it is possible to fish in winter with such vessels "as the Dutch fish with; but that he is not at all acquainted with "the other seas, not having been in them."

Here the doctor furnishes another striking proof of his unfitness for discussing the subject of the fisheries. It is an easy matter for any person to draw up, at his desk, a set of visionary schemes, upon subjects of which he may be almost totally ignorant. Such people may carry on their deceptions for a time, till brought to the ordeal, when all their pretentions vanish. The doctor did not know that the size of the fish is in any respect connected with the season of the year in which they are caught—and in the subsequent answer—is forced to acknowledge, that his knowledge of the fishing grounds is confined to one channel only. Respecting the important question asked by the committee, it may be observed, that though the north-west channel be extremely boisterous in November and December, the season of the full-grown herrings on the Scottish as well as the Irish coast, yet there are intervals when the weather is neither boisterous nor calm; being what may be called good fresh weather, with a small swell of the sea, and it is then that the herrings are taken in the greatest quantities. As the season, men, from long experience, are generally good judges of an approaching storm, this fishery might be safely and successfully carried on during these temperate intervals, providing the fishers could be persuaded to build and equip some large vessels, after the Dutch models, with lee-boards and buoy-ropes, for the Shetland fishery in summer, the Hebride open sea fishery in the autumn, and when practicable, in winter. The north channel being surrounded with high lands, frequently indented with capacious bays or lochs, vessels, if taken abruptly in a storm, may soon find shelter under these lofty shores, or in the land-locked bays, to which they may be directed by lighthouses.

The doctor being asked, whether it is his opinion that the fishery in the British seas can ever be brought to such perfection as that it could be carried on with profit to the undertakers, without any bounties or public aid whatever? he answered, "He certainly is of that opinion; he conceives that if any business is "of such a nature, as to require the continual aid of public support, it should be abandoned as hurtful to the community; but "this is very far from being the case with the British fisheries."—If all branches are to be abandoned that require the continual aid of the public, we must abandon the whale and pilchard fisheries, which experience hath proved would be totally lost to these kingdoms, were the bounties withdrawn. The same may be observed of the linen and other valuable branches of manufacture, which would be transferred to foreign countries, were government to withhold the bounty, trifling as it is, upon the exportation of these articles. In this respect the British government copy the example of all wise nations, antient and modern, with whom the encouragement of trade and manufactures, by means of public aid, and that with a liberal hand, hath been considered as the primary maxim of political government. It is by the judicious application of public money that mankind emerge from a state of savage nature, to civilized potent empires, of which the modern states, as France, Russia, Austria, Sweden, Denmark, Holland, and Prussia, furnish striking examples. Thus, according to Dr. Anderson's ideas, the history of mankind exhibits, in this respect, one continued chain of political errors. But of all the blunderers that the world hath seen, the inhabitants of the little sister kingdom are the greatest. By their liberality and perseverance, during these last 50 years, poverty, sloth and wretchedness, have greatly subsided; and should the same parliamentary exertions be continued 50 years longer, that country will rank amongst the second states in Europe, for civilization, trade and opulence.

They have lately extended their bounty on the herring fisheries from 20 to 30 shillings per ton, on all vessels from 20 to 100 tons, though many of such vessels have only to step out of Loch Foyle into Loch Swilly, and there take or buy the herrings, and then run away with them, in bulk, to Derry, to be packed in barrels

for

for the West India market; while the busses are returning back to Loch Swilly, to fetch new cargoes*.

The doctor being asked, whether he thought that the fish caught in the British seas, by British subjects, could, in any circumstances, be afforded so cheap, as, without public aid, to bear a fair competition in an open market, with fish of the same kind from Holland, Sweden, Norway, or any other country? he said, "If the question means to apply to fish in general, and is not meant to be confined exclusively to any particular kind, he does, without hesitation, give it as his opinion, that were the people who inhabit the islands and coasts of Britain, in such situations and circumstances, as to be able to avail themselves to the utmost, of the natural advantages they possess, *their fish could be afforded cheaper than other fish of equal quality, from any other part of the globe*."—We were just now told by the doctor, that the great herring fishery in the north-west channel of Scotland is not practicable by decked vessels, during the months of November and December; if so, which is partly the case at this season, the Irish have a decided advantage over the Scots in the winter fishery, from the certain arrival of the herrings in their land-locked bays, and within a narrow tract of coast, where they are taken by boats as well as decked vessels without ceasing, in such quantities as would seem incredible to persons unacquainted with the herring fisheries; while the Scottish vessels, during the greatest part of this valuable season, have to navigate a long voyage round the mull of Cantire on the south, or the Pentland firth on the north; voyages of 150 or 200 miles upon an average, before they reach the north-west channel, where, instead of an immediate fishery, they frequently spend many weeks in fruitless researches for the shoals, and sometimes return empty, after having expended 300l. in the outfit and wages during the unsuccessful trip. Such are the unalterable natural advantages of the Irish winter fishery over that of Scotland; while the liberal bounties and fishery laws of the former kingdom, also operate greatly in their favour.

The comparative state of the Scottish herring fisheries, with those of Sweden and Norway, is still more against the former. The Swedish fisheries, like the Irish, are contracted within a narrow point, which, fortunately for Sweden, lies in the neighbourhood of Gottenburgh, one of the first commercial cities in that

* Londonderry is situated upon Loch Foyle, 5 miles from Loch Swilly, 17 from Mulroy, and 21 from Sheep Haven, all of which waters are occasionally crowded with herrings. Londonderry is a place of considerable commerce, particularly with America and the West Indies; which, with its excellent situation for the fisheries, aided also by the liberal bounty of 30 shillings per ton, gives it great advantages over the Scots fishers, who, if the bounties be withdrawn, and the childish system of premiums, as proposed by Dr. Anderson, adopted, will undoubtedly transport themselves to a country ready to receive them, and all useful members of society, with open arms.

 kingdom

kingdom, and from whence the herrings are immediately conveyed to the markets of the Baltic, and the East Sea. But the peculiar advantage of the Swedish fisheries over Scotland and all other nations, lies in the extraordinary facility by which they are taken, and in such quantities, that besides supplying Europe and the West Indies with 200,000 barrels annually, millions of herrings are boiled merely for the oil, which, though small in quantity, and of indifferent quality, brings in some years a return from foreign states, nearly equal to the annual value of herrings exported from Scotland, upon an average. Dr. Anderson must also have known that the Swedish herrings are taken at little or no charge.

" The herrings are caught among the islands or rocks, none at " sea, the nets not being calculated for that purpose; besides it " is unnecessary, while they are in such plenty within the rocks." *Answer to Mr. Byers's Queries.* Another letter from Gottenburgh says, " they are in such abundance on the coast of Sweden, " that they are catched at no expence, as they set into little inlets " amongst the rocks, and, by enclosing them with a large net, " they take out as many as they please, with little bag nets: " they sell the herrings at Gottenburgh, for 9 or 10 shillings per " barrel, cask and salt included; so that they have cut the Dutch " entirely out of the trade, in supplying the different markets in " the Baltic, as they can be sent from Gottenburgh to all the mar- " kets in the Baltic, at a very easy freight. I think it my duty, as " an individual, to furnish any information in an inquiry of this na- " ture. *But I fear it would require a very high bounty to enable " us to dispute the market with the Swedes.*" Besides the ready method of catching what quantity of herrings they can use, either cured or for oil, the charge of cask and cooperage in Sweden is only 1s. 10d. in Scotland it exceeds 5s. It was owing to these advantages, that the Swedes were enabled to land their herrings on the keys of Dublin and Cork at 14s. per barrel, whilst the Irish-taken herrings could not be purchased under 20s. without loss to the fishers. In 1776, the quantity of herrings imported from Sweden, amounted to 56,400 barrels.

In order to check the foreign, and to encourage their own fisheries, the Irish parliament, in 1777, laid a duty of 4s. per barrel on all Swedish herrings, and, in 1785, the duty was extended to 10s. If therefore, the Irish found it necessary to lay a duty of 10s. upon every barrel of Swedish herrings, how could Dr. Anderson pretend to assure the committee, " that without public aid " or bounties, the Scottish fish could be afforded cheaper than " other fish of equal quality from any other part of the globe?"

Respecting white fish, I can, from the best mercantile authority declare, that we are undersold at foreign markets, by the Norwegians, who lie immediately on the great fishing grounds of the northern ocean, and whose expenditure in building and equipping decked vessels, with stores, wages, casks, &c. scarcely amounts to half of the expence in any part of Great Britain. How can Dr. Anderson reconcile his assertions to these facts? or by what species of magic can our people meet the Irish, Swedes, and Norwegians gins, particularly the two laſt, at foreign markets on equal terms, without the aid of the public? Will the building of cities in the Highlands, bring the fiſh to the gates of theſe cities to be taken at pleaſure; or will the building of large towns, on theſe barren ſhores, reduce the price of proviſions and labour? Unleſs the doctor can, by ſupernatural means, effect theſe great ends, we muſt either grant liberal bounties on our fiſheries, or, as the doctor adviſes, "abandon them, as hurtful to the community."

The doctor is ſo very inconſiſtent on the ſubject of bounties and premiums, that we are at a loſs to comprehend his real meaning; in one place he gives it as his opinion, that until the cities, towns, or great villages ſhall be built *upon his plan*, "bounties and premiums for the fiſheries, muſt be accounted in a great meaſure "an uſeleſs expenditure of the national treaſure, which he ſhould "not be willing, unleſs in particular circumſtances, *to adviſe*. "And that when theſe towns are built, and mankind brought together, *there will be no occaſion for public ſupport*, *by any mode* "*whatever*."

In another place he does not think it adviſeable to withdraw the public aid at once. He thinks it ought to be continued for ſome time longer, until the people ſhall be collected in the cities and towns, as propoſed above. Being deſired by the committee to explain himſelf further on this head, and to ſtate the ſpecific meaſures that he thinks would the moſt effectually, and in the ſhorteſt time, put that fiſhery into ſuch a train, as that it could afterwards go on of itſelf, without any public aid whatever; ſuch deference paid to the doctor's judgement on this important ſubject, merited a moſt reſpectful, as well as a copious anſwer, of many pages; of which we ſhall only give the outlines of the plan. Beſides temporary bounties to wherry-rigged veſſels from 15 to 60 tons burden, following the fiſheries in any part of the Britiſh ſeas between the mull of Galloway on the weſt, and Inverneſs on the eaſt-coaſt, but no further ſouthward, he propoſes

A ſet of 10 different premiums to boats, amounting in all to £.	100
Ditto —— ditto —— ——	600
Ditto to veſſels of 15 tons and upwards. "In a few years," ſays he, "the bounty on the tonnage, which "requires a much greater fund, and is leſs calculated "to promote induſtry, may be with ſafety withdrawn, and theſe premiums continued, under ſuch "farther reſtrictions as experience may point out as "neceſſary."	1000
A ſet of 10 premiums for the beſt cured white herrings	300
Ditto for the beſt cured red herrings —— ——	300
Ditto for the beſt cured dry white-fiſh —— ——	300

Then follows ſome plans of premiums to individual families in the Highlands, by which "5000l. a year, thus applied, would "ſettle annually 2000 families, or 10,000 perſons—thus continued "for 20 years, would amount to 200,000 perſons, not to take "into the account the increaſe by natural procreation." Probably another

another 200,000, provided the doctor shall send requisite annual supplies of provisions from the moon or elsewhere, for such a body of people in a desert country.

"Of these 200,000 persons," continues the doctor "one "tenth are fishermen, as originally settled.—that is 20,000— "And if it is supposed, that each of these fishermen, on an ave- "rage, have, in these 20 years, bred up one son to the business, "the whole number reared up by the application of 5000l. per "annum, would in that period amount to 40,000.—Of course, "supposing 10,000l. thus applied annually, the number of men "thus trained to the sea would be 80,000."

Then follows another estimate of premiums to boats and wherries, amounting in all to 3,500l. In the notes, a set of premiums are proposed to the boats of each town in the Hebrides, another set to the five best fished boats in the whole coasts or islands of Scotland, and lastly another set to busses. The inspection and management of the whole would probably require 1000 additional officers, whose salary at 20l. each, would amount to a greater sum than hath been paid to the busses, upon an average of years, since the commencement of the bounty, without answering any valuable purpose; besides the train of frauds, jobs, and perjuries which this intricate, if not unintelligible system would occasion over the maritime parts of the kingdom. To these premiums, boats, and the necessary fishing apparatus are to be given to all the persons who shall engage in that employ.

After some further reasoning on the subject, the doctor seems so confident of the great merits of his plan, that he intreats the committee not to check the torrent of their rapturous approbation, till they have closely surveyed all its beauties with the eye of reason, when they may feast away at pleasure.

"In stating," says he, "to the committee the effects that may "be expected to arise from the proper application of these small "sums, the witness is sufficiently aware that these effects will seem "*so disproportionately great, as almost to exceed belief.*—He must "beg, however, that gentlemen, *before they allow themselves to be* "*swayed by such general prepossessions, will attentively examine the* "*facts, as stated, and draw the conclusion that unbiassed reason* "authorises."

And being asked, should those fisheries, and the consequent improvement on the coast, be carried to the perfection the witness thinks them susceptible of, would not the national revenue be augmented thereby? and if so, what does he think might be the amount of the additional revenue which might be thus obtained? The doctor, after some analogical reasoning on this head, says, "the revenue will be augmented by this arrangement, at least *one* "*million per annum.* Nor would this be a sickly revenue, liable to "fluctuation and decay, but it would be an increasing fund, that "would grow greater and greater, without trouble or expence, "as the prosperity of the people increased. And here it is pro- "per to take notice, that although for the sake of distinctness,

"it

" it has been stated, that a small annual sum should be apparently " [illegible] of the public revenue of the country, for the purpose " of promoting these fisheries, yet, it now appears, that instead " of requiring money to be paid by the other subjects of Britain, " for the support of those engaged in this undertaking, there " would only be wanted a very small portion of the money that " the fisheries themselves would produce, to be applied *for some* " *time* for the purposes therein specified, and a very large overplus " would remain to be applied to the common expences of the state."

Here, in our humble opinion, the committee closed the examination rather abruptly. It might have been asked, That as the doctor had stated the number of people which might be collected on these shores, in the course of 50 years at 100,000, besides the increase by natural procreation, the whole, upon a moderate supposition amounting to 300,000, what measures would be adopted for supplying this great body of people with provisions, since it is evident that, in the present thinly inhabited state of the west coast the natural produce of grain is scarcely sufficient to keep one third part of the natives from perishing through want.

To this question, the doctor would probably have answered; "That as these shores abound in fish of every species known in the northern latitudes; as the cetaceous, the cartilaginous, and the spinous, two millions of people, (the supposed population in that country 100 years hence, agreeable to the established principles of calculation,) might be abundantly supplied in wholesome prolific food. For instance, herrings at breakfast; codfish, ling, tusk, dogfish, turbot, skate, soles, flounders and mackerel for dinner; lobsters, crabs, oysters, muscles, cockles, and shrimps for supper. These dressed in all the different modes of cookery would afford an agreeable variety suited to every taste and palate, the voluptuous epicure not excepted.—It might have been asked, How are the inhabitants to be supplied with bread?—Nothing more easy. The Norwegians, a hardy race, inhabiting the same latitudes as the Hebrideans, mix the sawings of fir with burnt fish bones; this, when baked into thin cakes, will prove both a nutritive and a pleasant substitute for the Scottish bannock, or the English loaf. Thus the bounty of the surrounding ocean will furnish the tables of the labouring people, without any [illegible] aid from government, for I would not advise a lavish expenditure of the national treasure, unless in cases where it is absolutely unavoidable, as the purchase of sawings, which the government agents stationed in the Hebrides may procure at a small expence from their neighbours of Labrador, and lodge in stores for the general use of the community.

It is true, there may be delicate palates among the higher classes of merchants and citizens, who must be humoured in their tastes, to prevent their withdrawing themselves with their property to luxurious England; I therefore have proposed to introduce a better system of agriculture on these western shores, by which the soil will produce at least tenfold more than the present crops;

while at the same time the rains, about which English writers have given exaggerated reports, will become less frequent, and there is not a doubt but that, with steady perseverance, the periodical rains may be brought on earlier in the season, by which the harvest will be more plentiful, and safely housed. To effect this happy circumstance the face of the county must undergo a thorough change; bogs, marshes, and fenny lands must be drained; mountains, as the paps of Jura, Cuchullin, the mountain of the Sun, and the hill of the old Hag, must be be blown up, by which a double advantage will be gained; the clouds meeting no interruption will be more favourable to the husbandman, while the stones which composed these eminences, will furnish materials for building the cities. With regard to the management and reclaiming of lands, these subjects are fully handled in my book upon husbandry, of which the honourable committee must have heard; these copies being circulated amongst the Hebrideans, and the coasts of the mainland, will give a new face to nature.—The many extensive fields of these fair islands, and even the hitherto unprofitable grounds, will raise luxuriant crops of wheat, whereby the rich, the delicate, and the sick may be plentifully furnished with wheaten bread, with pudding, and with pastry, while the straw and the chaff will afford nutritive sustenance to the cattle and sheep through the winter."

It may be be alledged that many horses will be necessary in the cities which the reporter proposes to the honourable lords of the treasury, and this honourable committee, and that such cattle may, in some seasons, feel a scarcity of straw; but this objection will vanish, when it is considered that goods in these islands will be chiefly conveyed by water carriage. For instance, a merchant in the city of Boisdale, in Uist, commissions a last of herrings, or any given quantity of fish, from the city of Dunvegan, in Skye; the goods will not, cannot, be sent by land carriage, but by daily vessels passing from town to town; and thus there will be little or no call for those expensive animals in the Hebrides, for the purposes of trade. None of that whipping, cutting, and beating, so common in your Watling-streets, your Thames-streets, and your Wappings; none of that swearing, d———g of eyes and limbs, so offensive to the ear and the sight, will be heard or seen amongst the happy cities of Hebrides. The wealthy inhabitants will indeed require many sets of horses, for whiskies, chaises, chariots and coaches, from which government will derive a considerable revenue, but as the small species of that noble animal, is now become fashionable among the British quality, there will be no occasion for importing your large, high-fed English horses; the Hebrides breed vast numbers of the shalty kind called garrans, some of whom do not exceed three feet at full growth. Their tails almost touch the ground; their mains are long, and the hair of their foreheads cover the greatest part of their faces. They are bred chiefly in the neighbourhood of the laird of Boisdale, a gentleman to whose hospitality the reporter is under such high obligations, as he

can

can we otherways repay them by suggesting his acceptance of a city upon the estate of Bolsdale, which though somewhat distant from the European continent, is, consequently, so much nearer the American world; and a beneficial trade may be carried on between both hemispheres, of which the city of Bolsdale will be the centre. It will be a pleasing sight to see the laird, as superior of the soil, drawn in his coach by six of their little [illegible] parading the streets of Bolsdale in all the pride of royal state; and, while the principal merchants shall be flocking to change in their carriages and four, the ladies will be shopping, or paying their morning visits with pairs; for I would not advise more, on account of the high spirit of these creatures.

Having thus suggested a further explanation of the doctor's plan of towns, I shall now mention in his own words, his proposal for "opening a communication for facilitating the little inter-" "nal commerce of the country already alluded to, (meaning "the main land) and for conveying intelligence from place to "place expeditiously and regularly. Here little more would "be wanted but *such a path as a horse could travel on with* "*ease and safety*." It is very extraordinary that the doctor should propose to colonize the western shores with some hundred thousand people, and at the same time limit the travels and intercourse with these people, to a horse road only. We may, however, account for this inconsistency, from the doctor's ideas of economy respecting the expenditure of the public money. To this, as before observed, may also be ascribed his not pushing the business of the northern island, till that country should be able to carry it on without public aid.

But there seems to be no end to the doctor's absurdities. We shall, therefore close our observations after stating the two following particulars: I had in my evidence (which was prior to the doctor's) introduced the subject of the fisheries, by tracing the history of the herrings in their annual migrations from the northern seas to the southern parts of Great Britain and Ireland, where they disappear; this being the testimonies of the most eminent writers in natural history, corroborated by the Dutch and all practical fishermen, who frequent these seas; and particularly by the Baltic traders, who frequently observe the herring shoals, proceeding southward, attended by millions of fowls, and always at a fixed season of the year. This, the doctor, in his usual spirit of contradiction, attempted to confute, in a long and disgusting harangue, which had not the effect on the minds of the audience that he expected. He begins thus, "It is generally believed, "that herrings breed *only* in the northern icy sea." The doctor hath no authority for that assertion, it being generally believed, that herrings breed also in the British seas, consequently his arguments were totally unnecessary. Then follows a dissertation on what he calls *the various historical opinions concerning herrings*, which he seems to have copied from the words of those who preceded him in their evidence before the committee, and were unanimous respecting the annual migration of herrings.

 Another

Another particular connected with the preceding subjects, merits notice. The doctor, who sets his face against all well received opinions, or works, and the authors of them, labours by invidious insinuations, to raise his own importance at the expence of one of the most useful men of the age. "In these islands, and "along the west coast of Scotland," says the doctor in his report, "there are many of the finest natural harbours that are to be "seen in the world; but these, *from the want of proper surveys*, "are not yet thoroughly known."—"All the charts of those "coasts," says he in another place, "are full of inaccuracies "and errors, that tend to endanger the safety of any vessel that "shall attempt to sail by them."

Respecting those heavy charges against a person of reputable character, and amiable manners, we shall give a short abstract from a late publication, entitled *Justification of Mr. Murdoch Mackenzie's Nautical Survey of the Orkney Islands and Hebrides, in Answer to the Accusations of Doctor Anderson.*

"As the nautical knowledge of the Orkney Islands, and the "western coasts of Scotland, was of great importance to the navi-"gation of Britain, Mr. Mackenzie, a man of science, conceived "the plan of making a survey, for the direction of mariners un-"acquainted with those seas. This he executed, with regard to "the Orkneys, at his own expence. The merit of the perfor-"mance was conspicuous. The success of the undertaking "attracted the attention of the public. Mr. Mackenzie was "afterwards employed by government to extend the survey; and "he in a manner spent his life time in that service. The national "benefit derived from his labours can only be known from the "estimation in which his charts are held by mariners; but, to a "man of knowledge, the simple inspection of the charts, is suf-"ficient to convince him with regard to the pains and labour em-"ployed in that undertaking.

"Dr. Anderson, a man who had no pretensions to the know-"ledge of nautical surveying, or to the use of charts, made a "public attack upon Mr. Mackenzie's works. He represented "the charts as extremely erroneous, and dangerous to mariners; "and he insinuated, that the survey had been an imposition on "the public. The printer of the Caledonian Mercury, received "his friend (cousin) doctor Anderson's accusation into his "paper. A public correspondence was then commenced through "that channel, and papers were alternately received from both "sides,

"But the printer having now, for reasons best known to him-"self, refused to receive an answer to Dr. Anderson's last letter, "which was intended to contain a number of certificates from "many gentlemen of Liverpool, Leith, &c. who will be allowed "to possess the greatest professional knowledge, the friends "of Mr. Mackenzie, and of truth, therefore, think it necessary "to publish the whole of the correspondence, which, when "brought under view, will expose the conduct of doctor Ander-"son,

"son, and justify the character of Mr. Mackenzie, whose behaviour, in relation to the public, will ever be ready to meet a fair enquiry."

Mr. Mackenzie continued in this employ, till age and infirmities obliged him to resign the business to his nephew, who is now surveying the west coast of *Great-Britain*, the only part which the uncle had not completed. After having thus served his country and mankind in the most essential manner, with fidelity, persevering application, and universal approbation, he is not allowed to close a useful life in peace, but brought forward and stigmatized in a public news-paper, as an impostor, not one of whose charts, the doctor believes has been "delineated from actual surveys, "but imagines they must have been sketched by the eye only, and that even in a hasty and superficial manner." *Dr. Anderson's first account*, November 3, 1784.

A N S W E R.

SIR, *November* 17.

"Mr. Mackenzie, by the infirmity of years and bodily ailments, unable to give application to what must require thought and attention of mind, finds himself ill qualified to enter the lists, or even to attempt an answer, to the author of a paragraph in your paper of the 3d. of November. But, conscious of his own integrity, he begs leave to assure the public, that with accuracy, fidelity, and care, he executed the trust reposed in him, of carrying on a nautical survey, in consequence of instructions received from the lords of the admiralty; in which he has pointed out the best tracks, and the properest anchorage, as far as necessary for the safety of shipping. And he submits the merit of his survey, the work of many years, upon the only proper test, the approbation of those *alone* who are most interested, and best qualified to judge, *seamen*, the masters of vessels of all kinds, who, after the continued use of the said surveys from 10 to 30 years, have never once found fault, so far at least as has come to his knowledge. On the contrary, as a proof of their accuracy, there has arisen amongst seamen, with regard to the use of these charts, a proverbial expression, which, the circumstances he is in at present, authorise him to repeat, *that he who has Mackenzie's charts, when navigating those coasts, needs no pilot*.

"At the same time, if any rock or shoal has happened to escape Mr. Mackenzie's most laborious search and diligent inquiry, (which is far from being impossible) Mr. Mackenzie thinks he has a right, in justice to the public, who employed him, and for the general interest of mankind, exclusive of any consideration for himself, to call upon Dr. Anderson (who he believes to be the author of the paragraph) to condescend upon those errors and neglects, which may be dangerous to seamen who trust in those charts, and which, it is pretended, that Dr. Anderson has discovered, in order that those corrections, if

"found

"found just, may be inserted in the draughts, for the purpose "of any future publication."

The doctor begins his second letter in a vaunting style, which, when we consider the age, and the feelings of the man whom he accuses, does no great honour to the doctor's humanity; and we shall soon perceive greater reason to form conclusions respecting the doctor's moral principles. He begins his second letter thus, "Dr. Anderson is sorry that Mr. Mackenzie should have felt "himself so much hurt, &c." Any reader will readily allow the propriety of Mr. Mackenzie's letter, and the candid manner of expressing himself, whether by his own pen, or that of a friend. His language is mild, his arguments are stated upon facts, and he only wishes, that the doctor would point out the errors, if any do really exist, in order that they may be corrected for the public benefit.

The doctor thus called upon to speak out at once, says, that "many years ago, Mr. Mackenzie published a set of charts under "the title of *Orcades*; the last of which maps contains a chart of "Lewis: (a part of the Hebrides) In that map, the rock called "*Skerinoe*, near the Schant islands, is laid down about 4 miles out "of its proper place. In a future survey he made of the west "coast of Scotland and Ireland, that rock of Skerinoe is laid "down nearly in its proper place: He therefore, had then dis-"covered his error, and very properly corrected it." Let us now hear the answer made by Mr. Mackenzie's friend to this mighty charge.

"SIR

"I beg leave, through the channel of your paper, to recall "the attention of the public to doctor Anderson's accusation of "Mr. Mackenzie's surveys, the public being highly interested "in judging how far those accusations of a work of such magni-"tude and importance, be either on the one hand true, or on the "other false. Dr. Anderson has represented those charts as "erroneous and dangerous; and has insinuated, if not declared, "that the public money had been mis-spent, in being laid out for "surveys, that were nothing but a species of imposition. In sup-"port of this charge, the doctor has condescended upon one parti-"cular, of which the public is now to judge. But, to enable "those, who never had an opportunity of examining the sub-"ject, it will be necessary to give a short account of the ori-"ginal of those surveys.

"The survey of the Orkneys was the first undertaken by "Mr. Mackenzie. It was made at his own expence, and pub-"lished at his own risk. In this work there is also a chart "of the Lewis, which he *in part* surveyed. These charts "were found so accurate, so useful, and so well received by "the public, that Mr. Mackenzie was employed by govern-"ment, to survey the west coast of Britain, and the coast of Ire-"land. In this general survey, Mr. Mackenzie begins with the "Lewis, the survey of which had not been *completed* in his pri-"vate labours; consequently, of this there is published a more

"perfect

"perfect chart.—The charge against the accuracy of Mr. Mackenzie's first publication will be best estimated by reading what Mr. Mackenzie has there said in relation to the Lewis. In page 3d there is a chapter entitled, *Manner of taking the Survey of the Orkneys and Lewis, with the Perfections and Imperfections of the Charts.*—There, having described his manner of taking the survey of the Orkneys, he thus proceeds:—

"The Lewis was surveyed in the same manner, only most of the lesser islands there were done by the eye, *the coast between Loch Shell and Loch-fin Fort, by information*; and no soundings taken but within the bays. Now, it is to be observed, the rock Skerinoe and Schant islands lie precisely on the coast between Loch Shell and Loch-fin Fort.—Therefore, the sunk rock Skerinoe could not be surveyed in this chart; and Mr. Mackenzie has warned every man who is to use his charts of this; that so the mariner may avoid the dangers of sailing by the chart of a coast which has not been surveyed."

The reader, though unacquainted with maritime affairs, will easily perceive the weakness, if not worse, of this unprecedented and unwarranted accusation. Among the numerous instances of the doctor's propensity to detraction, this is the most frivolous and illiberal. Disappointed and foiled in this instance, he reiterated fresh charges against the old man, and again was called upon to explain himself by specifying the particulars.

"Now," says Mr. Mackenzie's advocate, "as I hope to have satisfied the public, that the only error specified in Dr. Anderson's vague accusation is perfectly groundless, and the chart complained of irreproachable on the part of Mr. Mackenzie, I think I have a right, both as a well-wisher to the public, and a friend of Mr. Mackenzie, to call upon Dr. Anderson to wave his principle of delicacy on this occasion, and publish those errors by which the lives and fortunes of many of his country-men are every day exposed to danger. The doctor may rest assured, that Mr. Mackenzie's feelings have not been disturbed by what he has already published, nor is there any reason to believe they ever will be affected by what farther he can say; for, if it be a discovery of any value, as a work of this kind cannot be warranted free of imperfection, Mr. Mackenzie will never regret the improvement of his charts; but, if it be only a trifling criticism, or any unjust accusation, the doctor will only expose himself to ridicule and contempt."

Here the doctor is again put to his shifts, and hath the mortification to find himself once more beaten off the field. He pretends to criticise upon distances and bearings laid down in the charts, without having ever made a trial of the one or the other, upon the principles of science, of which, indeed, he was utterly incapable, like other quacks, who are ever boasting of their superior abilities and discernment, while, at the same time, they know little of the subjects which they pretend to elucidate. "But," says the friend of the accused, "before answering directly to the

"charge,

" charge, there is a previous question, not with regard to what right " the doctor has to challenge; every one has a right to challenge " an error, by which the lives and fortunes of others are endan- " gered; but the question here proposed, respects *the capacity of* " *the challenger*; how far he has proper information with regard " to the subject on which he founds his accusation. Dr. Anderson " has not told what instruments he had employed, or what time " he had spent in making those numerous observations: But, " without giving satisfaction with regard, at least, to the probable " means of information, no person has a right to offer a criticism " on the work of a master who made it the business of his life. " As truth, however, fears no scrutiny, we shall at present wave " this privilege of a defender."

Then follows the defence, wherein the doctor's accusations are fairly stated one by one, and ably answered, without equivocation, or quibbling with words. The doctor begins to sicken, whilst his antagonist gathers fresh strength upon every attack. "The " doctor seems to forget himself," says he, "when he talks of put- " ting an end to all further altercation—does he consider as alter- " cation, his being called upon publicly to make good his calum- " nious assertions?" At length, the printer interposes, and after allowing his cousin the last word, puts a negative on any thing farther that may be offered on the subject from either party. Mr. Mackenzie's friend, who seems to be of the true Fingalian blood, finding the Mercury door shut against him, and the doctor snugly lodged within, reprints the whole controversy in a pamphlet: thus issuing from an unsuspected quarter, drags the trembling culprit from his lurking hole, and forgetting the dignity of L. L. D. says, "here is a piece of impudence, which nothing but bad " principles could suggest, and which nothing but the deepest " sophistry could cover. In opposition to Mr. Mackenzie's actual " survey, he gives, for facts, downright falshoods.—Dr. Ander- " son has made the most violent attack upon the property of a " person who never injured him; he has made the most insi- " dious, as well as cruel attack, upon the fame of a well deserv- " ing citizen: Therefore, he must either prove that he had " made the *survey*, on which he grounds his accusation, or he " must be condemned as bearing false witness against his neigh- " bour. I call the attention of the public to this cause, where " truth, and the dearest rights of mankind, are concerned. That " which is Mr. Mackenzie's case to day, may be the case of any " other man tomorrow. If the world will not stigmatize the " person who most unprovokedly has violated truth, and has " wilfully transgressed the most sacred law of society, there " would be no principles of morality in man.——I have repre- " sented Dr. Anderson's facts, I believe, in their proper light; " and I have now to tell him, that there are other parts of his " conduct of which he should more ashamed; *first*, of having " wickedly devised evil against his neighbour without cause; and, " *secondly*, of having foolishly departed from the path of truth,

" in

"in expectation of supporting his calumnious assertions. What benefit he promised to himself for thus transgressing the law of natural benevolence, implanted in the heart of man, and never violated without some reason, he best can inform. I believe he now repents, because his purpose has been frustrated. When he settles the account with his conscience, it becomes not me to inquire; but an injured public will not fail, I hope, to resent the open violation of that which is right and amiable in the eyes of all other men." These remarks are so applicable to the doctor's recent behaviour towards other victims of his malignity, that they seem the language of inspiration for rescuing innocence and integrity from the secret machinations of this reporter of facts. While the blood of the Caledonian champion was thus boiling in his veins, reinforcements arrived from all quarters, in defence of the man who had wore out his constitution for the preservation of those useful men, the sons of Neptune. "The friends of Mr. Mackenzie," says his advocate, "having now said what was thought necessary, in justification of themselves, when attacked by Dr. Anderson, in his last letter, they will close the whole by (what must be admitted to be the best evidence possible in support of Mr. Mackenzie's survey) certificates from those who are most interested, and who alone have a title to judge—commanders and masters of vessels,—and branch pilots." Some of these certificates are jointly signed by a number of commanders in the same port, as follows:

Liverpool, Jan. 18, 1784. "We commanders and masters of vessels in Liverpool, trading to Norway, Hamburgh, the Baltic, &c. being informed that malicious remarks have been sent abroad, reflecting on Mr. Mackenzie's charts of the West Coast and islands of Scotland, do hereby certify to all whom it may concern, that we have always found these charts sufficiently exact for navigating ships with safety among the islands, or between them and the main land; and, by his improved method in them, the great diversity of high and low lands, cliffs, shores, &c. are so remarkably distinguished, as to make them easily known, so that we can proceed with more confidence, and have found them safer guides than any other charts we have ever seen." Signed by 23 commanders.

Two certificates are from Stockton to the same purpose, and expressing a surprize that any one should report the charts to be erroneous, and strongly asserting their correctness. Various certificates and letters from different ports in Scotland, particularly Leith, signed by 3 masters of custom-house yachts, 18 commanders and pilots. A certificate from port Glasgow, signed by the commander of the king's cutter, and 5 ship-masters, who navigated the northern seas. Various certificates from individual commanders of cutters, traders, and pilots; one of which says, "I hear that one Dr. Anderson has been finding fault with your draughts of the West of Scotland, and has wrote against them in the news-papers. This surprised me very much; for you must have know that I was born in one of these islands, and accustomed to shipping from my youth, and since that have been master of a vessel and pilot for 40 years; have had the charge of king's cutters and many merchant-ships through the Highlands, and as far as Liverpool, when your draughts were aboard, and never had reason to find fault with them, nor ever heard any captain or ship-master say they found them wrong; on the contrary, every one of them, as well as myself, approved of them much, as the best they ever saw. I own, indeed, they have done prejudice to the pilots; for, to my knowledge, many of them that used to be well employed, and well paid, before your charts came out, are now obliged to stay at home idle, or enter before the mast, because masters through the Highlands, to the West of England and to Ireland, sail by your draughts without taking a pilot. I believe Mr. Anderson is not well acquainted with sailing or sea charts, or he would not have fallen foul of such a performance. Stronoway pilots have suffered much by your draughts, as hath the Orkney pilots; for, formerly, few ships attempted to go westward from Stronaway without pilots, and now very few of us are employed, the ship-masters telling that they can do very well with Mackenzie's draughts. I am a well-wisher to all honest men, and sir, your most humble servant."

Another letter runs thus:—"Good sir, reading in the newspapers a violent attack made on you and your charts of the West Highlands, I can say it is a false and cruel attack. I have been pilot of his majesty's ships, and other respectable merchant ships belonging to Liverpool, and elsewhere; and, by depending on your charts, through the Orkney islands, and often through the West Highlands, to and again, have been successful, and trust in Almighty God to continue to be successful, as I get an honest and very good livelihood by pilotting vessels."

A letter from Kirkwall, capital of the Orkneys, is thus:—"Sir, I am extremely sorry to see you lately attacked on some part of your surveys, and I think it very surprising, that such a number of years have elapsed, these neglects you are charged with was not found out sooner, where there has been a constant course of shipping and experienced seamen, till a Dr. Anderson would do it. It is a known fact in this country, that before your surveys of the west of Britain and Ireland were published, there were from 10 to 15 pilots employed in Stromness, by shipping going to Liverpool and Ireland, and more needed, if they could have been had; and since that, no capable ship-master, going to these places, takes a pilot, that has your survey. I have frequently heard sensible masters of ships say, none who understood a map, needed a pilot where you surveyed, if he had your's. But I really think, Sir, that Dr. Anderson has imagined you in Abraham's bosom, and that he did not expect an answer. It is common for those employed as he is, *to find fault with others that have gone before on the same plan (however right) to raise their own merit, which always proceeds from ambition, avarice, and mercenary motives.*"

 Besides

Besides these testimonies, I have to mention Captain Kyd's evidence before the committee on the British fisheries. He hath been stationed these last 34 years, in his majesty's cutters, upon the eastern coast of Scotland and the Orkneys; and being examined respecting Mr. Mackenzie's charts, (Dr. Anderson, I believe, present) he recommended them, as the most accurate, and serviceable to the navigation of these seas, he had ever met with.

I do not perceive his evidence on this head in the report, though I believe it stands on the minutes from which the report was made. In a private conversation with this gentleman, he declared Mr. Mackenzie's charts of the Orkneys to be, in his opinion, the most accurate that any nation could produce. I have also been informed that the Dutch consider them in the same light, calling them a blessing to their country.

During the course of my inquiries amongst seafaring people in Ireland and the west of Scotland, I never heard any person speak, directly or indirectly, against these charts, on any point whatever. On the contrary, they were uniform in their encomiums on the charts, and the author of them. Some of the people having occasionally attended Mr. Mackenzie while taking the surveys of their coasts, represented him as a pains-taking honest man, who did justice to the public, though the weather was often unfavourable for that business. Sir Lucius O'Brien spoke in parliament of Mackenzie's charts of the Irish coast in the highest style of panegyric.—"And this," says he, "I consider as a very useful favour, for which this nation is in a considerable degree indebted to the noble lord who presides at present (1776) among the the lords commissioners of the admiralty."

Much more could be added on this head, but it is unnecessary. How, therefore, can Dr. Anderson reconcile to his honour and his conscience, the following assertion in a public newspaper, "That he soon found that no person could rely upon Mr. Mackenzie's charts of the western coasts of Scotland with safety—that he is convinced not one of the harbours has been delineated from actual surveys, but imagines they must have been sketched by the eye only, and that even in a hasty and superficial manner." In these and other assertions, he stands alone—contravened and confuted by those who are the most competent judges in the British kingdoms, as well as foreign states. Thus the false alarm respecting a subject of very great importance to the commerce of these kingdoms, falls to the ground, whilst the devoted victim to artful perfidy, and a depraved heart, will be gratefully remembered by posterity. I shall now leave the doctor to his own reflections, under the further mortifying information that his insidious arts have in a great measure failed of the ends which he proposed to himself, at the expence of many of his countrymen, and for which he seems to sacrifice the welfare of that country. Let him take this final advice, that, in every condition of life, honesty is the best *policy*, even though it should be the certain means of temporal misfortunes.

FINIS.

*** *The Binder is desired to take notice, that the Second Volume begins with* B B *page* 369

ERRATA

Page 32, line 22, *for* provision, *read* provisions.
—— 55, —— 9, *for* was *r.* were.
—— 78, —— 40-41, *for* Lock *r.* Loch.
—— 79, —— 25, *for* commissioners, *r.* commissioner.
—— 81, —— 23, *for* 82 *r.* 80.
—— 84, —— 37, *for* numbers *r.* number.
—— 110, —— 25, *for* them, however, *r.* them, may however.
—— 120, —— 24, *for* Shuma, *r.* Shuna.
—— 129, —— 26, *for* dina, *r.* dinna.
—— 129, —— 30, *for* fortues *r.* fortunes.
—— 133, —— 37, *for* murders, *r.* murder.
—— 136, —— 30, *for* and, *r.* at.
—— 138, —— 3, *for* Dunnot, *r.* Dungsby.
—— 144, —— 8, *for* be, *r.* besides.
—— 167, —— 31, *for* 1777, *r.* 1677.
—— 270, —— 34, *for* jumping, *r.* by jumping.
—— 348, —— 21, *for* prewent, *r.* prevent.
—— 349, —— 28, 31, 33, 35, *for* curve, *r.* cruive.
—— 408, —— 9, *for* on, *r.* no.
—— 409, —— 11, *for* run, *r.* runs.
—— 414, —— 34, *for* Nidan, *r.* Ridan.
—— 441, —— 18, *for* Island, *r.* Islands.
—— 457, —— 2, *for* Glenalk, *r.* Glenalg.
—— 528, —— 35, *for* meeckle, *r.* meekle.
—— 569, —— 36, *for* west, *r.* Longitude.

www.ingramcontent.com/pod-product-compliance
Lightning Source LLC
Chambersburg PA
CBHW030740230426
43667CB00007B/788

* 9 7 8 3 7 4 3 3 5 3 8 4 8 *